I0644876

Monastic Education in Korea

Contemporary Buddhism

MARK M. ROWE, SERIES EDITOR

Architects of Buddhist Leisure: Socially Disengaged Buddhism in Asia's Museums, Monuments, and Amusement Parks
Justin Thomas McDaniel

Educating Monks: Minority Buddhism on China's Southwest Border
Thomas A. Borchert

From the Mountains to the Cities: A History of Buddhist Propagation in Modern Korea
Mark A. Nathan

From Indra's Net to Internet: Communication, Technology, and the Evolution of Buddhist Ideas
Daniel Veidlinger

Soka Gakkai's Human Revolution: The Rise of a Mimetic Nation in Modern Japan
Levi McLaughlin

Guardians of the Buddha's Home: Domestic Religion in the Contemporary Jōdo Shinshū
Jessica Starling

Morality and Monastic Revival in Post-Mao Tibet
Jane E. Caple

Buddhist Tourism in Asia
Edited by Courtney Bruntz and Brooke Schedneck

Monastic Education in Korea: Teaching Monks about Buddhism in the Modern Age
Uri Kaplan

Monastic Education in Korea

Teaching Monks about Buddhism in the Modern Age

Uri Kaplan

UNIVERSITY OF HAWAI'I PRESS
HONOLULU

Paperback edition 2021

Printed in the United States of America

26 25 24 23 22 21 6 5 4 3 2 1

Library of Congress Cataloging-in-Publication Data

Names: Kaplan, Uri, author.
Title: Monastic education in Korea : teaching monks about Buddhism in the modern age / Uri Kaplan.
Other titles: Contemporary Buddhism.
Description: Honolulu : University of Hawaiʻi Press, 2020. | Series: Contemporary Buddhism | Includes bibliographical references and index.
Identifiers: LCCN 2019048006 | ISBN 9780824882389 (hardcover) | ISBN 9780824883577 (adobe pdf) | ISBN 9780824883584 (epub) | ISBN 9780824883591 (kindle edition)
Subjects: LCSH: Buddhist monks—Education—Korea (South) | Buddhist education—Korea (South)
Classification: LCC BQ162.K6 K37 2020 | DDC 294.3/7509519—dc23
LC record available at https://lccn.loc.gov/2019048006

ISBN 978-0-8248-8983-8 (pbk.)

University of Hawaiʻi Press books are printed on acid-free paper and meet the guidelines for permanence and durability of the Council on Library Resources.

All photographs are by the author.

Cover image: Class time at a female monastic seminary. Courtesy of Buddhist Television Network (BTN).

Dedicated to my father, who had been my most avid reader

Contents

List of Tables

Series Editor's Preface

IN THIS COMPREHENSIVE AND HIGHLY NUANCED "BIOGRAPHY of a curriculum," Uri Kaplan masterfully demonstrates the profound connections between monastic education, the global impact of Buddhist studies, "rhetorics of innovative modernity," and shifting monastic identities in contemporary Korea. Through detailed interviews with teachers and students, combined with extensive ethnographic work at Buddhist seminaries and monastic graduate schools, Kaplan traces how modern discourses of preservation and renewal have transformed not only Korean Buddhist education, but the tradition as a whole. Of the many valuable insights that emerge from this study, its exploration into how contemporary Korean Buddhism has tended to replicate the form and content of modern Buddhist studies could significantly shift the way researchers approach their work: "Rather than scholars going into the monasteries to find out what Buddhism is all about, it is more often the Buddhist monastics who are searching for Buddhism outside of their clusters and in our modern libraries, and then, (reversely) transmitting this Buddhism back home." By tracing the modern history of Buddhist curricula, Kaplan reveals a rich new vein for understanding the practice of being a monk in the world today.

Acknowledgments

I WOULD LIKE TO THANK MY FAMILY for being there for me even after so many years far away from home.

Writing a book is no easy task, and I am grateful for the kindness and counsel I received from mentors, colleagues, and friends during the years of work on this manuscript. Richard Jaffe's amicable advice and meticulous comments, corrections, and suggestions on previous drafts surely made the chapters richer and more presentable. Hwansoo Ilmee Kim's unrelenting encouragement and trust, as well as his practical assistance during my fieldwork, were crucial for the completion of this work. Robert Buswell's expert suggestions were of great value, and may have saved me from future embarrassment. David Morgan's generous assistance has been vital in helping me sharpen some of the theoretical structures of the book. I would like to express special gratitude to Cho Sungtaek and Sem Vermeersch for kindly facilitating my research while in Korea. Needless to say, any errors that remain in the following pages are my own.

Generous grants from the Korea Foundation (2008–2009), the Kyujanggak Institute of Korean Studies at Seoul National University (2015–2016), the Academy of Korean Studies (2016), and the Freiberg Center for East Asian Studies (2017) provided me with precious time to focus on fieldwork and writing.

Last but not least, I would like to express my great appreciation and gratitude to the numerous Korean Buddhist monastics and laypeople who shared their monastery quarters, classrooms, documents, thoughts and sentiments, and numerous cups of tea (and coffee) with me, without ever expecting anything in return. George Clayton Foulk, perhaps the first Western traveler to have visited Haeinsa in 1884, wrote that "the priests are the very best people of Korea,"[1] and I often found myself sympathetic with this weathered statement. Many of these kind individuals will remain anonymous here, but I do wish to acknowledge a few by name: Sŏkchung, Kim Pyŏng-ju, and Ko Myŏng-sŏk of the Chogye administration; Chongmuk, Wŏnsan, and Chunhwan of Haeinsa; Harim of Mit'asa; Myŏngo of Tonghaksa; Hayŏn of Pongnyŏngsa; Ch'ŏnmun of Pŏmŏsa; Suam and the office staff at the Tongbang Buddhist School; Hyŏnjin,

Chino, and Tŏksŏng of T'ongdosa; Chijŏng, Wŏn'gyŏng, and Pŏpch'an of the International Buddhist School; Sŏngjŏng and Kŭmgang of Sudŏksa; Pŏppon of Pŏpchusa; Tongju of the Traditional Korean Buddhist Ritual Academy; Sŏn'gam, Chimyŏng, and Suwŏl of the Elementary Chan Hall; Sŏnmin and Chigak of Sŏnamsa; Chŏngŏn of Paegyangsa; Tŏgwŏn of Ssanggyesa; Sangjin of the Anjŏng Buddhist University; Kwangdo of Kuinsa; and Tongjae of Hwagyesa. May you all attain enlightenment!

Monastic Education in Korea

Introduction

What Should Buddhist Monks Know about Buddhism?

THIS BOOK SPRANG OUT OF A SET of simple, pragmatic questions. First, what do Buddhist monks and nuns know about Buddhism? And further, what, if anything, *should* they know? How might their particular understanding of their religion differ from the Buddhism described in our modern textbooks? And ultimately, how have such perceptions of the tradition been constructed and reconstructed over time? Obviously, even after confining the inquiry primarily to the Korean setting, answering such questions still involves significant methodological difficulties. Familiarity with Buddhist texts and praxis—and insights about them—clearly varies to a considerable degree between individual monastics, and interviewing them all would require several consecutive rebirths in the realm of human research. Instead, examining the textual curricula of Buddhist monastic seminaries—which are now unified and mandatory for all home-leavers in Korea—may be the best way to catch a glimpse of what monastics are taught to believe their religion is all about. In other words, looking at what Korean Buddhist professionals pick out of their enormous canonical and non-canonical literature as the focal points of their training (as well as at what they leave out) would paint the most authoritative picture of what the tradition considers to be its core orthodoxy. Examining curricula may thus yield the best evidence for the identity of a whole tradition, and tracing shifting curricula may reveal the contentions, adaptations, and reinventions of that tradition over time.

I should probably state from the very beginning—with the hope of not disappointing any readers—that this study will not offer a sweeping, conclusive answer to the question of what Buddhist monks should know about

Buddhism. Rather, my intention lies in directing the spotlight toward the complexities inherent in trying to answer such a question in the first place. The cultural depository of Buddhism today includes over four thousand canonical texts, as well as thousands of non-canonical historical works, modern books and textbooks, oral traditions, and more recently, an increasingly growing body of online material. The sheer diversity of this mass of information, much of it less than fully coherent, makes the pedagogical choices of monastics ever more difficult. This book examines the negotiations of contemporary Korean monastics with their historical curricula, educational systems, and religious roles and identities, in the face of the great influx of new Buddhist ideas and practices entering Korea in today's increasingly globalized world. The debates and choices made in the process of the canonization and de-canonization of their pedagogical agendas illustrate the ways that monastics have to decide, over and over again, which texts and doctrines constitute the core of their Buddhist tradition.

To be sure, this process of educational reconstruction brings to the fore additional interesting questions. Should monks see themselves primarily as meditation practitioners or as teachers and propagators? Should they all be able to recite Classical Chinese Buddhist texts or should they be fluent in English? Does one become a better monk by understanding various Buddhist doctrines, or by learning to live and work humbly and diligently within a group? Is Buddhism better interiorized and understood through memorization of texts or by conducting research projects? Which Vinaya should monastics commonly study? Should Chan monastics know how to meditate in the Vipassanā style? Should Korean monks know the history of Buddhism in Tibet? These and other similar dilemmas dealt with by contemporary curriculum reformers illustrate the ways in which the modern pressures of globalization and localization—foreign hegemonies and nationalism—infiltrate monasteries and force Buddhist home-leavers to make difficult decisions regarding the direction they wish to take. As we shall see, such decisions are often highly contentious, illustrating the internal bureaucratic complications and some of the realpolitik involved in the operation of large Buddhist monastic organizations.

This work is essentially fashioned as a biography of a curriculum. It centers on the birth, institutionalization, and fall of the "traditional" Korean Buddhist monastic curriculum over the course of the past five centuries. It illustrates how a particular sixteenth- and seventeenth-century pedagogic program was reimagined in the course of the twentieth century to become the sole unified Korean monastic program, only to be criticized and utterly reformed in the twenty-first. Through a detailed analysis of such modifications, I attempt to demonstrate how Korean Buddhist reformers today tend to imitate the pedagogical practices and canonize the textual totems of the contemporary international discipline of Buddhist Studies, and how, by doing so, they ultimately transform Korean Buddhist orthodoxy from a particular kind of Chinese-centered scholastic Chan, to the broad, inclusive, pluralistic, Indian-focused religion we usually find in our English-language introductory textbooks about the religion. It seems that rather than scholars going into the monasteries to find out what Buddhism is all about, it is more often the Buddhist monastics who are searching for Buddhism outside of their clusters and in our modern libraries, and then, (reversely) transmitting this Buddhism back home.

Scholars have long noted that the formal Buddhist canons were inadequate for understanding the actual identities of Buddhists on the ground, and have offered to examine the "ritual canons,"[1] "practical canons,"[2] and "curricular canons"[3] instead, as the actual bodies of texts preserved, studied, and ritualized in particular communities. The inherited Korean depository of Buddhist texts—the lengthy formal *Koryŏ Canon*—has been treated in the past millennium more as a national talisman for subduing enemies and dispelling astral disasters than as a collection of texts to be studied in its entirety.[4] Instead, it was other, sometimes non-canonical texts, that constituted the "curricular canons," recited, explicated, and brooded over in lecture halls. As we shall soon see, various admonition texts replaced the formal Vinayas in regulating behaviors in Korean monasteries, and a few selected treatises—rather than some of the more well-known canonical sutras—formed the orthodox core of the traditional seminary programs. Nevertheless, in modern times, the "practical canons" of Korean Buddhism have begun shifting toward the formal canons, or at least toward the formal Buddhist canons as imagined by the dominant academic works of modern Buddhist Studies. If the formal canons did not really matter to the average monastic prior to the twentieth century, they were made to increasingly assume a more central position in Buddhist monastic learning in modern times. It is this process of conflation of the "practical," "formal," and "academic" Buddhist canons that gradually transforms Korean Buddhism from a regionally focused creed into a global pluralistic religion.

Yet, before we delve into discussions of textual curricula, perhaps the more fundamental question to consider is whether Chan practitioners—and Korean monastics generally do see themselves as belonging to the Chan (pronounced *Sŏn* in Korean) tradition—should engage in textual learning at all. In the *Śūraṃgama Sutra,* for instance, an apocryphal Chan text that has been widely read in Korean Buddhist seminaries for several hundred years, the Buddha explicitly criticizes Ānanda for having "excessive learning" (多聞), which he compares to talking about food without ever tasting it.[5] The fact that the Chan tradition has often endorsed fervent anti-textual rhetoric, while at the same time producing a huge mass of texts, has by now nearly become a cliché. Nevertheless, since the Tang Dynasty and throughout the ages, there was also another—more compromising—style of Chan, one that granted "words and letters" a crucial place in its monastic training. It is this type of Chan that has been historically dominant on the Korean peninsula, where leading monastics often stressed the importance of balancing their training in both Chan meditation and (textual) learning (*kyo* 教).

As will be clear by the end of this book, textual learning has become ever more central in the training of Buddhist monastics in contemporary Korea. In fact, graduating from one of the fifteen or so four-year seminary programs has by now become the prerequisite for ordaining with the Chogye Order, and is a qualifying criterion for joining a meditation retreat in one of the Chan Halls. A variety of monastic graduate schools has proliferated in the twenty-first century, fostering monastic specialists in Vinaya studies, rituals, Theravāda Buddhism, and Buddhist English. Diverse seminars on issues ranging from Buddhist preaching skills and temple management, to science, history, philosophy, psychology, cinema, cooking, Christianity, and so forth, are also regularly organized by the Order. In addition, a system of examinations has been developed in order to confirm that all monastics are familiar with the curricular orthodoxy, and to ensure that higher-ranking sangha bureaucrats are selected according to objective standards.

Doing Fieldwork in Korean Buddhist Monasteries

In order to paint a comprehensive picture of Buddhist monastic education in Korea, research for this book has not been confined to one particular methodological paradigm. Historical investigation and textual analysis were used side by side along with semi-structured interviews and lengthy fieldwork in Korean monasteries.[6] Aside from spending a considerable amount of time digging through internal seminar protocols and other related reports at the Chogye Order's archives in Seoul, I conducted "multi-locale" or "multi-sited" ethnography in monastic seminaries on the peninsula. As explained by George Marcus, "multi-sited" fieldwork is not bound to a single location, and is thus able to "follow the thing"—the "thing" in this case being monastic education—wherever it goes, allowing a better grasp of a social phenomenon rather than of a particular site.[7] Between 2012 and 2016 I made continual lengthy visits to all eighteen of the currently operating official Buddhist seminaries in the country and to the majority of the monastic graduate schools.[8] I interviewed some of the teachers and students on-site and collected data regarding their programs and schedules. In addition, in the fall of 2013 I audited classes for a semester at the largest T'aego Order seminary in Seoul, and whenever possible, also joined monastic continuing education (*yŏnsu kyoyuk*) programs organized by the different Orders.

Commenting on her own fieldwork in Japan, Helen Hardacre noted that formal introductions were often very important for establishing connections with religious groups in the country.[9] I likewise began my research using personal connections to arrange meetings with seminary teachers, but soon learned that in Korea, at least, that was unnecessary, and sometimes hindering. Arriving at a monastery with a formal appointment ensured, of course, that someone was going to be waiting for me, sometimes bearing gifts, willing and able to pour some tea and talk. The problem was that what was usually said in such formal occasions remained mostly in the realm of the proper "party line." Personal opinions and sentiments were kept very much private, and additional information about the realities of the seminary was not shared. Arriving as a complete stranger with a smile was often more beneficial. Korean monasteries are open public spaces and monastics are generally kind and welcoming, and in almost all cases I was able to simply show up at a seminary unannounced and find at least one teacher who was willing to share his or her experiences and thoughts with me with a high degree of frankness and generosity, show me around the cluster, and provide me with a room to stay for a couple of nights. In fact, my own foreign appearance, ponytail and backpack, as well as my familiarity with Buddhist terminology in the Korean language, made me a novelty in the eyes of many monastics, and they were often at least as curious and intrigued about speaking with me as I was in talking to them. They frequently viewed our meetings as an additional opportunity for propagation, some explicitly encouraging me to spread the teachings of Korean Buddhism in my home county.

Nevertheless, some limits could not be overcome. Richard Irvine mused that his own fieldwork in a Benedictine monastery was somewhat like "playing at being a monk," as he was not ordained himself and his existence was always peripheral rather than participatory.[10] Korean monasteries commonly attempt to maintain some spatial boundaries between the lay and the ordained. Eating, sleeping, and meditation are almost always done separately, but other limits apply as well. Although I was allowed to enter the classrooms and examine textbooks, as a layperson, I was very rarely permitted to actually join classes in monastic seminaries. When I tried to protest this exclusion, I was often told that my presence would be disturbing to the highly impressionable novices. It is hard to tell whether this was just a pretense, though I did have better luck joining some graduate monastic classes, where the students were fully ordained and have had more time to mature in their monastic practice. In some monasteries, teachers told me that if I was so interested in joining classes, I should just shave my head. They did not show much concern about the possibility of my disrobing right after concluding my research. The majority of those who disrobe do so in the very early stages of their monastic careers, and as one seminary teacher told me, "after a year or two in robes on the mountain, you will not be thinking of disrobing any longer."[11]

As far as I know, there has only been one case of an anthropologist ordaining with a local sangha for research. That particular researcher joined the Thai sangha for six months in 1968 as a temporary monk. He later argued that this greatly facilitated his fieldwork, although there were certain disadvantages, such as limitations on traveling to other monasteries.[12] As an outsider to the monastic world, my participation in the seminaries was peripheral at best. Ordaining as a novice, I would have undoubtedly been able to illustrate in more detail the day-to-day life of one particular seminary, but I would not have been permitted to travel from institution to institution and present a broader, more inclusive, bird's-eye view of monastic education in Korea. In fact, during my visits, I was sometimes asked by seminary teachers about the situation in other schools, thus in a way becoming an informant myself, the interviewer changing into an interviewee. Some seminary teachers were apparently less informed about other schools' programs than I gradually came to be, and at times queried about it and expressed interest in reading this book once it was completed.

In a rather entertaining piece titled the "Ten Lies of Ethnography," Gary Fine pointed out that although anthropologists commonly express constant sympathies for their subjects, there are certainly times of suspicion and even enmity.[13] I have surely faced some suspicion from seminary monastics, who were often worried about bad press and weary of my invasive questions. Some monastics attempted to present an overly ideal picture of Korean Buddhism, whereas I inquired about tensions and problematics. This book is patched up of these conflicting goals and motivations. To be sure, teachers at the seminaries proved to be much easier to talk to than were novices, who were generally facing significant pressure and strict discipline. When I tried to engage them in conversation, they were sometimes reluctant to talk, ushering me to their teachers instead, or pointing toward the office and quickly hurrying away to tend to one of their endless duties. One time, as I attempted to ask a seminary student about his life, he frowned and reproached me, saying "isn't this frivolous speech?!" ("*hamburo iyagi aniyo?!*").[14] Students of the various monastic graduate schools and at the Elementary Chan Hall (see chapter four) were usually more willing to talk, but the more meaningful exchanges I had with seminary novices have been outside monastic walls, when I accidently met them on the bus or in the city. Foreign monastic students, too, were generally much less hesitant to talk to me openly about their life at the seminary, some finding respite in speaking some English, even just for a little while.

This makes it quite clear that the monastic informers presented in this book were certainly not passive data providers, but agents with particular agendas and decisions about what they would like and what they would not like to share. Parts of this book, however, would undoubtedly still be uncomfortable to some, and at times, I have had to make difficult decisions regarding what information to incorporate and what to exclude from this monograph. My general rule of thumb has been not to quote anyone without explicit permission, and to try to only use data that would cause no harm to particular individuals—despite potentially being uncomfortable for the sangha as a whole.

Buddhist Education in Contemporary East Asia

This book has been stimulated by several pioneering works on Buddhist monastic education in other Asian localities. Of particular note are Anne Blackburn's study of Sri Lankan Buddhist textual practices and Justin McDaniel's fascinating treatment of Southeast Asian monastic education, which sharpened my conceptions of religious curricula as canons and the politics involved in their construction.[15] Georges Dreyfus, who went through fifteen years of monastic education in Tibet and lived to tell us about it, inspired me to look closer at the staged progression of a particular curriculum in tandem with the pedagogical methods used in its instruction.[16] Others have written on Buddhist education in Asia, and before delving into the intricacies of monastic textual practices in Korea, it may be useful to review some of the information—as fractional as it may still be—that has been gathered on parallel clerical schooling in neighboring China, Japan, and Taiwan, which share a common Chinese-character-based form of Buddhism. Though only a short summary of the state of Buddhist monastic learning in the larger Sinitic world, my hope is that this background will serve to highlight the particularities of Korean seminaries discussed in the subsequent chapters of the book.

To begin with, Buddhist education in Japan has been relegated for the most part to the sectarian universities, which were established at the end of the nineteenth and the beginning of the twentieth centuries.[17] These Buddhist-affiliated schools were gradually secularized during the course of the twentieth century, and only trifling percentages of their students today are aspiring priests coming from temple families.[18] Apart from secular degrees, the various Japanese denominations usually require some additional study and practice in a training monastery in order to obtain certification as priests. This period seems to range from several months to two years, but very little has been published about the actual curricular programs involved. What we do know is that in Sōtō Zen monasteries this training often includes lectures on the writings of Dōgen and Keizan, and that even in Rinzai Zen monasteries—envisioned as extremely anti-textual—the kōan curriculum sometimes involves individual sutra study and the writing of commentaries.[19] A 2002 survey among Rinzai Myōshin-ji clerics found that only about a quarter attained a degree from a Buddhist-affiliated university, and approximately half spent over two years in a training temple.[20] In addition, many—though certainly not all—Kōyasan-affiliated Shingon priests go through a rather rigorous one-year seminary program on the mountain after graduating from college, which consists of classes in rituals, Shingon history, Sanskrit, preaching, and Buddhist culture, and involves stern peer pressure and hazing.[21] In order to become a resident priest and take over a family temple in the Jōdo School one must pass an exam, either while attending a sectarian university or by registering for a one- to three-year evening school or correspondence course at one of the sect's offices.[22] Although the Tendai School also operates several seminaries, it is uncertain how many of the denomination's priests actually go through any significant period of education there.

For China, research on Buddhist pedagogy has mostly concentrated on the early twentieth century, and we still know very little about contemporary monastic educational institutions and programs. Holmes Welch,[23] Don Pittman,[24] Raoul Birnbaum,[25] and more recently Rongdao Lai[26] have presented detailed accounts of the attempts to modernize sangha education in China in the 1920s and 1930s by building new seminaries with broader Buddhist and secular curricula modeled on Japan's sectarian universities.[27] Most (if not all) of these seminaries closed down during the political turmoil of the 1950s, and it is only since the 1980s that seminaries for the Chinese sangha began to proliferate once again.[28] The central governmentally funded university of the Chinese Buddhist Association (Zhongguo foxueyuan 中國佛學院) was first founded in Beijing in 1956, but closed down only four years later, after producing approximately four hundred graduates. It began operating again in 1980, along with other sangha schools, many of which were built in the south of the country.[29] The central university currently offers a four-year Buddhist curriculum with additional secular subjects for the Buddhist elites, and also operates two branches in Suzhou and Nanjing. As of 2014, there were at least fifty-eight Han Chinese Buddhist seminaries operating on the mainland—still a small number considering China's huge population—as well as similar institutions serving Buddhist monastics of the Tibetan and Southeast Asian minorities, located predominantly in southwestern China.[30]

Sueki Fumihiko studied one of the new seminaries established in the late 1980s, the Jiuhuashan Foxueyuan (九華山 佛學院), which had selective admission procedures and rather high tuition fees, thus making its forty-five enrolled monastic students in the early 1990s the cream of the sangha.[31] Others have examined several seminaries operating in the vicinity of Hangzhou and Suzhou and discovered that their current curricula have been influenced a great deal by Tibetan Buddhist material and Japanese academic works.[32] I have had a chance to visit one historically significant new Chinese monastic institution, the seminary of Wannianchansi (萬年禪寺) at Mt. Tiantai, which offered a comprehensive, four-year Buddhist curriculum for fifty monks in 2014.[33] The head teacher explained to me that, like the Jiuhuashan Foxueyuan mentioned above, the institution admits only a small number of Tiantai monastics, and most others do not receive any substantial textual education during their monastic careers, apart from memorizing the liturgy.

More work has been done on contemporary Buddhist organizations in Taiwan. The first Buddhist seminary was opened in 1948 near Taipei, and by the late 1990s, approximately ninety Buddhist schools were operating on the island.[34] While the popular Tzu Chi Buddhist movement does not run its own monastic seminaries (though it does run a medical school and a secular university), other groups certainly do.[35] Foguangshan operates ten seminaries in Taiwan, housing hundreds of students, both lay and monastic. It also runs branches in Malaysia, Australia, and South Africa, as well as two secular universities. Yet, seminary education is not an official requirement for ordination in this organization.[36] Dharma Drum Mountain, in particular, seems to emphasize education, and its monastic school, established in 2001, is probably the only large Buddhist institution in East Asia outside of Korea that enforces a mandatory four-year monastic seminary curriculum for all its aspiring novices.[37]

Buddhist monastic education in Korea stands out from this group in several ways. For one thing, as examined in chapters two and three, it is the only East Asian Buddhist curricular program that has been unified nationally for at least a century, perhaps longer. Even after the separation of the Chogye and T'aego Orders in 1970, the seminaries of both of these dominant institutions generally maintained the same traditional curriculum, which has roots in the seventeenth century. Unlike in Japan, secular university education is only pursued by small percentages of the sangha, and mountain seminaries continue to dominate the scene. Additionally, making the four-year seminary textual program mandatory for all Chogye monastics in the 1990s, made this community one of the most textually fluent Buddhist sanghas in the contemporary Mahāyāna world. Unlike in neighboring countries, the Korean Buddhist core monastic educational programs are neither elitist nor marginal. They are unified and all-encompassing, influencing the perceptions of virtually each and every home-leaver in the nation today. This makes these curricula particularly significant as mirrors for understanding what Buddhism really means for monastics on the peninsula.

Chapter Overview

Chapter one serves as an introductory backdrop providing context for the entire monograph. Essentially, it presents an archeological breakdown of the fixed set of texts that comprise what has come to be known as the Korean monastic "traditional curriculum." It traces the historical construction of this educational program, and perhaps more importantly, scrutinizes the prevalence of intertextual referencing among its components and the kind of ideologies that have been placed at its central core, molding it into a single, coherent whole. I supplement this discussion with a short translation of a seventeenth-century text, the first historical doctrinal overview of this curriculum. I also offer an analysis of premodern printing records and monastic biographies, which shed some light on the nature of Buddhist pedagogical programs in existence prior to the twentieth century.

Chapter two illustrates how this particular historical syllabus was institutionalized in the modern era to become the sole, unified (and later, mandatory) Korean national program. It examines various attempts to reform and modernize sangha education in the twentieth century, focusing on the establishment of Buddhist institutions of higher learning and independent female seminaries. The chapter then portrays day-to-day schedules and practices at the seminaries, providing ethnographic snippets from the actual lives of monastic students. It closes with a discussion of the crucial 1994–1995 Chogye Order bureaucratic restructuring that made seminary education mandatory for the entire sangha, requiring the preliminary study of texts before any Korean Chan monastic may join a formal meditation retreat.

We reach the climax of our story in chapter three, which delineates the very recent, twenty-first-century, far-reaching reforms of the traditional curriculum. The chapter introduces the new required Buddhist syllabus and the rather animated battle between the Chogye administration and some of the seminary teachers surrounding its operation. The limited set of Classical Chinese texts that comprised the traditional curriculum has been substituted, for the most part, with vernacular Korean textbooks on broader Buddhist themes, while new pedagogical practices, such as final examinations and thesis writing, have been introduced into the mountain seminaries. I attempt to demonstrate how such reforms reflect the ways local Asian Buddhists tend to imitate the hegemonic ideals and practices of modern Buddhist Studies, and how this new program essentially transforms Korean Buddhist orthodoxy from a particular kind of Chan to a more general, inclusive, and international form of Buddhism. Although the discussion centers on the dominant Chogye Order, which presently operates fifteen seminaries and over twenty graduate schools for home-leavers, the chapter concludes with a survey of the pedagogical practices and institutions of the two other significant Buddhist monastic organizations in Korea, the T'aego and Ch'ŏnt'ae Orders.

Chapter four explores the proliferation of graduate schools and other specialized learning institutions for the sangha. It examines the recent establishment of Vinaya Schools, early-Buddhism academies, Madhyamika-studies institutions, ritual institutes, and English-language seminaries. These new establishments are intended to train monastic specialists in multiple kinds of Buddhism, and, in the process, they make Korean Buddhism a more pluralistic, diversified religion than it ever was before. The increasing conspicuousness of foreign Buddhist monastics in Korea adds to this pluralizing tendency, and their distinct experiences in acculturating to Korean monastic life in general and to seminary study in particular are discussed toward the end of the chapter.

Chapter five links educational structures and achievements to monastic administration. It demonstrates how new rank-examination systems revolutionize monastic hierarchies in Korea by positioning the passing of exams—rather than seniority, number of retreats, or spiritual development—as the principal criteria for ordaining and for holding higher positions in the bureaucracy. In order to make sure all students had a fair chance of success in these new tests, the Chogye Order has recently unified and centralized the postulant education system, creating a new postulant canon of required texts. It also established a system of continuing education seminars required for all those wishing to sit for the higher sangha examinations. The chapter provides several examples of the kind of questions asked in the various clerical exams, and overall, illustrates the way monastics are evaluated according to their ability to utilize Buddhist doctrines in their roles as teachers, propagators, administrators, and spiritual cultivators.

1

The Traditional Curriculum

1. *Admonitions to Beginners:* Raising the intention toward enlightenment and practicing precepts, meditation, and wisdom.
2. *Admonitions to the Gray-Robed Monks:* Subduing restless affections and safeguarding against unwholesome action.
3. Dahui's *Letters:* Shunning unwholesome understandings and revealing correct views.
4. Zongmi's *Chan Preface:* Correlating the three traditions [of Chan and learning] and bringing them back into one.
5. Chinul's *Excerpts:* Distinguishing sudden and gradual [approaches to practice] and revealing ineffable awareness.
6. Gaofeng's *Chan Essentials:* Raising great intentions and breaking down the *gongan* [literally: infiltrating into the entrance].
7. *Śūraṃgama Sutra:* Abandoning muddy thought-recollections and giving rise to refined wisdom.
8. *Awakening of Faith:* Opening the two gates [of *saṃsāra* and nirvana], which are based on the one mind.
9. *Diamond Sutra:* Breaking down the two attachments [to self and dharmas] and revealing the three kinds of emptiness [of self, dharmas, and emptiness itself].
10. *Sutra of Perfect Enlightenment:* Cutting off ignorance to reveal the Buddha nature.
11. *Huayan Sutra:* Gathering the numerous dharmas to illuminate the one mind.

Head of the Central Sangha College, Chongbŏm, explaining the progression of the traditional curriculum.[1]

THE EXCERPT ABOVE LISTS THE TEXTS THAT constitute what came to be known as the "traditional" Korean Buddhist monastic curriculum, and summarizes succinctly—though rather abstractly—their individual functions in the overall training program. This comparatively small group of texts was chosen out of the immense body of existing Buddhist literature and gradually assembled by several monks between the sixteenth and eighteenth centuries to form what would later become the particular type of orthodox Korean monastic Buddhism. The list is usually divided into four stages. The first stage is made up of admonitions literature (usually referred to as the *Ch'imun* class,[2] texts 1 and 2 in the list above), which I will argue has constituted the "practical Vinaya" of Korean Chan.[3] Next, the *Sajip* (四集, Fourfold Collection, texts 3–6), a compilation of four treatises written by Chinese and Korean Chan teachers, was put together to form the second stage of the curriculum. The third stage is comprised of study of the *Sagyo* (四教, the Four Sutras, texts 7–10): the *Śūraṃgama, Diamond,* and *Perfect Enlightenment* sutras, as well as the *Treatise on the Awakening of Faith in Mahāyāna,* which was evidently elevated to sutra status here. The *Taegyo* (大教, Higher Learning, text 11)—the last stage of the curriculum—positioned the *Huayan Sutra* at the pinnacle of this canon, and occasionally involved additional study of Chan genealogies and *gongan* (公案) collections.

It is these works, rather than the formal *Koryŏ Canon,* that have constituted the textual totems towering over Korean Buddhist monastic learning over the past several centuries. As later chapters will demonstrate, they continue to play a major role in contemporary debates on curricular reforms. I would thus like to devote this first chapter to briefly introducing these works and examining the contextual networks and historical associations that tie them all together into a coherent single program. After drawing short sketches of the chosen texts and their prevalence in Korea and in the greater region, I will examine their intertextuality and consider the specific picture of Buddhism they depict to those who study them in tandem. A survey of the printing circulation of the curricular texts will conclude this introductory chapter. Although the program was assembled gradually beginning in the sixteenth century and evidently used by several monastics starting in the seventeenth, the chapter will illustrate that—contrary to a view common in Korean Buddhist circles—there is no evidence that it constituted the single universal Buddhist curriculum in the late Chosŏn period. Indeed, the next chapter will demonstrate that it was only in the course of the twentieth century that it was reimagined and fixed as the orthodox Korean traditional curriculum.

The First Stage: Admonitions Literature

The *Dharmaguptaka,* or *Four-section Vinaya* (*Sifenlu* 四分律)—regularly associated with East Asian Buddhism—is missing from the traditional Korean Buddhist curriculum. Also missing are the *Brahma Net Sutra* (*Fanwangjing* 梵網經), with its fifty-eight bodhisattva precepts, and the texts of the Pure

Rules (*Qinggui* 淸規) genre, which are often viewed as independent Vinayas of Chan monasteries.[4] It is indeed true that monastics formally accept the *Dharamguptaka prātimokṣa* during ordinations and are generally aware of its main prohibitions; yet, evidence suggests that more extensive study of this lengthy and complex text was rarely done on the peninsula until very recent times. Rather, a different Vinaya-type genre appears in the first stage of the Korean monastic syllabus, one that we should certainly pay more attention to: that of admonitions.

When I speak of admonitions literature, I am referring to a group of treatises that present themselves as such by using titles such as *kyŏng* 警, *kyŏnghun* 警訓, *kyŏngmun* 警文, or *kyŏngch'aek* 警策, commonly written by various East Asian Buddhist masters for disciplining their pupils. The most fundamental text in the entire Korean traditional monastic seminary program is probably the *Admonitions to the Gray-Robed Monks* (Ch. *Zimen jingxun;* K. *Ch'imun kyŏnghun* 緇門警訓; hereafter *Ch'imun*).[5] The central position of the *Ch'imun* in Korean Buddhist learning becomes evident when one considers that, historically, most monks have not gone through the entire curriculum, but discontinued their studies after studying for only a year or two—in other words, after studying the *Ch'imun*. As is illustrated in chapter three, the *Ch'imun* is also one of the few texts that has made it intact through the recent Chogye Order reforms, and it is still (at least partially) studied by most Korean novices today. It is also the only Vinaya-related work studied in the T'aego Order seminary at Sŏnamsa and in the Korean Ch'ŏnt'ae School seminary at Kuinsa.

The *Ch'imun* is primarily a compilation of short treatises written by various Chinese Chan masters, but it also includes writings by Tiantai and Pure Land teachers.[6] One hundred and seventy-two such treatises were compiled into the first nine-fascicle *Ch'imun* edition created in 1313 by Zhixian Yongzhong (智賢永中) in Yuan China. Yongzhong claimed that his compilation was based on an earlier admonitions text, *Precious Admonitions to the Gray-Robed Community* (*Zilin baoxun* 緇林寶訓), which was compiled in 1255 by Zexian Yunqi (擇賢蘊齊).[7] In 1348, only thirty-five years after its initial publication, T'aego Pou (太古普愚, 1301–1382), returning from a two-year visit to China, brought the *Ch'imun,* along with an edition of *Baizhang's Pure Rules,* back to Korea. Pou held the highest monastic political position—that of State Preceptor (Kuksa 國師)—in late-fourteenth-century Koryŏ, and used his influence with the explicit aim of reconstructing and organizing the sangha according to these new Chan disciplinary expositions.[8] A little over a century later, in 1470, a Ming Dynasty Chan monk by the name of Rujin (如巹, b. 1425) republished the *Ch'imun* with an additional fascicle, and it is this longer, ten-fascicle edition, that became the standard text in late Chosŏn and in modern Korea.[9] At least eleven separate woodblock editions of this *Ch'imun* were published in sixteenth- and seventeenth-century Chosŏn alone.[10]

There is some evidence suggesting that such admonitions collections were used in the instruction of novices on the Chinese mainland as well. The 1341 Yuan Dynasty text *Pure Rules of a Village Temple* (*Cunsi qinggui* 村寺清規) proclaimed that new monastics were first to be instructed in the (above-mentioned) *Precious Admonitions to the Gray-Robed Community,* as well as in some other short expositions found in the *Ch'imun,* such as *Guishan's Admonitions* (*Guishan jingce* 潙山警策) and Yongan's *Record of the Monks' Hall* (*Sengtang ji* 僧堂記).[11] In Korea, it seems probable that the *Ch'imun* was used at least by students of the Pou lineage, beginning in the fourteenth century, but it is generally believed that it was actually Pou's fourth-generation disciple, Paekam Sŏngch'ong (栢庵性聰, 1631–1700), who was most responsible for popularizing the text. Sŏngch'ong was a prominent teacher in his day and was involved in the publication of several other curricular texts, such as the whole *Sajip* collection, the *Huayan Sutra,* and the *Awakening of Faith.*[12] In 1695, Sŏngch'ong composed the first and only available *Ch'imun Commentary* (*Ch'imun kyŏnghunju* 緇門警訓註). In its introduction, he stated that this was a great text for the instruction of beginners, crucial for admonishing and keeping novices in line.[13]

Anne Blackburn has shown how certain Buddhist communities in Ceylon trained novices using handbooks and summaries rather than the actual Pāli Canon.[14] In a similar way, the *Ch'imun* makes for a comprehensive beginner's textbook and is used as such, instead of the formal Vinaya, in Korean seminaries. It assembles short introductory essays on practically everything a new monastic trainee should master: rules and precepts, instructions for communal life, samples of vows of earlier teachers, short meditation instructions, hymns, historical records of Chinese kings praising the Dharma, and encouragements for study by famous monks. The majority of the chapters are authored by Song Dynasty Chan masters, but some date back to earlier times, such as a few pieces written by Daoan (道安, 312–385).[15] In the only available content analysis of the *Ch'imun* to date, Sin Hoe-jŏng argues that out of the original 203 essays of the *Ch'imun,* 121 (60 percent) were Vinaya-related, 46 were meditation-related, and 68 were wisdom-related.[16] Teachers I have talked with in Korean monastic seminaries often explain that these essays should be seen as the advice of elders and models of good monastic behavior rather than as strict rules and regulations. A prominent female monastic teacher reportedly said that the *Ch'imun* is to Buddhists what the *Analects* and the *Mencius* were for the Confucian aristocracy (*yangban* 兩班).[17] It assembled the fundamental paradigmatic instructions of the sages, which were meant to be followed by later generations.

Early-twentieth-century Korean Buddhist reformers critiqued the length and repetitious nature of the *Ch'imun* and attempted to create shorter, more palatable versions. Pak Han-yŏng's (1870–1948) first attempt to limit the *Ch'imun* to its most essential forty-three chapters did not catch on, but

An Chin-ho's (1880–1965) 1936 abridgement became the orthodox seminary edition for the rest of the twentieth century.[18] Along with other well-known Korean Buddhist reformers, such as Han Yong-un and Kwŏn Sangno, An was one of the first graduates of the Myŏngjin school—discussed in the following chapter—and it was he who ventured a complete rearrangement of the text into sixty-seven chapters under fourteen general categories. This compilation begins with a group of six chapters under the title of Admonitions (*Kyŏng-hun* 警訓), which is considered to be the most significant section, appearing first in the volume and most widely studied in seminaries today. Next in order are categories titled Urging Study (*Myŏnhak* 勉學), Bequeathed Instructions (*Yugye* 遺誡), Guidelines (*Chammyŏng* 箴銘), Letters (*Sŏjang* 書狀), Records (*Kimun* 記文), Introductions (*Sŏmun* 序文), Vows (*Wŏnmun* 願文), Chan (*Sŏn-mun* 禪文), Instructions to the Community (*Sijung* 示衆), Hymns (*Kech'an* 偈讚), Apologetics (*Hobop* 護法), Miscellanea (*Chamnok* 雜錄), and Appendices (*Purok* 附錄).

The first chapter in the *Ch'imun* is *Guishan's Admonitions,* which is one of the few essays in the entire compilation that had been (partially) translated into English.[19] Guishan (溈山, 771–853) was a disciple of renowned Chan master Baizhang, and his *Admonitions* essay circulated independently as an instructional text for beginners in China. It also seems to have played some part in the disciplinary instruction of new monastics in modern Vietnam.[20] The second essay of the *Ch'imun* is taken directly out of Zongze's eleventh-century *Rules of Purity for the Chan Monastery* (*Chanyuan qinggui* 禪苑淸規), and presents a summary of Chan monastic management offices and positions.[21] Another noteworthy essay in the collection is Huiran's (慧然) "Raising Vows" (*Fayuanwen* 發願文), which made its way from the *Ch'imun* straight into the morning and evening chanting liturgy of some of the major Korean monasteries, including Haeinsa and Chŏngamsa.[22]

As many prominent Chinese Buddhists in history received a classical education, it is not surprising to find numerous references to Confucius, Mencius, Xunzi, and other Confucian thinkers throughout the *Ch'imun*. Some authors admonish Buddhist novices using the well-known adage from the *Analects* to "restrain yourself and return to the rites" (*keji fuli* 克己復禮),[23] while others refer to Xunzi's scales and rectangles (*guiju* 規矩), which are needed to rectify the sangha, as "even jade cannot be made into a bowl without carving, so does a man cannot know the Way without study."[24] Contrary to the focus of the Indian Buddhist Vinayas on material possessions and sexual and dietary restrictions, these East Asian (Confucian-inspired) admonitions seem to be more interested in prodding Buddhist monastic novices to study hard, be prudent in speaking, and live harmoniously with others. As such, they resemble parallel Confucian texts on basic decorum, such as the *Dizi gui* (弟子規) taught in China and the *Saja sohak* (四字小學) studied in Korea.[25] Such an ethical focus on living harmoniously in the community is often singled out by seminary teachers as the most important value to be learned by Buddhist novices at the beginning of their monastic careers.

The *Ch'imun* is a long and comparatively difficult text. It contains a large number of rare and challenging Chinese characters, some of which are utterly indecipherable. The fact that its essays were written in different time periods and use diverse grammatical structures and terminology certainly does not make this compilation easier to read. Buddhist seminary teachers often argue that this text is not read at the beginning of the curriculum just for its content, but it is used as a kind of Chinese character primer and Buddhist terminology lexicon in preparation for reading more philosophical texts in later stages of the program. In other words, the *Ch'imun* serves as a kind of crash course in reading Chinese Buddhist literature, and after struggling with it at first, novices discover that they can read other curricular texts with relative ease. Some Korean monastic teachers also maintain that reading through the exhortations of the patriarchs in the *Ch'imun* helps increase novices' faith and confidence in the Buddhist path.[26] In 2008, the Chogye Order published a new, shorter edition of the *Ch'imun* in forty-four essays (*Sinp'yŏn Ch'imun* 新編緇門), in an attempt to further simplify the collection.[27] In a Chogye seminar held in the year 2000, a monastic teacher from Pŏmŏsa argued that seminaries should not focus only on Chinese admonitions, but that a "Korean *Ch'imun*" should be fashioned as well.[28] A Korean admonitions collection, however, has actually been in use for centuries.

The *Admonitions to Beginners* (*Ch'obalsim chagyŏngmun* 初發心自警文; hereafter *Ch'obalsim*) is a collection of three essays written by dominant Korean Buddhist teachers, which has sometimes accompanied the *Ch'imun* in the early stages of the curriculum, though in the twentieth century it was usually studied by postulants before they entered a seminary. The three texts are now all available in English translation in the *Collected Works of Korean Buddhism*. The first is Wŏnhyo's (617–686) *Arouse the Mind and Practice* (*Palsim suhaengjang* 發心修行章).[29] This short, 706-character text does not go into much detail, but provides general encouragements to practice, admonishments against breaking the precepts, and warnings regarding harmful desires. The next essay, Chinul's *Admonitions to Neophytes* (*Kye ch'osim hagin mun* 誡初心學人文) is more specific.[30] Its content is divided into three parts: admonitions for beginners (keeping the ten precepts, staying away from corrupt friends, getting along with others and respecting their privacy, walking, eating, and speaking solemnly, etc.); admonitions to fully ordained monks on the communal life (staying out of fights, refraining from frivolous talk, eating in a timely manner, and refraining from over-associating with the laity); and admonitions on the right frame of mind for Chan practice (refraining from doubt, laziness, etc.). It was written by Chinul in 1209 with the specific goal of regulating and disciplining his community in Susŏnsa; and eventually it began to circulate in other monasteries as well.[31]

The popularity of Chinul's *Admonitions to Neophytes* soon inspired other Korean Buddhist teachers to compose their own admonitions treatises. In the mid-fourteenth century the Korean Tiantai master, Unmok, published the *Tiantai Admonitions* (*Ch'ŏnt'ae marhak Unmok hwasang kyŏngch'aek* 天台末學雲默和尙警策), and, in the early fifteenth, the Chan monk Yaun (野雲) composed the third and final text that made it into the *Ch'obalsim* collection: the *Self Admonitions* (*Chagyŏngmun* 自警文).[32] This essay is centered on ten general warnings. They are similar to Chinul's *Admonitions* (refraining from over-associating with the laity, refraining from frivolous speech, etc.), but involve somewhat more sophisticated language and poetry. Wŏnhyo and Chinul's compositions circulated separately for a time, and in 1567, the three essays were assembled and published together for the first time under the title of *Ch'obalsim* in Ssanggyesa. After 1612, the three were always published together as a collection—in thirteen separate editions prior to the twentieth century. Once the new Korean *Hangŭl* script was invented in the fifteenth century, these essays were among the first to be published in the vernacular.[33]

All in all, it seems reasonable that the monastic career should begin with some education regarding the rules of the communal life in the monastery. This is also the case in Buddhist communities elsewhere.[34] As we have seen, the initial disciplinary instruction in Korea was not done through the study of the formal Vinayas or Pure Rules literature, but with the aid of Chinese and native Korean admonitions compilations. The focus of this admonitions genre is not dietary, sexual, or property-related, but rather restraining one's speech and action within a community to avoid strife, and encouraging novices to strive in their study and practice. Ironically, though, as will be closely examined in later chapters, contemporary Korean Buddhist modernizers have criticized the *Ch'imun* for being "too Chinese," calling for a romantic return to the canonical Indian Vinaya, a "return" to a Korean Buddhism that may have never really existed.

The Second Stage: Chan Treatises

After completing the admonitions stage of his or her education, the monastic novice was now ready to move on to the next stage, that of the Fourfold Collection of Chan treatises (四集; hereafter *Sajip*). This collection of four essays is viewed as introductory material to the doctrines and practices of Chan, studied before one could proceed to read the sutras—understood to be the actual words of the Buddha—in the later stages of the curriculum. Such gradual progress from commentaries to sutras is not unique to the Korean monastic program. Some of the Tibetan Buddhist curricula, for instance, allocate years to the study of commentarial texts (*śāstras*), and only afterward—if at all—advance to sutra examination.[35] The significance of these particular four treatises for understanding what Korean Buddhism stands for is thus immense, as they were the ones selected to instruct the still-flexible minds of novices and point them toward the orthodox way.

The four are often divided into two parts. The first two are Zongmi's (宗密, 780–841) *Chan Preface*[36] and Chinul's (知訥, 1158–1210) *Excerpts from the Dharma Collection and Special Practice Record with Personal Notes* (hereafter *Excerpts*[37]), which are essentially expositions of the various Chan lineages and doctrines, and are thus sometimes labeled as "teachings." The next two are Dahui's (大慧, 1089–1163) *Letters*[38] and Gaofeng's (高峰, 1237–1295) *Chan Essentials,*[39] which provide more practical instructions in the Kanhua (看話) Chan method of *huatou* (話頭, critical phrase) investigation, and are thus often labeled as "Chan."[40] This *huatou,* or *gongan,* practice is more commonly known in its Japanese pronunciation as kōan meditation. Only two of these four essays are found in the comprehensive modern Taishō edition of the canon, yet the other two have been more influential to the Korean tradition than most other texts in that authoritative collection of scriptures.

The first historical reference to teaching these four texts successively as a single program in Korea comes from the sixteenth century. It is found in Hyujŏng's (休靜, 1520–1604) records of his grand-teacher (the teacher of his teacher), Chiŏm (智嚴, 1464–1534), who reportedly explained:

> In guiding beginners, first establish knowledge according to reality using [Zongmi's] *Preface* and [Chinul's] *Excerpts*, and then sweep away the maladies of knowing and understanding using [Gaofeng's] *Chan Essentials* and [Dahui's] *Recorded Sayings*, and point toward the path of liberation.[41]

A later reference is found in the records of Kyŏnghŏn (敬軒, 1542–1632), who was a student of Hyujŏng, thus possibly pointing us toward the fact that the *Sajip* was first promoted within this particular lineage.[42] Kyŏnghŏn is said to have trained his disciples:

> First using the *Preface* and *Excerpts* so one can determine and unpack the (various) interpretations of the Buddha Dharma; and based on this strong foundation, one can later move on to the *Chan Essentials* and Dahui's *Letters*, which break though the maladies of knowing and understanding the Buddha Dharma.[43]

Both of these quotations demonstrate a fascinating Chan pedagogical method of using the four texts in succession—the first two for building knowledge, and the next two for destroying it. According to this rationale, Buddhist doctrines must first be learned and understood only to later be abandoned and shattered. Not long after Kyŏnghŏn, in the early seventeenth century, we begin to encounter Chan teachers referring to the four treatises as a collection entitled *Sajip,* as well as evidence of several monasteries manufacturing woodblocks for printing them together as a set. They were all published in tandem for the first time in Chirisan's Nŭngin Hermitage in 1603–1604, then again in Songgwangsa in 1608–1609, in Yongboksa in 1628, and in Yongjangsa in 1635.[44]

Zongmi's *Preface* was first transcribed in 857 during the Tang Dynasty, and a Dunhuang manuscript of the text from 952 is still extant.[45] It was published several times in China and in the Buddhist Xixia Tangut world, as well as twice in Japan in the seventeenth century within Kegon (華嚴) circles. Yet, it was by far more widely circulated in Korea, largely due to Chinul's interest in Zongmi.[46] Sixteen separate woodblock editions of this text were manufactured on the peninsula between the fifteenth and seventeenth centuries alone.[47] The main message of the text seems to be that Mahāyāna sutras should not be discarded by Chan practitioners, as they were the word of the Buddha and thus cannot be contradictory to the mind of the Buddha, which is Chan. Zongmi criticized in this essay the "misunderstanding" regarding Bodhidharma's slogan of mind transmission "not depending on words and letters,"[48] and argued that this phrase should only be understood as expedient means used by Bodhidharma to inform people that the moon (awakening) does not lie in the finger (sutras), yet the sutras were necessary for pointing us toward it.

The *Preface* goes on to correlate various sutras with the teachings of the different Chan houses, comparing the sutras to the inked string of the carpenter used as a measuring standard for Chan practitioners. Zongmi lamented in this essay the fact that, in his day, sutra scholasticism was often practiced in separate circles from Chan, and called for a sutra-based Chan practice. Accordingly, the first thing that was traditionally taught to Korean monastic novices who completed the preliminary admonitions course was that Chan was not separate from the words and letters of the Mahāyāna sutras, and that textual study was essential to their practice.[49]

The second great project of the *Preface* was comparing and contrasting the Chan and Tiantai lineages of the day. Using the frameworks of gradual and sudden approaches to practice, Zongmi designated the various teachings as viable skillful means, but seemed to favor the position of the Heze lineage, in which sudden awakening was a necessary precondition for correct cultivation. Without such preliminary awakening, Zongmi argued, one would not be able to know what to base his or her practice on.[50] He explained that just as the sun rises suddenly yet the frost melts gradually, as a child is born with all limbs intact but only gradually learns to use them, and as an aristocrat who grew up in the wilderness suddenly returns home yet gradually learns ritual and music—

while one realizes his or her Buddha nature suddenly, he or she still has to gradually remove their "beginningless habit-energies" (*wushi xiqi* 無始習氣) in order to become fully enlightened. This Heze-Chan sudden-enlightenment-followed-by-gradual-cultivation (*dunwu jianxiu* 頓悟漸修) model proposed by Zongmi has become the hallmark of the traditional curriculum, and consequently stood at the center of Korean Buddhist discourse for centuries.

Much of the popularity of Zongmi in Korea was owed to Chinul. It was Chinul who brought Zongmi and his Heze syncretic sutra-based Chan ideology—which lost its popularity in China in the eleventh century—back from the dead and into mainstream Korean Buddhism.[51] Robert Buswell described Chinul's *Excerpts* as his magnum opus. Written a year before his death, it was composed with the purpose of serving as a handbook for students.[52] It is the only native Korean text in the *Sajip,* yet it essentially continues to discuss the various Chan houses using the same Zongmi-related themes of the sudden and the gradual, discussed above. In fact, it is not presented as an individual thesis, but as a commentary on another, lost, Zongmi text, *The Dharma Collection and Special Practice Record.*[53]

Chinul cited Zongmi's (negative) assessment of the main Chan schools saying that the Northern School regarded everything as false, the Hongzhou School regarded everything as true, and the Oxhead School regarded everything as nonexistent. He provided the analogy of the Mani jewel, which remained luminous no matter what color it reflected, yet the Hongzhou insisted that the colors were the jewel, the Northern School attempted to remove the colors, and the Oxhead School proclaimed that both the colors and the luminosity were nonexistent.[54] He reiterated Zongmi's sudden-awakening-followed-by-gradual-cultivation model, arguing that it was the most fitting program for the present degenerate age (*malbŏp* 末法). Chinul then turned to focus on cultivation practices. He allowed that chanting (*yŏmbul* 念佛) and sutra study were both useful practices for those of lesser faculties, that cultivating faith with the *Huayan Sutra* was beneficial for those of middling faculties, but that practicing no-mind (*munyŏm* 無念) and *huatou* investigation were the most valuable undertakings for those of high faculties.[55] His version of Buddhism taught to novices in Korea was thus multi-praxis, allowing multiple ways of cultivation for the sangha. Nevertheless, no-mind and *huatou* meditation were posited at the peak of his scheme, and it is this type of meditation practice that stands at the center of the next two *Sajip* treatises.

Kanhua Chan, with its focus on *huatou* meditation practice, is generally thought to have been invented either by Dahui or by his teacher, Yuanwu Keqin (圜悟克勤, 1063–1165), and first popularized in Korea by Chinul.[56] The third essay in the *Sajip,* Dahui's *Letters,* consists of the last six fascicles (25–30) of Dahui's *Recorded Sayings,* and includes sixty-five letters he had written to forty-two people—two monks and forty members of the literati (*shidafu* 士大

夫).[57] This work has been particularly popular in Korea, which is evident from the fact that two out of the three extant commentaries to the compilation were written on the peninsula.[58] Dahui presided over the two most important monasteries in China at the time, and some of his correspondences were with prominent Confucian literati, such as Liu Zihui (1101–1147), who was the teacher of young Zhu Xi (1130–1200), head minister Zhang Shangying (1043–1122), and several direct students of the Cheng brothers.[59] Thus, although the *Letters* has become a crucial text in monastic training in Korea, it was probably originally compiled for propagating *huatou* meditation to lay practitioners and Confucian scholars.[60]

"Quiet sitting" (*jingzuo* 靜坐) had become somewhat of a popular practice among Song scholar-officials, and Dahui's foremost objective in many of the *Letters* was to condemn such endeavors and recommend *huatou* investigation instead.[61] Morten Schlütter explained that Dahui's critique of quiet sitting or "silent illumination" (*mozhao* 默照) should be seen in the context of the competition between the Linji (to which Dahui belonged) and the Caodong masters (who recommended silent illumination) over the political support of the literati.[62] The *Letters* states over and over again that quiet sitting is mere idleness, and that authentic practice was not related to sitting or lying down, to quiet or noise, but should be done at all times, in everyday activities, and even in dreams. "To make the Buddha sit is to kill the Buddha," Dahui insisted, and warned that those who were attached to sitting would never grasp the principle.[63] One well-known legend depicts Dahui burning the woodblocks of the *Blue Cliff Record*—written by his own teacher no less—perhaps in order to reprimand his students for simply "learning" the different *gongan* cases instead of actually holding them constantly in their minds. Lists were unnecessary, and one *huatou* was sufficient—Dahui's favorite clearly being the *huatou* in which "Wu" (無) was the answer to the question of whether a dog has a Buddha nature. He referred to this well-known *huatou* thirty-four times in letters to twenty-five different individuals.[64] In comparison, he only referenced other *huatou* in his communications with four people. In explaining *huatou* practice, Dahui was also perhaps the first teacher in Buddhist history to reconceive doubt (*yiqing* 疑情) not as a hindrance, but as a vital driving force in the investigation, necessary for breaking through regular thinking patterns toward enlightenment.[65] The last essay in the *Sajip* collection, Gaofeng's *Chan Essentials,* expanded on these ideas.

Like the *Letters,* the *Chan Essentials* is principally a collection of teachings to the laity on correct *huatou* practice. The work consists of twenty-nine chapters: thirteen sermons to large (lay) audiences, three private interviews, two letters, and some biographical information, all collected by one of Gaofeng's lay disciples between 1288 and 1295.[66] Ironically, although this text has never found its way into a standard edition of a formal Buddhist canon, it was published in Korea more often than any of the other *Sajip* essays. Thirty-three separate editions of this work were produced from its first engraving in 1354 until the end of the eighteenth century.[67]

Gaofeng is generally recognized as the eighteenth patriarch of the Linji Chan lineage. His sermons illustrate a more sudden approach to practice than what we have seen in the other *Sajip* essays. In fact, in contrast to the textually based scholastic Chan of Zongmi and Chinul, the introduction to the *Chan Essentials* states explicitly that these teachings were not based on words and letters (*buliwenzi* 不立文字), and it is generally understood that the work embodies a sudden-awakening-sudden-cultivation (*dunwu dunxiu* 頓悟頓修) approach to practice.[68] Perhaps after going through the more gradualist essays by Zongmi, Chinul, and Dahui, students were now deemed ready for a more sudden pedagogic approach. Then again, it is possible that the main intention behind adding this text to the program was for its extensive pragmatic instructions in concrete *huatou* practice, rather than for its theoretical standpoints.

At the core of the practical method depicted in this treatise stand the "three essentials" (*sanyao* 三要) of *huatou* contemplation.[69] The first essential is the "faculty of great faith" (*daxingen* 大信根)—a confidence in the soteriological power of this Kanhua Chan method itself. The second, which is Gaofeng's most original addition to Dahui's methodology, is a "drive of great fury" (*dafenzhi* 大憤志), bringing such an intense urgency to practice that it "is just as if you've come across the villain who murdered your father." The third essential, resting on the first two, is the "feeling of great doubt" (*dayiqing* 大疑情), which gradually engulfs a person until there is no separation between oneself and doubt and one becomes one chunk (*yipian* 一片) of doubt. If all goes well this chunk is ultimately blustered and one enters the "no-mind samadhi" (*wuxin sanmei* 無心三昧) of enlightenment.

More than other parts of the curriculum, the *Sajip* collection highlights the particular Korean flavor of Chan. It is a Buddhist cocktail that had been concocted by Chinul, who in his *Excerpts* blended the textual Chan and the "sudden-awakening-followed-by-gradual cultivation" approaches of Zongmi and the Heze School with the Kanhua Chan soteriological praxis of Dahui (and later of Gaofeng). It is a particular type of Chan that is not based on quiet sitting, but on sutra learning and on raising doubt with the aid of a single *huatou* during all activities of daily life. These *Sajip* treatises were used as hermeneutical tools for the later study of the sutras. In other words, it is through the lens of these basic approaches to Buddhist practice that novices would have been likely to comprehend the teachings of the Mahāyāna sutras, which comprise the next two stages of the curriculum.

The Third Stage: The Four Sutras

After completing the admonitions and *Sajip* courses, novices going through the traditional curriculum finally advanced from learning the words of the patriarchs to learning the words of the Buddha. Four sutras were selected to form the *Sagyo* course by seventeenth-century teachers, and I suspect that these particular sutras were chosen because they were the favorites of the *Sajip* authors, and they are generally believed to confirm the basic ideologies the *Sajip* authors wished to promote. The four are the *Diamond Sutra, Śūraṃgama Sutra, Sutra of Perfect Enlightenment,* and *Awakening of Faith in Mahāyāna*—the latter, although strictly speaking a treatise and not a sutra, was regarded essential enough to be added to this central group of texts. It is important to note that several well-known Mahāyāna sutras were left out of this curriculum, and, perhaps, the absence of the *Platform, Vimalakīrti,* and *Laṅkāvatāra* sutras is especially conspicuous, possibly owing to their more subitist soteriological visions.[70] It is also remarkable that at least three of the four (all but the *Diamond*) are believed to be Chinese apocryphal texts, composed in seventh- to eighth-century China, rather than "authentic" Indian translations. In the following, I am only able to present short outlines of the place of these formidable texts in Korean Buddhist history. Readers are encouraged to delve into their teachings elsewhere in one of their now-readily-available translations.

The *Diamond Sutra* is part of the Perfection of Wisdom genre and has been central to most East Asian Buddhist traditions.[71] In Korea, it was the second-most frequently printed Buddhist text between the fifteenth and seventeenth centuries.[72] In early-fifteenth-century Korea, Kihwa (己和, 1376–1433) assembled five representative commentaries to this sutra into a collection and added an introduction. This compilation, known in Korea as the *Ogahae* (五家解), includes commentaries from Chinese teachers from the sixth to the twelfth centuries (Zongmi among them), and has commonly been studied alongside the sutra itself in Korean monastic seminaries.[73] The modern Chogye Order Constitution (Chonghŏn) points to this sutra, and to this sutra alone, as the foundational teaching of the school.

The *Sutra of Perfect Enlightenment* is a rather short Chinese apocrypha on which at least four commentaries were written in the eighth century.[74] It became especially well known after Zongmi's praise for it in the ninth century, and his commentary on the text inspired the additional composition of several sub-commentaries. It was first mentioned in Korea only in the eleventh century by Ŭich'ŏn (義天, 1055–1101), who wrote a short essay on it, and it was often cited later by other Korean leading monastics, such as Chinul, Hyesim, Pou, and Hyujŏng.[75] It is structured in such a way that the early chapters depict a more sudden approach "pointing directly to one's mind," while the later chapters describe various means with a more gradualist perspective. Like some of the other curricular texts, chapters out of the *Sutra of Perfect Enlightenment* sometimes made it into the liturgy (or ritual canon) of some monasteries. As of 2014, for example, the third chapter of the sutra, "Chapter of the Universal Vision Bodhisattva" (*Poan posal-pum* 普眼菩薩品), is chanted in its Korean translation in daily morning ceremonies at Wŏljŏngsa.

The contents of the *Śūraṃgama Sutra* bear some resemblance to the *Sutra of Perfect Enlightenment,* and James Benn suggested that the latter might be a summary of the essential points of the longer *Śūraṃgama.*[76] The two share the same first commentator (Weique 惟慤, in the eighth century), as well as the same metaphors of the fingers pointing at the moon, the disoriented person who confuses north and south, and the sky flowers (*konghua* 空華) representing optical illusions.[77] These analogies have become staples in Korean Chan circles. Disputes about the *Śūraṃgama*'s authenticity erupted in eighth-century Nara, and it has never gained much of a reputation in Japan since.[78] Although Zhu Xi, too, claimed it was a forgery, it still enjoyed great popularity in China during the Song and Ming periods, and at least eighty-six commentaries were written for it in the Middle Kingdom.[79] In fact, Wu Jiang argued that it was the most popular Buddhist scripture among the Ming literati, a factor that certainly may have contributed to its inclusion in the Korean program.[80] It remained central in modern China, and Yang Wenhui's well-known Jetavana Hermitage, which has become a prototype for other early-twentieth-century seminaries, centered its entire second-year curriculum on this text.[81]

The first Korean commentary to the *Śūraṃgama* appeared in 1265, and two additional ones were written during the Chosŏn period, one in the new *Hangŭl* script.[82] In fact, this text was arguably the first Buddhist sutra to be published in the (then) new Korean vernacular.[83] Kim Chin-yŏl provided a detailed analysis of the references in the text and argued that the sutra was composed in China between the years 714 and 723.[84] The text begins with the famous story of Ānanda being seduced by a prostitute on his alms rounds. As he returns to the assembly, the Buddha delivers a long sermon that centers on the impossibility of locating "the self," and from which several *huatou* have been extracted. The sutra is also famous for its admonition for strict vegetarianism, and includes the *Śūraṃgama Dhāraṇī,* which has become one of the most popular spells in East Asian Buddhism.

The fourth text, which was added to the *Sagyo* at a somewhat later date, is the *Awakening of Faith in Mahāyāna.*[85] It is attributed to Aśvaghoṣa, but it is generally accepted today to view it as a Chinese apocryphal treatise. A long-standing adage in Korean monastic seminaries characterizes the last two *Sagyo* works as "tedious *Awakening of Faith* and firm *Śūraṃgama*" (*k'ank'an Kisin, ch'adol Nŭngŏm* 칸칸기신, 차돌능엄), and indeed the *Awakening* is a rather scholastic exposition of the mind.[86] Wŏnhyo's early-seventh-century commentary is considered one of the three main interpretations of the text, and it has been particularly popular on the peninsula. The treatise was printed in seven different monasteries in the seventeenth century alone, and its schemata of the one mind and two gates is considered basic doctrine by most, if not all, Korean monastics and Buddhist scholars alike.[87]

The Fourth Stage: Huayan

The last stage and the ultimate apex of the traditional curricular canon was the study of the *Huayan Sutra* (華嚴經).[88] This text is given a special place in the Korean tradition, which is accordingly often understood to be Huayan-Chan. Historically, this sutra was sometimes accompanied in the last stage of the program by two additional Chan collections—the *Jingde Transmission of the Lamp* (*Jingde chuandenglu* 景德傳燈錄)[89] and the *Enlightened Verses* (*Sŏnmun yŏmsong* 禪門拈頌)[90]—but these texts were rarely studied in seminaries in the twentieth century, and are no longer considered to be part of the core traditional curriculum. Nevertheless, these three seem to have been regarded as the highest Buddhist teachings in fourteenth- and fifteenth-century Korea. The Great Code of Administration (*Kyŏngguk-taejŏn* 經國大典) of Chosŏn designated these specific three texts to be recited at the official national sangha examinations: the *Huayan Sutra* by doctrinal monks, and the two collections by Chan monastics.[91]

The lengthy *Huayan Sutra* is commonly understood to be a compilation of various shorter essays, the most well-known of which is the *Ten (Bodhisattva) Stages Sutra* (*Shidijing* 十地經), whose basic contents are also found in the *Śūraṃgama Sutra* of the *Sagyo*. There are two editions of the text: the earlier fifth-century sixty-fascicle compilation, and the seventh-century eighty-fascicle version. Seminary teachers in Korea determine individually which version to use in class. The *Transmission of the Lamp* was written in the early eleventh century and consists of 1,701 biographies of Chan masters, beginning with Śākyamuni himself. It provided monastics with a lineage, a history, and prototypes of enlightenment from which *gongan*s could be extracted. Finally, the *Enlightened Verses* is the first Korean native *gongan* collection, compiled by Chinul's disciple and successor Hyesim (慧心, 1178–1234). It is based on the *Transmission of the Lamp,* with additional cases extracted from the *Huayan, Lotus,* and other sutras. It is rather long, containing 1,463 *gongan* cases supplemented by explanations and poems.

Intertextuality

The Buddhist textual depository is enormous and Buddhist traditions must inevitably pick and choose particular texts to focus on in their liturgies and curricular programs. These choices are what make various Buddhisms distinct from one another. The questions to be asked then are why specific texts were preferred over others by a particular tradition, and what makes these selections stick together as a generally coherent set. We have already examined the way in which Chinul's distinct synthesis of Zongmi's soteriology and Dahui's approach to practice created a unified *Sajip* agenda. In this section, I analyze the main ideologies, metaphors, schemata, and intertextual mutual-referencing that provides the entire traditional Korean monastic curriculum its unified, particular flavor.

Probably the most dominant teaching that runs across most Korean curricular texts is Zongmi's "sudden-enlightenment-followed-by-gradual-cultivation," with its gradualist approach to Chan soteriology. It was commonly promulgated by Zongmi and Chinul, and Miriam Levering found an additional allusion to it in Dahui's *Letters*.[92] Mario Poceski found this same soteriology in the first chapter of the *Ch'imun, Guishan's Admonitions*.[93] Perhaps the most explicit reference to it in the curricular sutras is found in the *Śūraṃgama Sutra*'s statement that "although one is suddenly enlightened to the principle, actual manifestations of things are not suddenly eliminated, but are gradually extinguished."[94] Unsurprisingly, this passage was cited over and over by Zongmi and Chinul, and it is also found in other widespread Chosŏn Buddhist treatises, such as Hyujŏng's *Mirror of Sŏn* (*Sŏn'ga kwigam* 禪家龜鑑).[95] Although I was unable to locate explicit references to this approach in the *Sutra of Perfect Enlightenment,* Zongmi insisted in his commentary to it that it conformed to this same model, and it is his commentary that eventually became the most authoritative way to understand the text.

Robert Buswell explained how the *Huayan Sutra,* too, can easily be reconciled with the schema of "sudden-awakening-followed-by-gradual-cultivation." He elucidated that Chinul depicted the fifty-two stages of the *Huayan* as starting with initial sudden awakening to one's Buddhahood at the beginning of the ten faiths, and only after that gradually progressing through the ten abidings, ten practices, ten transferences, and ten bodhisattva stages, and finally to complete enlightenment.[96]

It is not only that almost all of the curricular texts conform to this model, but perhaps the curricular structure itself may be viewed as symbolizing a similar process. It begins with the *Sajip* texts' emphasis on *huatou* practice to inspire initial awakening, and only later turns to the study of the long gradual path of cultivation as depicted in the *Huayan Sutra*. Note that this process is illustrated yet again in Dahui's (instructive) biography, which depicts his first awakening as inspired by a sermon of a teacher (like a *Ch'imun* text), his second awakening as generated by investigating a *huatou* (as explained in the *Sajip*), and his final awakening as stimulated by reading about the eighth stage of the bodhisattva in the *Huayan Sutra* (as in the last *Taegyo* stage of the curriculum).[97]

The ideological fathers of the entire curriculum are the two *Sajip* authors, Zongmi and Dahui, whose teachings were synthesized by Chinul. Zongmi, in fact, makes his appearance in the curriculum a number of times: his *Preface* is part of the *Sajip,* his unknown *Dharma Collection and Special Practice Record* stands at the center of Chinul's *Excerpts,* his commentary to the *Diamond Sutra* is included in the *Ogahae* collection traditionally studied with the *Diamond Sutra* in Korean seminaries, and his commentary to the *Sutra of Perfect Enlightenment* is also often used in the course. To be sure, the *Sutra of Perfect Enlightenment* seems to have been his favorite sutra, and it is said to have sparked his own initial awakening. He proclaimed that although the *Huayan* is the most exalted sutra, this short text is the best shortcut to get to it.[98] He often borrowed metaphors from the *Śūraṃgama* (fingers and moon) and the *Awakening of Faith* (wind and waves) to illustrate his ideas. In short, the *Sagyo* sutras and the *Huayan* were the sutras most often commented upon and referred to by Zongmi, and perhaps for that reason they have been adopted as a set into the Korean curriculum. Zongmi has been regarded as a patriarch of both the Huayan tradition and of the Heze Chan School, and it is this blend of the sudden Chan and the gradual Huayan approaches that underlies the Korean program.

Like Zongmi, Dahui, too, seems to have embodied a sutra-based textual Chan approach. Miriam Levering has noted that his writings include a great deal of sutra references, which are generally missing from the recorded sayings of other Chan masters, such as Linji and Mazu.[99] In fact, his *Letters* makes generous use not just of any sutra, but particularly of the same set of curricular texts discussed thus far. The largest number of citations found in his essays comes from the *Huayan,* followed by the *Śūraṃgama, Diamond Sutra, Transmission of the Lamp,* and the *Sutra of Perfect Enlightenment.*[100] Aside from the *Letters,* three other essays by Dahui were included in the unabridged *Ch'imun* collection, and as noted earlier, his final awakening was inspired by the *Huayan Sutra.* Evidently, the same limited collection of texts dominated the writings and life experiences of both Zongmi and Dahui.

Chinul often referred to this same body of texts, in particular to the *Huayan Sutra,* to which his second awakening experience is attributed and on which he wrote a short essay.[101] He also often cited the *Sutra of Perfect Enlightenment* and the *Awakening of Faith.* It is Chinul's vision that holds the whole set of texts together. More surprising, perhaps, is the discovery that although Gaofeng's *Chan Essentials*—with its sudden, subitist approach to Chan practice—does reference the sutras far less than the other *Sajip* essays, whenever it does cite from the sutras, it tends to utilize passages from the same *Huayan* and *Śūraṃgama.*[102]

There is some indication that this set of texts was used in tandem in fourteenth-century Chinese Buddhist monasticism as well. A 1338 Pure Rules collection (*Chixiu baizhang qinggui* 勅修百丈淸規) provided a list of sutras to be chanted at special events, a list which parallels the Korean traditional curricular program to a considerable extant, with the only exception being an addition of one sutra. It specifies the *Huayan, Śūraṃgama, Diamond, Sutra of Perfect Enlightenment, Golden Light Sutra,* and the *Lotus*—which, as we shall see, was part of the *Sagyo* before it was replaced by the *Awakening of Faith*—as the core texts to be recited.

In sum, the *Sagyo* and *Huayan* sutras were the favorite texts of the *Sajip* authors, most notably Zongmi and Dahui. They inspired their awakenings, and were frequently commented on and cited by them in order to support their own agenda of a textual, sutra-based, *Huayan*-focused, "sudden-awakening-followed-by-gradual-cultivation" type of Chan. Later monastics would systematize this group of texts into a four-phase curriculum, but it is the founding ideology of Zongmi and Dahui and the sutras they favored that created the particular kind of Buddhism the Korean tradition was destined to become.

Ch'ŏnghak's Curricular Poem

The first and only premodern, in-depth analysis of what came to be known as the traditional monastic curriculum in Korea is found in a poem written by a relatively unknown monk by the name of Ch'ŏnghak (淸學, 1570–1654). Ch'ŏnghak left home at the early age of thirteen and became a monk at the nearby southern monastery of Porimsa (寶林寺). This cluster was a large Buddhist center at the time, mythologized as the first Chan temple on the peninsula. He avoided joining the monk troops fighting against the Japanese invaders in the late sixteenth century, preferring to perform austerities and pray for peace deep in the mountains. He later traveled to study under various masters, and upon his death his disciples buried his remains in a stupa at Porimsa and published a collection of his writings. It is here that we find his curricular poem, rather dryly titled *Sajip–Sagyo–Transmission of the Lamp–Enlightened Verses–Huayan Sutra.*[103] I provide a full translation of this poem below in order to exemplify how the core traditional curricular doctrines—and with them Buddhism as a whole—were understood on the peninsula four centuries ago:[104]

1. Gaofeng's *Chan Essentials*
If you want to know the essential focus of study,
Begin with the Chan mind of heaven and earth.
Like climbing a cliff without worrying about losing your life,
Like piercing through a diamond with no hesitation,
Like a brilliant shortcut that runs against the wake of a boat,
A piercing wisdom like a mosquito biting into an iron bull.

Establishing the three essentials [of faith, rage, and doubt] all together in the numinous tower of mind,
And not wavering even in face of fire or falling stars.

2. Dahui's *Letters*
Why argue about the correct lineage of Chan,
When the imposing sharpness [of Dahui] alone stands out from the crowd?
Not falling for the ten maladies of *huatou* practice[105] and purifying all dreams,
Raising [*huatou*-related] doubt morning, noon, and evening; cleansing your mind,
Understanding through words will make you sink into the underworld,
Investigating the "live word" [of the *huatou*] will get you out of the realm of ghosts.
Not letting in even a tiny fraction of other views,
And you still do not realize that only [Dahui] is the [true Dharma] heir?

3. Zongmi's *Chan Preface*
The entire teachings of the Buddha—
Zongmi reformulated and outlined.
He revealed the functions of the three teachings,[106]
And clarified their interconnectedness and one-taste,
The vow of wisdom overturns prior confusions,
Sitting Chan is a helpful skillful means on the way.
These few chapters open up a great path,
Sympathetically responding to all, they teach in detail.

4. Chinul's *Excerpts*
For those first entering the great wisdom of the Heze garden,
With extensive expertise of the various schools, [Chinul] leveled the road ahead.
Discerning between the hanging Mani jewel itself and the colors of blue and yellow [it manifested],
Holding a copper mirror to clarify [the difference between] essence and functions,
As if suddenly waking up in bed, and the dark dream is destroyed,
[And then continuing with] gradual cultivation and study to achieve good form,

And finally taking hold of the Chan sword, which can cut through frost,
And cutting off all shrubbery of sentiments [obstructing] the road ahead.

5. *Sutra of Perfect Enlightenment:*
[This Sutra tells of] bodhisattvas asking the Buddha about the practices that led him thus far,
And he entirely reveals the ultimate beyond the fleetingness of joy.
Ignorance quietened—this is the nature of true suchness,
Seeds of afflictions extinguished—this is the origin of liberation,
[In which] wisdom and delusion are completely inseparable,
And sentient and non-sentient beings are wonderfully hard to distinguish.
It has already been a long time since the myriad beings achieved Buddhahood,
Lying on a white cloud, complete enlightenment surrounds all!

6. *Diamond Sutra:*
The Buddha has already expounded on the principle entirely,
Why then did the Five Chan Houses[107] have to reiterate it?
The torch of the *Diamond Sutra* sheds light on the three types of emptiness,[108]
In the light of its wisdom the six perfections[109] are completed,
The various manifestations die out, yet it is not the end of manifestation,
The three types of mind[110] all enter [emptiness], yet these minds are not abandoned.
Hence the wisdom-eye that understands emptiness has been cleansed,
How could such saintly blessings be repaid any time soon?

7. *Śūraṃgama Sutra:*
If you wish to know how to overcome the afflictions,
Look through the bright window of the *Śūraṃgama Sutra*.
Evaporating the fog of emotion by searching for the mind in seven places,[111]
Clearing out the murky eyes by analyzing the eight transformations,[112]
The five aggregates[113] transform into the womb of the *Tathāgata,*

The seven elements[114] become a wonderful castle of
enlightenment.
Eliminating delusions and destroying malicious intentions,
Each and every thing brightens the original truth.

8. *Lotus Sutra:*
The ten directions[115] are completely revealed from the white tuft
of hair [between the Buddha's eyebrows],
And by this, men and gods cut through the distinction between
knowing and the objects known.
As [one grasps that] the myriad dharmas are all true: joy is
attained,
[Knowing that] the thousand distinctions are all wonderful is the
beginning of achieving bliss,
Rights and wrongs, causes and effects are all linked to the same
essence,
The worldly and sagely, pure and coarse are one and the same.
The myriad otherworldly Buddhas of the past, present, and
future—
Their teachings are basically the same as the teaching [of
Śākyamuni] on Vulture Peak.

9. *Huayan Sutra:*
The *Huayan Sutra* is the crown of the various teachings,
By all-embracing, the result is awakening, and everything is
linked together naturally.
The one and the many interpenetrate, lighting up a thousand
lights,
Phenomena and principles join together into one hanging moon,
Cultivating the six senses to advance through the ten stages of the
bodhisattva,
Practicing to attain great merit in this full lifetime.
Only by knowing that things do not differ from one another,
One directly attains the body of truth and there is no further need
for Chan!

10. *Transmission of the Lamp:*
The thirty scrolls of the *Transmission of the Lamp* explicate the
origins of the Way,
Detailed stories from previous generations are all included:
King Wu of Liang's questions to Bodhidharma release us from
our shackles,

The second patriarch wipes off our murky eyes with "no-mind,"
The circumstances of the patriarchs illuminate night and day,
Paraphrases from this group of sages clarify heaven and earth.
Leisurely studying these extensive verses and fathoming their gist,
Know that these living beings are all past Buddhas!

11. *Enlightened Verses:*
The Way is already abundant in the flow of the rivers and the lofty mountains,
And who will try to communicate it through words?
Yunmen with a single blow destroys the Thus-come-one,[116]
Linji's *gongan* "on the way"[117] and the "void-ness of Mañjuśrī,"[118]
The numinous dragon of the great seas is hard to catch,
Green Paulownia trees and great phoenixes[119] are hard to assemble.
Knowing that words are all frivolous,
Look to the ends of heaven, after the rains, the peaks appear!

Ch'ŏnghak's poem summarizes for us in a lyrical manner the contents of the curricular texts, and more importantly, brings to light which of the doctrines found within them were considered the most significant. It illustrates how novices going through this curriculum would end up understanding their tradition through the schemata of Gaofeng's "three essentials," Dahui's "ten maladies of *huatou* practice," Zongmi's accommodating attitudes to the various Chan houses, Chinul's "sudden-awakening-followed-by-gradual-cultivation," the original Buddhahood of the *Sutra of Perfect Enlightenment,* the emptiness of the *Diamond Sutra,* the inability to find a constant self in the "seven places," "eight transformations," and "five aggregates" in the *Śūraṃgama,* the equalization of all manifestation as joyful in the *Lotus,* the all-embracing interpenetration of all phenomena and principles and the ten bodhisattva stages of the *Huayan,* the history of the Chan school's patriarchs in the *Transmission of the Lamp,* and finally some *gongan* cases from the *Enlightened Verses.*

This program indeed encapsulates a very comprehensive picture of Mahāyāna Buddhism, but it is perhaps more interesting to examine what it does *not* contain. First, any kind of Vinaya-type literature is missing from this list, which means that the *Ch'imun* was added to the curricular program at a later date. In addition, the *Lotus Sutra* is portrayed in this version of the *Sagyo* and, as we shall soon see, it was replaced by the *Awakening of Faith* only in the eighteenth century. Most importantly, what are generally considered today to be some of the most basic Buddhist doctrines—the four noble truths, the eightfold path, and the twelve-linked conditioned origination schemata—received only peripheral mention, if they were mentioned at all,[120] and were virtually irrelevant for Buddhist monastics going through such a curriculum prior to the mid-twentieth century. It is hard to conceive of a Buddhism today that does not stem from these basic doctrines, and reparation of such "deficiencies" in the traditional curriculum are among the main reasons extensive reforms have been taking place recently in the Chogye Order's education system.

Historical Construction and Deconstruction

Now that we have familiarized ourselves with the list of traditional curricular texts and their central agendas, let us take a closer look at the way these works were gradually assembled to form a set program in the sixteenth and seventeenth centuries. In order to do so, we will make use of two kinds of evidence: first, records of temple woodblock manufacturing, which can direct us toward the texts that were circulating at different periods and in particular localities; and second, biographies of monks from the period, which at times point out the specific texts studied by actual individuals.

There seems to be much truth to J. Z. Smith's statement that canonization is "as much an affair of technology as [it is of] theology."[121] Although research on printing history in Korea is still in its rudimentary stages and there seems to be some inconsistency in the sources, its primary findings are valuable not only for indicating which texts may have been more popular and central in any given time period, but also for pointing out which texts were printed together, and thus technologically canonized, perhaps, as a set curriculum in particular locations. In general, it seems that Huayan-related publications were most popular during the Koryŏ period, and Chan text printing gained momentum in the early Chosŏn (fifteenth to seventeenth centuries).[122] In fact, there seems to have been a remarkable textual revival of Chan literature at the same time in neighboring China, and the new Korean interest in Chan publications should be understood within this broader East Asian context.[123] To be sure, the *Lotus Sutra* has continued to be the most frequently printed Buddhist work in Korea between the fifteenth and seventeenth centuries. Still, it is possible to detect a gradual increase in the publication of the traditional set of curriculum texts during the course of this period. Table 1 illustrates the printing frequency of selected Buddhist texts in the early Chosŏn Dynasty.

As indicated by table 1, aside from the *Lotus* and the *Diamond* sutras, the most widely printed Buddhist work in the fourteenth and fifteenth centuries was the *Six Sutras Collection* (*Yukkyŏng happu* 六經合部), which consisted of the *Diamond Sutra,* a chapter from the *Huayan Sutra* on Samatabhadra Bodhisattva's vow (*Puxian xingyuan pin* 普賢行願品), the *Śūraṃgama Dhāraṇī* (*Lengyan shenzhou* 楞嚴神咒), the *Amitābha Sutra* (*Amituo jing* 阿彌陀經), Avalokiteśvara's chapter of the *Lotus Sutra* (*Guanshiyin pusa pumen pin* 觀世音菩薩普門品), and a confession ritual text for Avalokiteśvara (K.

Table 1 Most Frequently Printed Texts in Early Chosŏn

Text	14th–15th Centuries	16th Century	17th Century
Lotus Sutra	9	35	68
Diamond Sutra	9	11	11
Śūraṃgama Sutra	4	3	7
Sutra of Perfect Enlightenment	–	2	5
Awakening of Faith in Mahāyāna	–	1	7
Huayan Sutra	?	1	?
Zongmi's *Chan Preface*	1	6	12
Chinul's *Excerpts*	1	8	12
Dahui's *Letters*	–	7	10
Gaofeng's *Chan Essentials*	–	8	10
Ch'imun	–	3	5
Enlightened Verses	–	4	–
Ch'obalsim	–	8	–
Mengshan Treatises	–	20	3
Hyujŏng's Treatises	–	–	18
Sutra on the Profound Kindness of Parents[a] (大報父母恩重經)	4	17	8
The Six Sutras Collection (六經合部)	6	–	–
Platform Sutra	1	3	–
Suryukchae Ritual Texts[b]	–	28	8
The Four Confucian Books (四書)	8	12	60

Source: Data for this table was extracted from information found in: Son, "16–17 segi Pulgyo chŏngch'aek kwa Pulgyogye ŭi tonghyang," and "16 segi Chosŏn ŭi Pulsŏ kanhaeng."

a The *Sutra on the Profound Kindness of Parents* is a seventh-century Chinese apocrypha, which seems to have been popular in China as well. Over fifty copies were discovered in Dunhuang. It focuses on the debt of sons to their loving mothers, and Zongmi quoted large portions from it in his writings. For a detailed analysis see Alan Cole, *Mothers and Sons in Chinese Buddhism,* chapter 7.

b The *Suryukchae* (水陸齋, Water and Land Ritual) is a ritual intended to ease calamities by guiding departed souls to the land of bliss (with the rationale that suffering often sprang from dejected souls). It was widely practiced in early Chosŏn, but was discontinued in the sixteenth century and replaced by a Confucian parallel rite to placate the souls of the un-mourned. It was re-established in modern Korea. See Hee-sook Nam and Inga Diederich, "Publications of Buddhist Literary Texts: The Publication and Popularization of Mantra Collections and Buddhist Ritual Texts in the Late Chosŏn Dynasty," 20–21; Henrik Sorensen, "Esoteric Buddhism Under the Chosŏn," 616–658.

Kwanseŭm posal yemun 觀世音菩薩禮文). This list is obviously different from the above curriculum, but it does include parts of the *Diamond, Śūraṃgama,* and *Huayan* sutras, which stand at the center of the program to come. Perhaps this was the most popular Buddhist textual program (or the "ritual canon") of fifteenth-century Korea.

Up until the early sixteenth century, most Buddhist woodblock manufacturing on the peninsula was organized and controlled by the government. Yet, with the increasing tendency of the central Chosŏn administration to marginalize Buddhism,[124] publications were gradually relegated to private enterprises taken up by individual monasteries. Ironically, cutting off ties with the central government did not curb Buddhist textual production but rather seems to have stimulated printing on a larger scale than ever before. Whereas in the fifteenth century, woodblock manufacturing for eighty-four Buddhist texts was sponsored by the government (mainly during the reign of King Sejo, 1455–1468) and woodblocks for sixty-four texts were made in individual temples; over three hundred texts were privately published in monasteries later in the sixteenth and in the seventeenth centuries.[125]

Indeed, rather than hamper Buddhist textual production, privatization seems to have brought a great increase in woodblock manufacturing, and this is especially true in regard to Chan treatise publications. Still, according to the available printing records, the most popular Chan treatises in sixteenth-century Korea were not authored by any of the *Sajip* writers, but by another Chinese monastic by the name of Mengshan Deyi (蒙山德異, 1232–1308).[126] Mengshan was a contemporary of Gaofeng who attracted the attention of numerous Korean students, but his influence withered after it was Gaofeng, and not he, who received official Linji transmission in 1288.[127] In fact, Son Sŏng-p'il explained that Mengshan was especially popular in Korea among monastics of Naong's (懶翁, 1320–1376) lineage, which during the sixteenth century, and especially after the Japanese invasion (1592–1598), gradually lost favor to the T'aego-Hyujŏng lineage, which led the fighting efforts.[128] Therefore, as can be easily traced from table 1, Hyujŏng's treatises and the *Sajip* texts replaced Mengshan as the most widely published Chan texts in the seventeenth century. Interestingly, however, Mengshan was not completely forgotten in Korean Buddhist education circles. His essays are still studied, not in the regular monastic seminaries, but as a part of the new Elementary Chan Hall curriculum for novices.[129]

As we have seen, the *Ch'imun* was not mentioned in Ch'ŏnghak's poem, and there is very little evidence that it was used in the sixteenth century. One exception to that is the monastery of Ansimsa (安心寺), which in 1575–1576 published not only three of the *Sajip* texts in tandem (the *Letters, Excerpts,* and *Chan Essentials*), but also the *Ch'imun, Diamond Sutra,* and *Sutra of Perfect Enlightenment*.[130] Another temple, Hwaamsa (花岩寺)—

located only a few hours' walk from Ansimsa on the same mountain, called Kosan (高山)—published two *Sagyo* texts along with the *Śūraṃgama* and *Lotus* sutras, possibly making this mountain the first stronghold of the traditional curriculum. In addition, there is evidence that Hyujŏng—perhaps the most prominent monastic figure of the sixteenth century, whose association with the *Sajip* texts was already pointed out above—made use of all the *Sagyo* texts, though not exclusively. Records illustrate that Hyujŏng taught the Ten Basic Sutras and Treatises (*Sippon kyŏngnon* 十本經論), which included texts that, in time, became part of the fixed curriculum (*Diamond, Śūraṃgama, Huayan, Sutra of Perfect Enlightenment, Lotus, Enlightened Verses, Transmission of the Lamp*), but also other texts, such as the *Vimalakīrti Sutra*.[131]

The popularity of the traditional curricular texts grew in the seventeenth century. At least four different monasteries manufactured woodblocks for the four *Sajip* treatises together as a set, often in tandem with at least some of the curricular sutras. One of these projects, for instance, was initiated by a rather unknown monk by the name of Hyesun (惠淳), who led an eight-year project in Yongboksa between 1628 and 1636, manufacturing woodblocks for twenty-six Buddhist texts, including not only the entire *Sajip* and *Sagyo*, but also the *Admonitions to Beginners, Enlightened Verses,* and several works by Hyujŏng.[132] The preface to his 1628 edition of the *Chan Essentials* explains that Hyesun instigated the project in order to restore peace to the peninsula following the Japanese invasions of the late sixteenth century, and it is unclear whether he ever intended to use the texts for educating novices. Nonetheless, we do have more explicit records showing that Ch'ŏnghak—the author of the curricular poem presented above—and four additional monastics, utilized, for pedagogical purposes, the entire program of the *Sajip, Sagyo* (with the *Lotus Sutra* instead of the *Awakening of Faith*), and *Huayan,* along with the *Transmission of the Lamp* and *Enlightened Verses* collections, though admittedly not always in the same order of study.[133] One of Hyujŏng's disciples, Ŏn'gi (彥機, 1581–1644), for example, is said to have reversed the order of study: beginning with the *Huayan,* progressing to the *Sagyo* sutras, and culminating with the *Sajip* treatises at the end.[134]

It has been pointed out that the Korean Neo-Confucian curriculum was also assembled in the sixteenth and seventeenth centuries and may have influenced Buddhists to create a parallel system.[135] Private Confucian academies (*sŏwŏn* 書院) began to proliferate in sixteenth-century Korea, and, as pointed out by Lee Jong-su, the Buddhist and Confucian systems were comparable both in the length of the programs (Buddhists ten to twelve years; Confucians thirteen to fifteen years) and in the general gradual progress from more elementary schooling to higher studies.[136] This may be so, but it is not much, and I believe a more interesting mimesis can be detected. The Korean Neo-Confucian curriculum was based on Zhu Xi's model, which progressed from the

Four Books (*Sishu* 四書)—believed to have been either written or edited by the ancient patriarchs—and into the Five Classics, or five *jings* (*Wujing* 五經). In a similar way, the core of the Korean Buddhist curriculum was fashioned to begin with a collection of four treatises written by selected patriarchs, followed by five nominated sutras—five *jings*. In other words, it seems that the four treatises of the *Sajip* mirrored the Confucian Four Books, and the five sutras (*jing*) of the *Sagyo* and *Huayan* replicated the Confucian Five Classics (*jing*). Perhaps the inclusion of the *Ch'imun* at the beginning of the Buddhist program was similarly influenced by the use of Zhu Xi's *Elementary Learning* (*Xiaoxue* 小學) as the preparatory text in the Confucian programs—both being preliminary collections of short essays (in the case of *Ch'imun*) or quotations (in the case of the *Elementary Learning*) from the patriarchs of their respective traditions. Zhu Xi's impact in Korea, thus, seems to have stretched far beyond the domain of Confucian pedagogy, providing the basic frameworks for the construction of the Buddhist monastic curriculum as well.

As political circumstances altered in eighteenth- and nineteenth-century Chosŏn, we find a decrease in the number of Buddhist publications alongside a boom in Confucian book printings.[137] Still, it is possible to locate a few allusions to the monastic curriculum in the biographies of monks from the period. Apart from an increased use of the *Ch'imun*, the *Awakening of Faith* replaced the *Lotus* in the *Sagyo* set in some eighteenth-century monastic biographies. Yet, it is only from the nineteenth century that all *Sagyo* records contained the *Awakening of Faith* instead of the *Lotus*.[138] The reason for this curious shift in the *Sagyo* is not entirely clear, but it may have something to do with the stronger referential affiliation of the *Awakening of Faith* with Zongmi and Chinul.

It is important to emphasize that this was by no means the sole Korean Buddhist curriculum in existence before the twentieth century. Contrary to what seems to be the general understanding in Korean Buddhist circles, although this program has its roots in the sixteenth and seventeenth centuries, it had not been fixed and popularized nationwide before the modern period. An analysis of the education-related biographical information of over 130 monastics of the late Chosŏn period illustrates that very few—12 to be exact—are recorded to have been involved in the study or teaching of, at a minimum, the *Sajip, Sagyo,* and *Huayan* scriptures as a set.[139] Even as late as the nineteenth century, only five of the fifty monks referenced in the list had undergone a program that involved both the *Sajip* and the *Sagyo*. Other curricular programs existed as well. The prolific Kŭngsŏn (亘璇, 1767–1852), for example, rejected the literary-based Chan of the Heze school and promoted a shorter sudden-Chan-focused curriculum, progressing through the *Diamond* and *Platform* sutras alongside the *Chan Essentials* and *Enlightened Verses*.[140] Records show that the early-nineteenth-century monk Hyejŭp (惠楫, 1791–

1858) began his studies with the *Ch'imun* and the *Sajip* at the age of nineteen, but then, instead of progressing to the fourfold *Sagyo* sutras, moved on to study the so-called Fivefold Teachings (*Ogyo* 五教), which are generally depicted as Vinaya, Nirvana, Buddha nature, Huayan, and Yogācāra, but may also refer to a different list of sutras.[141]

The next chapter will demonstrate that it was actually twentieth-century Korean Buddhist scholars who labeled our specific program the traditional Korean monastic curriculum, and who may thus be responsible for the institutionalization and popularization of this model. It was still later—toward the end of the twentieth century—that this curriculum finally became the mandatory educational program for all Korean Buddhist novices, yet, it was rapidly and utterly revised at the start of the new millennium.

2

Monastic Education in Twentieth-Century Korea

TRADITIONS ARE OFTEN FASHIONED IN RETROSPECT. THIS well-worn insight of Hobsbawm and Ranger, found in their influential book *The Invention of Tradition,* seems to have had a lesser-known precedent in the writings of Tang Chinese scholar Liu Zhiji (661–721), who remarked over 1,300 years ago that "the past is constructed by us" (自我作古).[1] Aptly restated by Stuart Chandler, "modernity neither replaces nor supersedes tradition; it creates a new rendition of it."[2] It is thus perhaps not very surprising to discover that, ironically, the sacralization of the "traditional" Korean curriculum seems to have been made possible by the new "modern" history writing of the early twentieth century. Pioneering Korean Buddhist historians, most notably Yi Nŭnghwa (1869–1943), Kim Yŏngsu (1884–1967), and Kwŏn Sangno (1879–1965), were the first to investigate the origins of the curriculum studied in their day. Influenced mainly by Japanese prototypes of modern Buddhist historiography—evincing a sort of religious Stockholm syndrome[3]—their projects involved attempts to systematize a national Chan lineage, and they each pointed out different historical figures as central in the construction of the traditional Korean national curriculum.[4] Their projects were essentially anachronistic, focusing on the history of the present rather than on the present of history. Their narratives were not free of political agenda; and motivated by nationalistic attempts to create a unified Buddhist history for Korea, they gave authority to a particular curriculum, rather than analyzed the pluralities of the past.

Both Yi Nŭnghwa and Kwŏn Sangno wrote their histories under the auspices of Ch'oe Namsŏn (1890–1957), who had spent time studying translations of Western philosophical works at Waseda University in Japan and was stimulated to find similar greatness in Korean Buddhist philosophy upon his return to the peninsula.[5] Ch'oe's own publishing house printed Yi Nŭnghwa's encyclopedic *History of Korean Buddhism* (*Chosŏn Pulgyo t'ongsa* 朝鮮佛敎

通史) in 1918. This book presented two slightly different curricular models, one involving a ten-year program, and the other an eleven-year syllabus. This schema has become the orthodox understanding of the national, traditional, monastic curriculum, and has been quoted and requoted in Korean Buddhist circles ever since. It is presented in full in table 2.

Yi, a French language teacher and an enthusiastic lay Buddhist researcher who authored and edited several books and magazines, has been called the "father of modern Korean Buddhist Studies." Unfortunately, as was common practice at the time, Yi often neglected to provide references and textual evidence for his claims, and scholars have argued that his historical research on the traditional curriculum consisted mainly of sending letters to contemporary monastic leaders at Hwaŏmsa and Sŏnamsa to ask them about it.[6] It is thus not impossible that Yi's curricular models reflect the ones used at these temples in the early twentieth century more accurately than they do any earlier historical models. To be sure, both sketches indicate that the core *Sajip, Sagyo,* and *Taegyo* courses were rather common at the time. Nevertheless, the *Ch'imun* was included only in the eleven-year model, while the ten-year program found the shorter *Ch'obalsim* collection sufficient for admonishing beginners. Yi's longer curricular model also offered a few other idiosyncrasies, such as the inclusion of the study of the *Precious Admonitions to the Gray-Robed Community* as well as both the *Lotus Sutra* and Hyujŏng's *Mirror of Sŏn* in the last stage of the program.

Modernity often involves conflicting forces and propensities. It has the tendency to simultaneously play on the rhetoric of the "long-standing" and the "traditional," as well as on that of the "novel" and "innovative." This chapter explores the ways in which modern dialectic strategies of both preservation and renewal—endurance and reform—made their mark on Buddhist education in twentieth-century Korea. On the one hand, the traditional curriculum (which now had a history and a name) was salvaged by being rationalized to focus on institutions rather than on charismatic teachers, and systematized through formal decrees and regulations to ensure its ongoing survival. By the end of the twentieth century, the traditional program had gained absolute authority, having been codified in law as the mandatory precondition for receiving the full precepts and formally becoming a Chogye-Order-affiliated monastic. On the other hand, the rhetoric of innovative modernity was used by several twentieth-century Korean Buddhists in their attempts to reformulate the traditional curriculum, to "match it to the changing times," and to create new types of Buddhist educational institutions. The establishment of the first female monastic seminaries, as well as the construction of various Buddhist colleges in the mid-twentieth century, could be viewed in this context. These trends will provide the background for the far-reaching curricular reforms of the twenty-first century, which will be explored in subsequent chapters.

Table 2 Yi Nŭnghwa's Traditional Curricular Models

Course	10-Year System		11-Year System	
Novice (*Sami-kwa* 沙彌科)	One year	1. Ten novice precepts 2. Chanting ritual texts 3. *Heart Sutra* 4. *Ch'obalsim*	Three years	1. Ten novice precepts 2. Chanting ritual texts 3. *Heart Sutra* 4. *Ch'obalsim* 5. *Novice Precepts and Decorum*[a] 6. *Ch'imun* 7. *Precious Admonitions to the Gray-Robed Community*
Fourfold Treatise Collection (*Sajip-kwa* 四集科)	Two years	1. Zongmi's *Chan Preface* 2. Dahui's *Letters* 3. Chinul's *Excerpts* 4. Gaofeng's *Chan Essentials*	Two years	1. Zongmi's *Chan Preface* 2. Dahui's *Letters* 3. Chinul's *Excerpts* 4. Gaofeng's *Chan Essentials*
Four Sutras (*Sagyo-kwa* 四敎科)	Four years	1. *Śūraṃgama Sutra* 2. *Awakening of Faith* 3. *Diamond Sutra* 4. *Sutra of Perfect Enlightenment*	2.5 years	1. *Śūraṃgama Sutra* 2. *Awakening of Faith* 3. *Diamond Sutra* 4. *Sutra of Perfect Enlightenment*
High Teachings (*Taegyo-kwa* 大敎科)	Three years	1. *Huayan Sutra* 2. *Enlightened Verses* 3. *Transmission of the Lamp*	3.5 years	1. *Huayan Sutra* 2. *Enlightened Verses* 3. *Transmission of the Lamp* 4. *Ten-Stages Treatise* (*Shidi lun* 十地論) 5. Hyujŏng's *Mirror of Sŏn* 6. *Lotus Sutra*
Optional (*Suŭi-kwa* 隨意科)	Four or more years of additional specialized study			

Source: Chongmuk, "Ch'ongnim ŭi chindan, naagal panghyang: Haein ch'ongnim chungsim ŭro," 220.

a The *Novice Precepts and Decorum* (*Shami luyi* 沙彌律儀) is a short text said to have been compiled in sixteenth-century Ming by Lianchi (蓮池, 1536–1615). It includes both the ten *Śrāmaṇera* novice precepts as well as 284 minor rules of decorum for communal monastic living. The novice precepts consist of the basic five (lay) precepts (not to kill, steal, be involved in licentious acts, lie, and drink) supplemented by additional rules against adornment with flowers and perfumes, dance, songs and entertainment, sleeping on high and broad seats/beds, eating between meals, and handling gold and silver.

Seminary Education in Colonial Korea

Han Yong-un (韓龍雲, 1879–1944) has certainly become the most renowned and studied colonial-era Korean Buddhist modernizer. In his 1913 classic, *On the Reformation of Korean Buddhism* (*Chosŏn Pulgyo yusillon* 朝鮮佛教維新論), he lamented the fact that monks in his day focused solely on studying short commentaries and the sayings of the patriarchs, perhaps referring to the *Ch'imun* and *Sajip* collections. He called for addressing three pressing needs in the education of the sangha: first, enriching the syllabus with general knowledge (*pot'ong-hak* 普通學) as a basis for later specialization; second, pedagogical reforms (*sabŏm-hak* 師範學) and the fostering of quality teachers; and third, sending monks to study abroad in India, China, Europe, and the United States.[7] Reforms in these three areas were indeed soon pursued.

The importance of supplementing Buddhist curricula with general secular subjects—such as science, philosophy, literature, and languages—in order to create more capable missionaries, was highlighted not only by Han Yong-un, but also by other early-modern Korean reformers, such as Pak Hanyŏng (1870–1948) and the previously mentioned Kwŏn Sangno.[8] In fact, modernist reformers in Japan and China at the time were also promoting a general education for their respective sanghas. Taixu's new Chinese Buddhist seminaries of the 1920s, for example, based their curricula on Japanese Buddhist sectarian colleges, and offered courses in general history, geography, the Japanese language, and even psychology.[9] In Korea, as early as the years 1906–1910, twenty modern primary schools (*pot'ong hakkyo* 普通學校) were established in various mountain monasteries throughout the country. These schools offered mixed classes for both monastic and lay youngsters and put together four-year curricula consisting of Buddhist doctrine, Korean language, Chinese characters, math, science, handicrafts, music, and perhaps the most modern subject of them all—sports.[10] This was all rather new, since unlike in Southeast Asia, where Buddhist temples had long functioned as primary schools for village children, there is no evidence of Korean monasteries' involvement in nonreligious primary schooling prior to the twentieth century.[11]

In 1911, the Japanese promulgated the infamous Temple Ordinance. This set of regulations is usually portrayed as an attempt to place Korean Buddhism under Japanese control—which it partially was—yet it could also be viewed as the first modern bureaucratization of Buddhism on the peninsula. Through it, a unified thirty-head-temples system was set up, and the committee of abbots of these thirty temples (Ponsan chuji hoeŭi 本山住持會議) became the de facto frontrunners of Korean Buddhism, leading discussions on management and educational reforms. It was this committee that in 1915 established a new graded education system based on the abovementioned monastic primary schools, supplemented with regional seminaries (chibang hangnim 地方學林) in the mountain monasteries, as well as with higher education in a Central Seminary in Seoul (Chungang hangnim 中央學林).[12] While monastic primary schools focused on general secular subjects, the regional seminaries offered a peculiar, three-year curriculum that rearranged the *Sajip* and *Sagyo* texts and supplemented them with language, history, sports, and introductions to the canonical *Dharmaguptaka Vinaya* and *Brahma Net Sutra*.[13] The regional seminary established in Pŏmŏsa in 1916, for example, taught introductions to the formal Vinaya, *Transmission of the Lamp,* the *Preface* and *Letters,* the *Diamond Sutra,* and the *Awakening of Faith,* as well as Korean grammar, Japanese history, and the history of the Korean Three Kingdoms period, all in the first year. The second year was devoted to the *Excerpts,* the *Chan Essentials,* the *Śūraṃgama Sutra,* and the history of the Koryŏ Dynasty, while third-year students studied the *Sutra of Perfect Enlightenment,* the *Laṅkāvatāra,* and the history of the Chosŏn Dynasty.[14] The core *Sajip* and *Sagyo* texts were all there, but were studied in a different order and were supplemented by various history courses and a new, rudimentary Vinaya unit.

The regional seminaries were meant to replace the earlier, traditional monastic seminaries, which were called *kangdang* (講堂) at the time. Forty-seven *kangdang* existed in 1913 but only twenty-five remained in 1917 after nearly half were converted into regional seminaries. Nevertheless, the earlier institutions maintained their popularity, and 542 students are said to have studied in these *kangdang* in 1917, compared to only 290 students who were enrolled in monastic primary schools, and only 222 who attended the formal regional seminaries.[15] Interestingly, the largest monastic seminaries of the early twentieth century were not located in the places those familiar with Korean Buddhism today would expect them to be found. To be sure, the largest seminary seems to have been T'ongdosa—still a central monastic institution today—which had fifty-eight students in 1918. Other early-twentieth-century popular monastic seminaries, however, have long gone out of fashion—Kŏnpongsa attracted fifty-seven students, Kŭmyongsa fifty-four, and Yujŏmsa forty-six—all practically disappearing from the scene by mid-century. Haeinsa, perhaps the most dominant monastery in the second half of the twentieth century, housed only five monastic students in 1918.[16]

This new, three-level education system did not last long. Partly due to financial difficulties and partly related to traditionalist anti-reform (or, according to orthodox Chogye Order history, "less-Japanese-influenced") counter-revolutionist sangha members, monasteries returned to their individual *kangdang* models in the late 1920s.[17] By 1937, there were 32 such monastic seminaries in the country teaching an overall number of 646 students, the largest located in Pusan's Pŏmŏsa.[18] Their curricula, however, seem to have been anything but systematized and unified. Evidence is scant, but the available data suggests that although the traditional curricular texts stood at the center of seminary education in colonial times, many, if not most seminaries, hosted teachers teaching only some of these texts, and very few monks, if any, went through the exact order of study as depicted by Yi Nŭnghwa above. Hwarang, for instance, tells the story of a particular early-twentieth-century monk who began his education in 1913 at the large Pŏmŏsa seminary, studying the *Śūraṃgama, Enlightened Verses, Transmission of the Lamp,* and the *Brahma Net Sutra* for a year, before moving to a different monastery to study the *Sagyo* texts for two years. He finally returned to Pŏmŏsa to study the *Huayan Sutra* for three years.[19] Note that the *Sajip* treatises were not part of this curriculum, and that the Chan anthologies were moved to the early stages of the program. This particular monk's education lasted for six years, and there is evidence that the T'ongdosa curriculum of the 1930s lasted seven years. It had no *Ch'imun* courses, but began with two years of *Sajip,* continued with three years of *Sagyo,* and ended with two years of *Huayan* studies. Both of these examples illustrate that at least some of the seminaries offered programs that were much shorter than the ones depicted in Yi Nŭnghwa's history.[20]

In the year 2000, an interview with Pŏmnyong, perhaps the only living monk who had studied in seminaries during the colonial period, was published by the Chogye Order.[21] In it, he recalled beginning his seminary education in Yujŏmsa in the mid-1930s, where he studied parts of the *Ch'imun* and *Ch'obalsim,* as well as Dahui's *Letters,* for about a year. There were over thirty students in the seminary at the time, which made it a comparatively large center of learning, yet there were almost no books available, and study consisted simply of copying the texts from the wood-engraved plates available on-site and attempting to memorize them. There were no formal classes, and two to three days a week students simply copied a page of text and attempted to memorize it. Pŏmnyong humorously reminisced that only one in ten succeeded in actually doing so. In any case, after less than a year of undergoing this kind of study, he traveled to the seminary of Sangwŏnsa and studied the *Diamond Sutra* with the *Ogahae* commentarial collection, as well as Chinul's *Excerpts.* This ended his formal textual education; he then went to sit in a Chan Hall.

Although this fascinating memoir is only the story of a single monk, it offers a highly revealing window to the realities of seminaries in the early twentieth century. Unlike the curricular histories described above that recount formal plans and policies, this individual account exposes a much humbler reality in which students simply had to make do with reading and copying the texts available in no particular order and with no unified time frame. We can probably deduce from this that monastic education prior to the twentieth century was often even more sporadic and unsystematic.

Proposals for monastic seminary curricular reforms continued to be issued throughout the 1930s, though none of them were actualized. In the March 1932 issue of the magazine *Pulgyo*, a monk by the name of Ch'ŏlun voiced a critique of the study of the "difficult" *Sajip* treatises at the beginning of the curriculum, and offered instead a program that would start with the *Ch'obalsim, Ch'imun,* and other disciplinary treatises, such as the *42-Section Sutra* (*Sishierzhang jing* 四十二章經)[22] and the *Bequeathed Teachings Sutra* (*Yijiao jing* 遺教經)[23]; then proceed to the study of various commentaries on the *Sagyo* sutras; and finally end with reading the more difficult *Huayan, Enlightened Verses, Abhidharmakośa,* and the *Sajip* texts of the *Letters* and the *Preface*.[24]

A more extreme seminary reform proposal was issued in the 1930s by the Scholarly Association of Korean Buddhism (Chosŏn Pulgyo hagin taehoe 朝鮮佛教學人大會), which included a number of Korean monastics who had returned from studying in Japanese universities and were very much influenced by the modern Buddhist Studies they encountered there.[25] These reformers proposed not only supplementing the monastic seminary with general history, math, science, and language courses, but also a complete reformation of the Buddhist part of the program. Instead of focusing on the learning of the treatises written by the patriarchs—the *Ch'imun, Sajip,* and commentaries on the sutras—they suggested the study of general introductions to various Buddhist traditions. Following modern Japanese scholarly trends and in absolute opposition to the way Buddhism was historically studied by monastics in East Asia, these reformers disregarded commentaries and treatises and called for an almost Protestant return to the real word of Buddha *Śākyamuni* as manifested in the sutras.[26] Their comprehensive curriculum of general introductions included, for the first time, classes on early Buddhism and the *Jātakas,* as well as survey courses on the teachings of Tiantai and Yogācāra Buddhism. Despite the fact that this curriculum proposal was never put into practice, it is worth reproducing it in full here, even if only as a premonition for the comprehensive reforms that would take place almost a century later, in early-twenty-first-century Korea. The proposal is presented in table 3.

The discussion thus far has been related to Han Yong-un's first proposition, which was the need to supplement sangha education with general secular knowledge. Han's second suggestion, the need to improve the quality of teaching, will be addressed in the next section, but before that, some words must be said about his last reform proposal: sending monastics to study abroad. At least 360 monastics left Korea to study abroad during the 35 years of colonial rule.[27] Most, of course, went to Japan, which was not only close geographically and linguistically, but also provided increasing opportunities for travel in colonial times. In fact, it is estimated that there were over 200,000 Korean university students in Japan between the years 1919 and 1942, and Buddhist monastics

able 3 The Scholarly Association of Korean Buddhism's 1930s Curricular Reform Proposal

First year	1. Buddhist Vinaya 2. *Jātakas* 3. Buddhist Treatises 4. The Essentials of the *Śūraṃgama* 5. Early Buddhism 6. History of Buddhism in Korea 7. Mantras and Rituals	8. Korean and Chinese Characters Composition 9. Japanese Reading and Writing 10. English	11. History and Geography of Korea 12. Calculation 13. General Science 14. Music 15. Sports
Second year	1. Understanding the Rules and Ethics of the Order 2. The Essentials of the *Huayan Sutra* 3. Buddhist Treatises 4. The Essentials of the *Diamond Sutra* 5. The Essentials of the *Awakening of Faith* 6. History of Indian Buddhism 7. Mantras and Rituals	8. Korean and Chinese Characters Composition 9. Japanese Reading and Writing 10. English	11. Japanese History and Geography 12. Algebra 13. General Science 14. Music 15. Sports
Third year	1. The Order and Social Ethics 2. The Essentials of the *Huayan Sutra* 3. The Essentials of the Major Buddhist Schools 4. The Essentials of the *Abhidharmakośa* 5. The Essentials of Tiantai 6. History of Chinese Buddhism	7. Korean and Chinese Characters Composition	8. Western History and World Geography 9. Geometry 10. General Science 11. Music 12. Sports
Fourth year	1. The Order and Social Ethics 2. The Essentials of Chan 3. The Essentials of the Major Buddhist Schools 4. The Essentials of Yogācāra 5. Buddhist Research Methods 6. History of Japanese Buddhism	7. Korean and Chinese Characters Composition 8. Japanese Reading and Writing 9. English	10. Western History and World Geography 11. Geometry 12. Agriculture 13. Music 14. Sports

Source: Kim Kwang-sik, "1930 yŏndae Pulgyogye ŭi kangwŏn chedo kaesŏn munje."

only constituted a small portion of this general trend. Eleven Korean monastics also left to study in China during that time, and two traveled all the way to Europe. Kim Pŏp-in (1899–1964) was one of the few monks who participated in the March First Independence Movement of 1919 before leaving to study philosophy in Paris in the 1920s, and Paek Sŏng-uk (1897–1981) received a PhD in Buddhist Studies from the University of Würzburg in Germany in 1924.[28] In Japan, the most popular institution among Korean monastic students was Komazawa of the Sōtō School, but some studied in other sectarian establishments, as well as in general non-Buddhist universities. Returning home after graduation, many monastics who left the peninsula as students of Buddhism returned as scholars of Buddhist Studies, reinterpreting their tradition through new, foreign hermeneutical lenses.[29]

At first, monastic leaders were excited to send as many of their disciples as they could to study in the "modern world," and major monasteries seem to have competed in trying to dispatch as many of their monks abroad as they could. Yet, by the 1930s there was much disillusionment. Some of the monastics who left ended up following Japanese Buddhist customs and marrying; others studied subjects unrelated to Buddhism and used this education to enhance their material status and to obtain a secular job; and some disrobed after graduation.[30] Still others returned with antagonistic attitudes toward the old-fashioned, "authoritarian," ignorant abbots who supported their study abroad in the first place.[31]

Attempting to address these issues, the abbots of the large monastic complexes of T'ongdosa, Pŏmŏsa, and Haeinsa met in 1937 and stipulated that all prospective study-abroad students should be stable graduates of the *Taegyo* course who have undergone several retreats, and should be obligated to send progress reports and hold a temple position for at least three to five years upon return. Plans aside, since most monastics pursued their foreign educations using their own economic means, many felt no responsibility toward their home institutions. Still, some did turn out to be the future leaders of Korean Buddhism, and their experiences in Japan undoubtedly shaped their perspectives on the way Buddhism should be practiced and studied back home. While away, they had been introduced to a wider variety of Buddhist traditions, and it is interesting to see how, beginning in the 1920s, after the first few monastics started returning from their studies in Japan, Korean Buddhist magazines—which had previously tended to focus on Chan—published an increasing number of articles dealing with other Buddhist doctrines popular in greater East Asia at the time, such as Abhidharma philosophy.[32] In the second half of the twentieth century, the number of Korean monastics studying abroad decreased drastically, but the Chogye Order today still invests some of its resources in fellowships to enable capable monastics to pursue graduate work in foreign countries.[33]

Early Initiatives of Buddhist Higher Education

Efforts were also made from the very beginning of the twentieth century to create a unified, central, modern Buddhist Studies institution of higher education, with the goal of nurturing specialists, monastic seminary teachers, and propagators.[34] The Myŏngjin School (明進)—its name alluding to new popular attitudes of progress and civilization—was the first of such pioneering institutions. The school was opened in 1906 in Seoul's Wŏnhŭngsa, inspired by the eight hundred or so Protestant missionary private schools that were proliferating in Korea at the time, as well as by Japanese Buddhist sectarian universities, first founded in the 1880s.[35] It was initiated by Yi Po-dam (b. 1859) and Yun Ch'i-ho (1864–1945), the latter being the first Korean to study in the United States, attending Emory University in the late nineteenth century.[36] Historian Yi Nŭnghwa was one of the lecturers at the school. The Japanese Pure Land (Jōdo) School, which was highly active both in Korea and in China from the late nineteenth century, sponsored this small institution.[37] Nevertheless, although Jōdo's *Amidism* was proclaimed as its doctrinal basis, the Myŏngjin School's curriculum included classes on a variety of Buddhist themes, as well as a selection of modern "general knowledge" courses in history, geography, science, and even law.[38] Its two-year program is detailed in table 4.

As table 4 illustrates, although the three Pure Land sutras were taught in the first year of the program, the Buddhist portion of the curriculum was quite comprehensive. The *Brahma Net Sutra* and the canonical *Dharmaguptaka Vinaya* were added to a broad Mahāyāna curriculum of Tiantai, Huayan, and mostly Chan-related sutras and treatises. Law and land-measurement skills were taught in order to help monks protect their monastic lands from governmental encroachment. The school accepted both monastics and laypeople, and for that reason, as well as for its association with the Japanese, it seems to have been rather controversial from the very start. Conservative sangha members protested the use of the new central Seoul temple of Wŏnhŭngsa for the school, and a monk by the name of Na Ch'ŏng-ho went so far as to establish a rival institution at Pongŭnsa.[39] Nevertheless, the first eleven students graduated in 1908, among them prominent modernist figures, such as the abovementioned Han Yong-un and Kwŏn Sangno, Independence Movement activist Yi Chong-uk, and An Chin-ho, who authored the abridged *Ch'imun* used in seminaries today.

In 1909, the school came under the direction of Yi Hoegwang (1862–1933), who was later condemned for attempting to ally Korean Buddhism with the Japanese Sōtō sect.[40] Yi changed the name of the school to Buddhist Teachers School (Pulgyo sabŏm hakkyo 佛教師範學校), thus pointing explicitly to its function. He also extended the length of the program to four years—matching it to the higher education systems of Europe and Japan—but due to economic

Table 4 The Curriculum of the Myŏngjin School

	First Year		Second Year	
	First Semester	Second Semester	First Semester	Second Semester
Courses (Five hours of class a day)	1. Dushun's *Huayan fajie guanmen* (華嚴法界觀)[a] 2. The three Pure Land sutras 3. *Brahma Net Sutra* 4. History of Religions 5. Arithmetic 6. History and Geography of Korea 7. Science (natural history/ biology) 8. Calculation 9. Agriculture 10. Japanese 11. Sports	1. Chegwan's *Outline of the Tiantai Four Teachings* (*Ch'ŏnt'ae sagyoŭi* 天台四教儀)[b] 2. *Laṅkāvatāra Sutra* 3. *Dharmaguptaka Vinaya* 4. Propagation Methods 5. Arithmetic 6. History and Geography of Korea 7. Science (natural history/ biology) 8. Land Measuring 9. Drawing 10. Japanese 11. Sports	1. *Huayan Sutra* 2. *Enlightened Verses* 3. *Nirvana Sutra* 4. Law 5. Philosophy 6. Arithmetic 7. History and Geography of Foreign Countries 8. Science (physics and chemistry) 9. Land Measuring 10. Japanese 11. Sports	1. *Huayan Sutra* 2. *Transmission of the Lamp* 3. Yanshou's *Records of the Source-Mirror*[c] 4. Law 5. Philosophy 6. Arithmetic 7. History and Geography of Foreign Countries 8. Science (physics and chemistry) 9. Economics 10. Japanese 11. Sports
Practice	Two hours a day of Chan meditation			

Source: Changik, "Hyŏndae Pulgyo ch'ulgacha toje kyoyuk ŭi kwaje," 116–117.

a This is a treatise on Huayan thought attributed to its first patriarch Dushun (杜順, 557–640). A subcommentary for it was produced by Zongmi. It generally expounds upon the four Huayan insights into the *dharmakaya/dhrmadhatu* (法界觀門): the phenomenon *dharmakaya*, the principle *dharmakaya*, the non-obstruction of phenomenon and principles *dharmakaya*, and the non-obstruction of phenomena *dharmakaya* (事法界, 理法界, 理事無碍法界, 事事無碍法界). A full English translation of this short treatise is found in: Alan Fox, "Dushun's Huayan Fajie Guan Men (Meditative Approaches to the Huayan Dharmadhatu)."

b The *Outline of the Tiantai Four Teachings* is a summary of Tiantai thought written in China in 960 by the Korean monk Chegwan (諦觀, d. 970). It has become the most dominant Tendai introductory text in modern Japan, and thus received considerable attention from Western scholars of Buddhism. Via the Japanese-influenced Myŏngjin curriculum Chegwan seems to have found his way back to his homeland. A full English translation of the text is available in: David Chappell, *T'ien-t'ai Buddhism: An Outline of the Fourfold Teachings*. Charles Muller provides a more recent translation of the text on his website at: http://www.acmuller.net/kor-bud/*Sagyo*ui.html.

c The *Record of the Source-Mirror* (*Zongjing lu* 宗鏡錄) is Yongming Yanshou's magnum opus. It was inspired by the scholastic sutra-based Chan of Zongmi, and includes several citations from the *Chan Preface*. It was later quoted by Chinul. For an analysis of this essay and its author and a partial English translation see: Albert Welter, *Yongming Yanshou's Conception of Chan in the Zongjing lu: A Special Transmission Within the Scriptures*.

difficulties compounded by inner dissension among Korean reformers regarding the Sōtō alliance, it was soon closed down, in 1910.[41] All in all, Myŏngjin seems to have been a rather humble first attempt at a centralized Buddhist institution of higher education. It barely survived for three years and only produced eighteen graduates. Still, it signposted the road ahead.

In fact, the Myŏngjin School seems to bear some unmistakable parallels to Yang Wenhui's famous and pioneering Jetavana Hermitage Seminary (Zhihuan Jingshe 祇洹精舍), which operated at the exact same time in China. Both were inspired by Japanese Buddhist sectarian university programs that taught a mix of Buddhist and general subjects for a handful of the Buddhist elite.[42] Both were revolutionary in creating mixed classrooms of laypeople and the ordained, and in allowing lay scholars to teach monastics about Buddhism, and both were criticized for it by more conservative monastics.[43] Both were at least partly formed in order to help protect monastic lands,[44] and both fostered students who would become the future leaders of their nations' Buddhist communities. Finally, both were short lived, yet, the Jetavana Hermitage became the prototype for the seventy-two Buddhist academies (Foxueyuan 佛學院) that operated in China from the 1920s to the 1940s, while the Myŏngjin School paved the way for other Buddhist universities that sprang up throughout twentieth-century Korea.

Most other Buddhist schools of higher learning that were established in colonial Korea were similarly rather small and temporary. The Buddhist Academy of Higher Education (Pulgyo kodŭng kangsuk 佛教高等講塾) was established in 1914 in the same Wŏnhŭngsa where Myŏngjin was formally located. Twenty-six students enrolled, but it was shut down in less than a year.[45] The Central Seminary (Chungang hangnim 中央學林) was established in 1918 with a curriculum that put additional emphasis on Japanese language and history classes; yet it closed in the early 1920s.[46] The Buddhist Specialists School (Pulgyo chŏnsu hakkyo 佛教專修學校) was opened in 1928 with thirty-one registered students, three English teachers, and new courses in Buddhist arts; and a year later, Pak Han-yŏng established the first Korean Buddhist Research Institute in Kaeunsa. Both were similarly short lived.[47] Attempts to establish stable institutions of higher education were made outside of the capital as well, and in 1927 the Tongguk Seminary (Tongguk kyŏngwŏn 東國經院) was opened in Yujŏmsa, proposing a ten-year program for future seminary teachers.[48] All *Sajip* graduates were eligible to enroll, and the curriculum was to begin with five years of sutra reading, continue with three years of special research, and end with two years of general Buddhist philosophy and history. Plans aside, this school, too, was dismantled before it was able to produce a single graduate.

The 1930s carried some optimistic winds of change for Buddhist higher education on the peninsula. The Central Buddhist Specialized School (Chungang Pulgyo chŏnmun hakkyo 中央佛教專門學校) was the first Buddhist school in Korea to receive official recognition and be given university status by the Japanese colonial government in 1930. Perhaps for this reason it was able to persist longer and attract a greater number of students. It handed out official graduate diplomas to a student body consisting of half monastic and half lay students, and boasted over two hundred alumni by 1940.[49] That year it was also renamed the Hyehwa Specialized School (Hyehwa chŏnmun hakkyo 惠化傳門學校), dropping "Buddhism" from its title in concurrence with the secularizing policies of the Japanese at the time.[50] As Japanese war efforts intensified in the early 1940s, Korean Buddhist students had to wear army uniforms to school and were often mobilized for military labor on vacations.[51] All the headmasters of the school were Japanese, as were eleven out of its thirty regular lecturers. It was closed down due to the war in 1944, and was only reopened again after independence in 1946, this time as Dongguk University.

From Buddhist Schools to Buddhist-Affiliated Universities

Once the central Buddhist institution was operating as Dongguk University, it took another step away from the Buddhist monastic world, and legally entered the modern national secular education system.[52] It was no longer focused on the sangha, nor was it strictly Buddhist, for that matter. To be sure, it still had a Buddhist Studies department, but it was now supplemented by departments of Korean Literature, English, and Sociology. By 1953, it established a Law School and a department of Agriculture. It also inaugurated a graduate school, and in the 1950s began issuing internationally recognized secular BA, MA, and PhD degrees. As it gradually established additional non-religious departments throughout the remainder of the twentieth century, it attracted increasing numbers of lay students, many of whom were not Buddhist at all. Today, religion rarely plays a part in the decisions of Koreans to attend this school. In fact, the university office presented me with recent statistics in which even in the Buddhist-related departments (there are now Buddhist Studies, Chan Studies, Indian Philosophy, and Buddhist Social Welfare departments), only 27 percent of the student body consists of monks and nuns. One may very well ask in what sense it is still considered to be a Buddhist institution at all.

Clearly, this is not an unusual phenomenon. Most European and American universities in the nineteenth century were led by Christian clergymen and held mandatory chapel services, and it was only during the twentieth century that the Bible was dropped from the syllabus and a secularized consensus replaced the religious one in higher education, though formally many maintain a denominational affiliation.[53] In Korea, too, there are currently thirty-three Protestant-affiliated universities offering almost completely secularized programs. The sectarian Buddhist universities in Japan seem to have gone through a similar process of curricular secularization in the twentieth century, and their student bodies today consist of only 2–10 percent of students coming from temple families on their way to join the clergy.[54] Some of the professors in these schools have expressed concern about the loss of their Buddhist identity, and institutions have attempted to address this problem by making "Introduction to Buddhism" a required course for all first-year students, and by providing space to practice Buddhism for those who wish to do so.[55] Dongguk University has responded similarly. All undergraduate students today are required to take two Buddhism-related courses before graduation. One is called "Meditation and the Self"; it is taught by a monk and includes actual sitting meditation practice. The other is called "Buddhism and the Human Being," and is focused on the study of basic doctrines. There is also a small temple on campus that offers weekend sermons and doctrinal classes for those interested.

Although secularized, Dongguk's main strength lies in offering the more academically oriented Korean sangha, an alternative to the monastic seminaries. Almost all of the university's monastic students reside in special dormitories where some communal practice is encouraged.[56] The Buddhist classes and seminars offered, though, are a far cry from the traditional text-focused study of the *Ch'imun, Sajip, Sagyo,* and *Huayan,* and are more in line with contemporary general histories and summaries-centered Buddhist Studies programs at Japanese and Western universities. Dongguk thus serves as a channel that connects the local sangha to the scholarly trends of Buddhist Studies elsewhere, and in the next chapter we shall see how these trends have recently begun to infiltrate Korean mountain monasteries. The school produced almost one hundred MA-holding monastics and twenty PhDs by the end of the twentieth century, and provides the most rigorous Buddhist research environment available in Korea today.[57] Its graduates often assume leadership roles in the Chogye Order, hold military positions as Buddhist chaplains,[58] or teach at one of the mountain monastic seminaries.[59]

Two other, much smaller Buddhist-affiliated universities have been established in Korea more recently. The small Chingak Order (眞覺) established Widŏk University in Kyŏngju in 1994, and the Korean Ch'ŏnt'ae Order began operating Kŭmgang University in 2004. Though technically not recognized as a Buddhist group, Won Buddhism also operates a secular university in Iksan, which was officially recognized as a degree-granting institution in 1971. Mention can also be made of the interesting case of Masan College, which began as a Buddhist school of higher learning set within the grounds of the Haeinsa monastery in the 1950s, yet was so thoroughly secularized in the 1960s that it finally lost all Buddhist affiliation and was legally recognized as Kyŏngnam University in 1971.[60]

In response to Dongguk University's gradual secularization, a new, purely monastic, central institution of higher education was established as an alternative. The Central Sangha College (Chungang sŭngga taehak 中央僧

伽大學) was first established in 1979. It opened admission to nuns in 1982, established a graduate school in 1989, and was finally recognized legally as a four-year degree-granting institution in 1994.[61] It remains the only Buddhist monastic degree-granting institution in Korea, though mountain seminary teachers sometimes express the hope that their schools will win recognition as universities in the future.[62] Similar Buddhist schools in India, Thailand, Singapore, and elsewhere also began issuing secular BA and graduate degrees in the second half of the twentieth century.[63] John Jorgensen argued that in its early years the Central Sangha College was a hub for monastic radicals and reformers, its ideology based on banned translations of the Marxist Buddhism of Sen'o Girō.[64] Today, however, it is more often imagined within the Korean sangha as the school attracting monastics who are interested in politics, and who hope to obtain management positions at the Chogye headquarters after graduation.

The Central Sangha College offers a creative middle way between the mountain monastic seminaries and Dongguk University. It is now located in a new modern campus rather than in a mountain monastery and, like Dongguk, it stepped away from the *Sajip-Sagyo* textual-focused curriculum of the seminaries to offer more general courses on topics including Buddhist culture, social welfare, temple management, and propagation methods. The school also promotes research and issues graduate degrees. Unlike Dongguk, however, only monks and nuns are allowed to enroll, and must live communally at the school and participate in weekly communal work and rituals. Today, all first-year students must live together in a "big room," and often hold communal *Diamond Sutra*–reading (*kangyŏng* 看經) sessions in the afternoons, as is done in the monastic seminaries. The student body is comparatively large, and in the past thirty years or so it has produced over one thousand alumni.

Seminaries in Postcolonial Korea

Unlike in Japan, where Buddhist-affiliated universities have become the customary pedagogical institutions for Buddhist clerics, mountain seminaries have continued to play a major role in Korea even after the establishment of Dongguk University and the Central Sangha College. Seminaries were closed down during the turmoil of the Korean War (1950–1953), but, beginning in the mid-1950s, major monasteries gradually began to reorganize schools based on the *Ch'imun-Sajip-Sagyo-Huayan* program, which by then had come to be widely perceived as the national Buddhist syllabus. Haeinsa's seminary was the first to reopen, in 1955, followed by the nun seminaries of Tonghaksa and Unmunsa. In the 1960s T'ongdosa, Yongjusa, Pŏmŏsa, and other, smaller temples established their own schools. By 1969 there were twelve seminaries operating on the peninsula with an overall student body of about five hundred monastics.[65] Hwaŏmsa's seminary was established in 1971 by a teacher from Pŏmŏsa, Pulguksa's school was established in 1975, and by the end of the 1970s there were already eighteen seminaries teaching over seven hundred students.[66] Chikchisa, Songgwangsa,[67] Ssanggyesa, Ch'ŏnamsa, and other monasteries established seminaries in the 1980s, but as some smaller seminaries closed down, the overall number of schools has remained in the range of sixteen to twenty since the 1970s. The majority of these seminaries were very small. Even the larger monastery of Pŏmŏsa, for example, produced an average of only six graduates a year between the mid-1960s and mid-1970s, while T'ongdosa graduated an average of about four alumni per year in the 1960s and ten per year in the 1970s and 1980s.[68] Haeinsa was somewhat larger, boasting over seventy students during the 1970s and over a hundred throughout the 1980s. The female seminaries, which will be described in more detail in later sections, have had larger student bodies.

It is important to note that these postcolonial monastic seminaries were anything but unified and systematized at first. Between the 1960s and the early 1980s each monastery ran its own program, centered mainly on the ideas of its head teacher (*kangju* 講主). Program lengths varied between two and six years in the different schools.[69] Monks were not obligated to join a seminary, and in fact it is estimated that less than half actually did. Others would simply join a Chan Hall or take on a position (*soim* 所任) at a temple. Often the decision of whether or not to join a seminary was not completely dependent on individual desires, but on those of the tonsure teacher (*ŭnsa* 恩師) assigned to every new postulant in Korea, who serves almost as a monastic substitute to the secular father (or mother) figure for the rest of his or her monastic career. Even those who did enter seminaries, often read through only parts of the *Ch'imun* and perhaps some of the *Sajip* texts before leaving the school.[70] Rarely did anyone study the complete *Sagyo* texts and the *Huayan Sutra*.[71]

Biographical anecdotes confirm this lack of systematization. Irhwan recalls joining Haeinsa's celebrated seminary when it reopened in 1955 along with close to fifty other students. He recounts studying the *Ch'imun, Sajip,* and *Sagyo* texts for about four years, but having to travel to T'ongdosa to study the *Huayan,* as Haeinsa did not have a teacher for that course at the time.[72] Chigwan, who was abbot of Haeinsa in the 1970s and head of the entire Chogye administration in the early 2000s, also went to Haeinsa in 1955 but studied only the *Sagyo* and *Huayan* there for three years. He then traveled to T'ongdosa to study the *Enlightened Verses,* but explains that there were no formal classes. He simply studied the text individually and went to see a teacher when he had specific questions to ask. He also recalls that in the 1960s Haeinsa systematized the curriculum into a four-year program, and that the only monasteries that taught the whole core traditional curriculum at the time were Haeinsa, T'ongdosa, and, for nuns, Tonghaksa.[73] Wŏnsan, who was the head of the Chogye Order's Education Department in the late 1990s, further emphasized the flexibility and lack of structure in the education system in the mid-twentieth century. He explained that each monastery had teachers specializing in different texts, and so students often traveled from seminary to seminary to study. He himself went through most of the traditional curriculum studying different texts in three different locations. He also remembers that students spent most of their time doing odd jobs at the monastery, and spent very little time actually studying.[74] Accordingly, it seems clear that in the 1960s the shift from a teacher-based apprenticeship education to a modern, institution-based school system had not yet been completed.

As always, there was no lack of reform proposals. In 1965, Chigwan, the head teacher of Haeinsa at the time, suggested adding additional basic Mahāyāna sutras to the curriculum.[75] Two years later, in 1967, the head of the entire Haeinsa community, Sŏngch'ŏl, proposed an innovative four-year seminary curriculum with a new emphasis not only on secular subjects, but also on Indian Buddhism. His plan included required courses in the Pāli language, the *Āgamas,* philosophy, education, Buddhist history, and religious studies, as well as electives in law, psychology, biology, culture, and music. He also suggested supplementing the Haeinsa seminary with a graduate school for training teachers. These plans, however, were not realized.[76] In 1972, the Chogye administration sponsored a survey of the situation of the country's seminaries and concluded rather humorlessly that the level of education was very low. In order to promote a better educational atmosphere, they suggested changing the name of the seminaries from the old-fashioned-sounding Lecture Hall (*kangdang* 講堂 or *kangwŏn* 講院) to the more modern-sounding Sangha Academy (*Sŭngga hagwŏn* 僧伽學院), and unifying the system into a six-year curriculum—split in half into three years of doctrinal learning and three years of Chan.[77] This proposal, too, was never realized.

In 1975, the Buddhist magazine *Sŏngnim* (釋林) devoted an entire issue to articles dealing with the education of the sangha. In it, Yi Ki-yŏng lamented the strict division between practice at Chan Halls and study at seminaries and argued for the need to devise a new system that integrated both.[78] Another article in that volume noted the economic difficulties of the Korean sangha, arguing that it could not rely on donations alone and that seminary education should therefore be supplemented by some sort of professional education that will allow home-leavers, paradoxically, to earn money in secular society in order to continue their religious work.[79] Later, in 1986, a prominent Korean lay Buddhist professor by the name of Chŏng Pyŏng-jo put forth another interesting reform proposal. First, echoing Yi Ki-yŏng, he suggested adding a textual study program to the Chan Halls during the retreat off-seasons, focusing on Chan treatises and histories. In addition, he put forth an eight-year curricular proposal for the seminaries. His program begins with a year of *Ch'obalsim, Śākyamuni*'s biography, religious studies, and Buddhist cultural history. The second stage was a three-year study of *Āgamas,* Vinaya, the *Diamond Sutra,* Chinul's *Chinsim-chiksŏl* (眞心直說), philosophy, Indian Buddhist history, and English. The third stage was another three-year study of the *Lotus Sutra,* the *Awakening of Faith,* Chan history, Wŏnhyo research, the history of Buddhism in China and Korea, and Sanskrit. The final year was to be dedicated to the *Huayan Sutra,* as well as to propagation methods and further research in Mahāyāna Buddhism.[80]

These reform proposals seem to have had much in common, that is, besides the fact that they were all lost in the trash bin of history. The early-twentieth-century emphasis on the desirability of monks learning secular subjects continued well into the 1980s, though the focus of the proposals shifted from the sciences to philosophy and (comparative) religion. Often the need to teach monks languages was emphasized as well, whether it was Japanese in the early years of the century or English and Indian classical languages in the postcolonial years. As in other traditionally Mahāyānist East Asian countries, Indian Buddhism, especially the *Āgamas* and Abhidharma, seems to have gradually become more important to Korean Buddhists over the course of the twentieth century. At the same time, I believe it is also possible to detect a weakened interest in Chan in favor of a more general sort of Buddhism, as well as a greater focus on the sutras instead of treatises. The only treatises left on Chŏng's proposal described above, for instance, were a number of native-Korean-written essays, perhaps in an attempt to further nationalize the curriculum. The foreign *Sajip* texts are completely missing from this plan. The following chapters will discuss how these new trends in what Korean Buddhists understood to be central to their tradition would finally break through into actual reforms on the ground in the twenty-first century.

During the final years of the twentieth century, the core traditional curriculum seems to have gradually become the basis of all institutions, and it was often supplemented by special weekend lectures on non-Buddhist topics. Haeinsa, for example, offered English classes and special lectures in philosophy, psychology, Buddhist history, and propagation strategies since the 1980s.[81] Hwaŏmsa at the time supplemented its curriculum with courses on Abhidharma philosophy and daily sports.[82] All nun seminaries added Hyujŏng's *Mirror of Sŏn* and the *Brahma Net Sutra* to their curricula in the 1980s.[83] By the early 1990s all sixteen operating seminaries structured their program around the core texts of the traditional curriculum, and most supplemented it with special lectures on various general topics. Eight of the seminaries offered Japanese language classes, and five taught English. Five schools offered special lectures on Buddhist history, and three on propagation and calligraphy. Computers and comparative religion were each taught in two institutions. Lectures on the *Āgamas* were given in two of the seminaries, and other schools held special classes on Mādhyamika and Yogācāra thought. In addition, *Zhuangzi* was read at Pulguksa, and the *Analects* at Ssanggyesa.[84] Finally, the martial art *Taijiquan* (K. *T'aegŭkkwŏn* 太極拳) has been taught at Ch'ŏnamsa ever since the seminary was founded in the mid-1980s.

Modern Debates over Sudden and Gradual Awakening

An additional curriculum-related development occurred in the mid-1970s, with the revival of the old sudden and gradual soteriological debate. The central figure in the debate was the head of the Haeinsa community in the 1970s and the head of the entire Chogye Order in the 1980s, Sŏngch'ŏl (性徹, 1912–1993). Sŏngch'ŏl critiqued the "sudden-enlightenment-followed-by-gradual-cultivation" model propounded by Zongmi and Chinul as compromising the absolute, simultaneous, immediate nature of real Chan enlightenment, and favored instead the more subitist model of "sudden-enlightenment-and-sudden-cultivation" (*dunwu dunxiu* 頓悟頓修).[85] Looking back at Zongmi's essays, Sŏngch'ŏl found that the initial "sudden awakening" was occasionally characterized as "understanding awakening" (*jiewu* 解悟) while the complete awakening at the end of the gradual practice was sometimes termed "confirmed awakening" (*zhengwu* 證悟).[86] Consequently, and in accordance with Dahui's critique of knowing and understanding (*zhijie* 智解) as harmful to *huatou* practice, Sŏngch'ŏl argued that Zongmi's "sudden awakening" should not be regarded as awakening at all, but simply as a kind of rational understanding that cannot be trusted as a basis for real Chan practice.[87] He likened using this "understanding" in practicing Chan to jumping into the fire while holding an armful of firewood.[88]

Sŏngch'ŏl backed his ideology with real action. In 1976, he took the gradualist "heterodox" *Sajip* essays of Zongmi and Chinul off Haeinsa's seminary curriculum.[89] In their place, he added two other texts to the *Letters* and *Chan Essentials*, forming a new *Sajip*. These were the *Platform Sutra* and a fourteenth-century text by the Ming Chinese monk Dazhu (大珠) on sudden awakening (*Dunwu rudao yaomenlun* 頓悟入道要門論), which generally confirmed his more subitist soteriological views. With these changes, the *Sajip* lost its original focus on Heze gradualist Chan, and was placed instead within the confines of what came to be the orthodox Linji lineage. One may wonder to what extent contemporary (Rinzai-influenced) Japanese Buddhist scholarship has had an impact on his views. One could also ask whether the *Huayan*, *Śūraṃgama*, and other more gradualist texts should not have been taken out of the curriculum along with the *Preface* and *Excerpts* to complete Sŏngch'ŏl's sudden-complete-enlightenment vision.

Sŏngch'ŏl has certainly been one of the most influential monastics in modern Korea, and his views have had a lasting impact. His new subitist *Sajip* collection remained on the curriculum of Haeinsa—perhaps the most dominant monastic center in Korea—well into the twenty-first century. It also seems to have influenced the perspectives of teachers in other seminaries. Until the 1990s, Hwaŏmsa's seminary, too, taught a similar program involving the *Platform Sutra,* Dahui's *Letters* and the *Vimalakīrti Sutra,* and neither the *Preface* nor the *Excerpts.*[90] As the next chapter will illustrate, my own fieldwork in seminaries demonstrates that although the *Sajip* has for the most part lost its place on the curricula, when having to choose among its texts, seminary teachers today tend to conform to Sŏngch'ŏl's vision and favor Dahui's *Letters,* and in some cases the *Chan Essentials,* over the gradualist essays of Zongmi and Chinul.

Female Seminaries: Stepping Down from the Hermitages

Perhaps the greatest revolution in twentieth-century Korean Buddhism was the gradual independence and growth of female monastic education, which had previously been marginalized or subordinated to the male seminaries. In premodern Korea, nuns were excluded altogether from the sangha examinations and from holding official Buddhist positions and titles. By the early twentieth century, however, several male seminary teachers allowed female students from the surrounding hermitages to join their classes.[91] The first female-only seminary was opened in Seoul's Pomunsa in 1936,[92] and there were a few other mostly unsuccessful attempts to open nun seminaries in Namjangsa, Mit'asa, and other small temples in the 1940s and early 1950s.[93] Gradually, nun communities began to step down from the surrounding satellite hermitages they inhabited and move into some of the larger central monasteries.[94]

Then, in 1956, for the first time in Korean Buddhist history, a nun by the name of Myoŏm received official "transmission to teach" (*chŏngang* 傳講) from her male teacher, Kyŏngbong, and began teaching classes in the newly founded female seminary of Tonghaksa.[95] Two years later, in 1958, Unmunsa's nun seminary was established by a male T'ongdosa monk, and approximately twenty similar nun schools were inaugurated in the same way in the 1960s and 1970s, though most did not last long.[96] The final breakthrough happened in 1985. Up until then, all nun seminary teachers received "transmission to teach" from male teachers, but in 1985 the first nun-to-nun transmission occurred in Unmunsa, symbolizing the final independence of the female seminaries from their male supervision.[97] Following that event, nun seminary student numbers grew rapidly, and since the early 1980s there have been consistently more female seminary students in Korea than male students. In fact, in the 1990s, female seminary student numbers doubled those of their male counterparts. While many male monastics skipped the seminary and went directly to a Chan Hall after their novice ordinations, almost all female novices were encouraged to begin their monastic careers at a seminary.

Scholars have attempted to explain the creation of new independent female monastic seminaries by pointing toward the leadership roles nuns took in the Purification Movement, for which they were "rewarded" with their own temples and seminaries.[98] Some explain that, because married clergy were expelled from the monasteries in the 1950s and 1960s, there was simply a lack of celibate monks to take over and maintain the clusters and nuns were given a chance to occupy some of the major temples, such as Unmunsa and Tonghaksa, which soon became the first female seminaries.[99] Sugyŏng argued that even earlier, during the Korean War, as monks were leaving the monasteries to join the military, seminary teachers tried to fill their empty classrooms with nuns, accepting them as disciples and giving them transmission to teach.[100] The overall zeitgeist of a more equal gender relationship in twentieth-century Korea was probably the most dominant factor in the changes, as it has been in many other religious communities in modern times.

Personal connections of some of the leading nuns also proved to be helpful. Perhaps the most dominant seminary nun in the twentieth century, Myoŏm—who was the first female to receive transmission to teach in the 1950s, taught in several major seminaries, studied at Dongguk's graduate school, and established the major seminary of Pongnyŏngsa in 1974—certainly had such connections.[101] Her father had been a prominent monk in colonial times. As the story goes, six years after his ordination he visited his ex-wife once in order to filially satisfy his aging mother's wish for a grandchild.[102] Thus Myoŏm was born. During the military turbulence of the late 1940s, her mother sent her to hide in her father's temple, where she met the monastic leaders of the day, was ordained, and even studied under Sŏngch'ŏl.[103] Her important role in the female monastic emancipation in Korea should not go unnoticed.

By the end of the twentieth century, there were five female monastic seminaries on the peninsula: the three large centers of Unmunsa—which has been the largest seminary in the country since the 1990s, continuously housing over two hundred students—Tonghaksa, and Pongnyŏngsa, which hosted over a hundred students each in the 1990s; as well as two somewhat smaller communities, Seoul's Samsŏn seminary, which opened in 1979,[104] and Ch'ŏngamsa's school, which has operated since 1987.[105] They all followed the traditional *Sajip-Sagyo* curriculum, supplemented by special lectures on Buddhist history and culture.

Each of the female seminaries is imagined a little differently by the community of nuns. Unmunsa is known as the working seminary, Tonghaksa as the scholarly seminary, Pongnyŏngsa as the strict disciplinary seminary, and Ch'ŏngamsa as the "freethinking" seminary. Sometimes female novices decide which school to attend according to these stereotypes. Although nuns often claim that their ordination gets them to transcend gender differentiation, during the 1990s, female seminaries—and female seminaries only—offered special classes in piano and flower arrangement, both clearly associated with feminine gender roles. Such courses were dropped from the programs in the twenty-first century. In 1992, the largest monastic library in the country—housing tens of thousands of books as well as modern multimedia rooms—was opened in Pongnyŏngsa. The first female monastic Vinaya School was established there in 1999, inspiring the inauguration of several other similar institutions in the twenty-first century.

Because there were fewer nun seminaries yet more nun students, female institutions tended to be more crowded than their male counterparts. But numbers are hardly the only difference. Female seminaries and nunneries in general tend to be situated in more secluded locations; Ch'ŏnamsa certainly being the most isolated of them all. The most striking peculiarity of the female seminaries, however, is the almost complete lack of lay employees. In Korean male Buddhist monasteries today, lay volunteers and paid workers do most, if not all, of the office, kitchen, construction, and farming work. In female seminaries, on the other hand, it is usually the students who do all of the non-professional labor. The new cohorts often do the cleaning, kitchen, and farming work, while the more advanced students are in charge of the office and managerial jobs.

In fact, when I visited Ch'ŏnamsa in 2014, some of the older nuns insisted that not only the students but the entire community worked together daily in the kitchen and in the gardens. When I asked nun seminary teachers about this inequality, they often explained that nunneries are much poorer than male monasteries, as lay female devotees (*posallim*) usually prefer to donate their time and money to the male temples. They explained that they simply could not afford to pay lay employees. Other female monastics I talked to seemed to have found comfort in the fact that, unlike in other Asian countries, they were allowed to ordain and manage their own temples in the first place, and stressed that they do not need to hire help as work is a vital Buddhist practice for novices. When I raised this concern with some of the male monastics, they sometimes lowered their heads abashed, admitting that perhaps their monasteries should be more like those of the nuns.

Communal Life at the Seminaries

Seminary teachers frequently stress that the most important practice in monastic schools is not the textual study itself. Although this has been changing recently, twentieth-century seminaries frequently had very little formal class time, very little class preparation, and no homework, reports, or exams. Rather, they say, the most essential aspect of seminary education is students' acculturation to "communal living" (*taejung saenghwal* 大衆生活). Seminary novices are obliged to live together in shared "big rooms" (*kŭnbang*), where they not only sleep together, but also study, chant, eat, and spend most of their time with each other (fig. 1). Sharing such a small space with other students is often portrayed as the toughest and most significant aspect of the training in the seminaries.[106] Personal privacy is given away completely, and in order to survive novices simply must smooth out their edges and "lower their minds" (*hasim* 下心).

This cultivation of humbleness bordering on self-negation, accompanied by order, cleanliness, quietness, and other qualities necessary to maintain peace in a very small room full of busy students, is viewed as the seminaries' most foundational educational objective. Fist fights do break out at times, and I have been told that monks are never expelled from a seminary due to negligence in study, but they occasionally leave as a result of social problems and difficulty adjusting to the suffocating communal conditions. "Sangha," after all, means community, and seminary education has focused primarily on molding the novices into a harmonious community rather than on the teaching of doctrines. "I am not really here to learn about Buddhism," a friendly seminary student told me on one of my visits to Pŏmŏsa in 2013, "I am here to learn how to be a monk!"

Michael Lampert has reported that the Disciplinarian (*dge bskos*) of the large Tibetan monastic school of Sera collects fines, intimidates via public reprimands, and sometimes even makes use of a strike or two of the leather whip to punish monks who play around or doze off during lectures.[107] Although no corporal punishment has been employed in Korean seminaries of late, learning to be a monk on the peninsula, too, involves adapting to very strict hierarchies and constant disciplinary reproaches. Seminary students of the first three grades choose a leader (called *ch'aljŭng*) who is responsible for the overall order in the big room. The higher *Taegyo* class leader is called *Ipsŭng* (立繩). His position allows him to punish lower-level students. This title originates in Song Chinese Pure Rules provisions, and in some contemporary Korean seminaries the slightest disrespect for the *Ipsŭng* is punishable by three thousand prostrations. Above the *Ipsŭng* in the seminary hierarchy stands the Study Supervisor (*Hakkam* 學監), who is the second-in-command below the head teacher and is responsible for the general order and discipline of the students.

Many of the *Hakkam* and *Ipsŭng* today seem to exercise their disciplinary rights quite generously. Common faults are lateness, disorganized attire, mistakenly wearing someone else's shoes (a common enough error as all of their shoes look the same), speaking or acting impolitely to one's seniors, improper walking and sitting postures, failing to show up to a scheduled task, failing to have one's name on a piece of clothing, wearing colorful underclothes, and a variety of other behaviors that may seem improper to the senior students. The standard punishment is prostrations in the Buddha Hall for a specific time

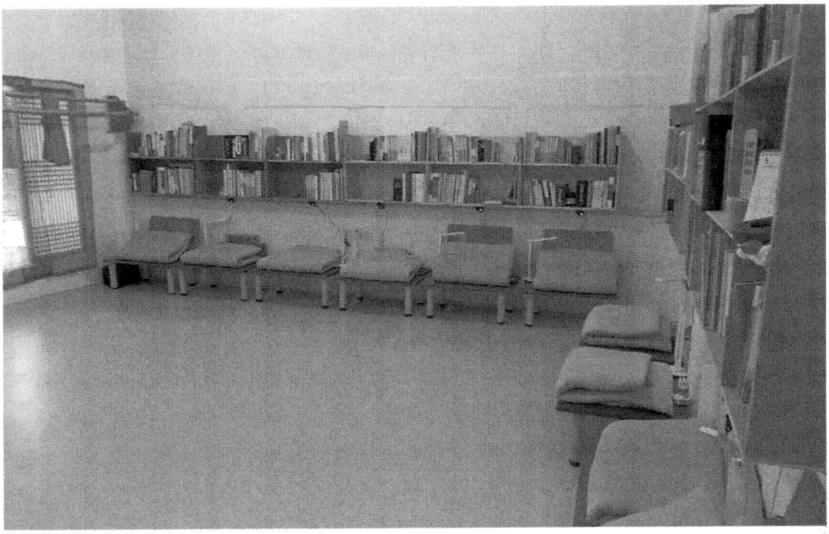

FIG. 1. The "big room" in Sŏnamsa's seminary.

period, which can range from thirty minutes to an all-night vigil depending on the severity of the offense. Some of the female monasteries punish with additional labor instead.

It is also quite common for the more senior students to assemble their minors for harsh public reproaches, a custom that reaffirms hierarchical distinctions and builds communal solidarity among students of the same big room. In addition, upper-class students every so often command those with less seniority to perform all kinds of sundry tasks for them. Like all Korean men, male monks have to serve in the military for two years either before or after ordination, and many compare the strict hierarchic relationships they have endured in the military to what they experience in the seminaries. Female monastics sometimes brag that their seminaries are much less hierarchic in nature, because they have no prior military experience.

As we have seen, in the early twentieth century seminary schedules were quite loose and flexible. Education was for the most part dependent on the personal proclivities of the head teacher, rather than on a systematized, fixed program. In the second half of the century, this teacher-based apprenticeship model gradually transformed into a modern, institution-based school system with set curricula and daily schedules, which were soon codified in newly written Pure Rules. In some of the schools, only as late as the 1980s and 1990s, regulated schedules of rituals, formal classes, sutra-chanting sessions, group debates, communal work, and formal monastic meals were organized for the first time.[108] In his discussion of monastic Buddhist life in Sri Lanka, Jeffery Samuels argued that the sangha learned monastic behavior less via textual study and more through what he termed "action-oriented pedagogy," which involved doing, performing, and speaking.[109] Similarly, in Korean monastic seminaries, class time has been limited, yet living through the strict busy daily schedules gradually transforms the awkward novices into steady-postured, solemn, and firm monastics.[110]

Schedules still vary to a degree, yet the core seminary daily program has been unified at least since the 1990s, and is as follows. Students rise at 3 a.m. and are responsible for all the preparations necessary for the morning rituals (*yebul* 禮佛). This includes making the rounds in the monastery to wake all humans and spirits by sounding the various monastic instruments (*toryangsŏk* 道場釋), as well as arranging the sitting pillows for the community in the main hall before the morning rituals, which usually begin around 4 a.m. and last for about twenty to thirty minutes. After the morning rituals, most seminaries hold a communal sutra-chanting session (*kangyŏng* 看經), which lasts between twenty and fifty minutes. Interestingly, in female seminaries this exact same activity is called *ipsŏn* (入禪), literally meaning "entering Chan," and thus stressing the meditational aspect of this communal chanting. The *Diamond Sutra* is the most common sutra read out loud in unison in many seminaries during these sessions. Some prefer reading *Guishan's Admonitions* or other parts of the *Ch'imun* instead, and in some schools the actual texts studied during that period in class are the ones chanted. This communal chanting is important not only for reviewing and internalizing the texts, but also for providing a chance for the vocal development important for monastic rituals, as well as for cultivating concentration and practicing breath control. It is also an opportunity to work on body posture, as sitting in the full lotus position is encouraged. Some seminaries hold such communal chanting sessions several times a day.

Both breakfast and lunch are usually taken in the big room in the formal four-bowl ritualistic style (*paru kongyang* 鉢盂供養), though dinner is eaten casually in the dining hall.[111] These four-bowl meals involve intricate rituals, which can take up to a full hour, and are aimed again to promote harmonious communal action, attitudes of humility and gratitude toward the food, and encouragement to practice harder.[112] Seminary students are also responsible for sounding the monastic instruments and arranging the halls before the evening rituals, and are the ones conducting the longer midday offering rituals (*sasi Pulgong* 巳時佛供) in the various halls of the monastery. Through repeated performance of these ceremonies, novices memorize the various *dhāraṇī* of the *Thousand Hands Sutra* (*Ch'ŏnsu kyŏng* 千手經)—which has been chanted at the midday rituals throughout the country since the 1970s[113]—and their bodily gestures, singing voices, and postures gradually become more "monkish." Although the numerous rituals, sutra-chanting sessions, and formal meals at the seminary clearly involve solemn concentration and are generally understood to be different types of cultivation (*suhaeng* 修行), there was no time at all allocated to communal Chan-sitting in any of the seminaries prior to the twenty-first century. As the novices are of the lowest position in the monastery—aside from the postulants, if there are any—much of their time has been dedicated to doing all sorts of odd jobs in the cluster, and they were not expected to meditate. In fact, cleaning and running errands is often what monks seem to remember most about their seminary lives. Some students are also selected to serve as personal attendants to the older monks in residence, a position that may be quite demanding yet involves an unmistakable measure of power and prestige.

Toward the end of the twentieth century, seminaries usually had about an hour and a half of formal class time after breakfast, five or six times a week. Classes were often held in the big room, once it was cleaned after breakfast. Classes began, as they still do today, with a short bowing ritual formally entreating the teacher to teach (*sanggangrye* 上講禮). As the traditional curriculum is focused on specific texts rather than on general surveys and introductions, classes were conducted in what is often called the "Confucian school method" (*sŏdang-sik* 書堂式), in which texts are read out loud line by line with the Korean pronunciation of the Chinese characters, and then translated into modern Korean. There was little discussion and few attempts to understand the context of the texts; study essentially meant reading and translating. Memorization supposedly played a major role in such study historically, as it has been elsewhere,[114] but by the end of the twentieth century only short parts from the *Ch'imun* were sometimes memorized in the seminaries. Some of the monks I talked to, who had attended seminaries in the late twentieth century, recall that they had to memorize a passage or two from the *Ch'imun* and recite it in front of the teacher every morning. The modern pedagogical shift away from the memorization of texts and into a more content-analysis-focused education had been completed by the turn of the century. Apart from the liturgy, there is no memorization at all in Korean Buddhist seminaries today.

Time was reserved in the afternoons for individual preparation for the next day's class, which basically involved trying to find the difficult Chinese characters in the dictionary. In addition, time was allocated in the evenings for short group debates (*non'gang* 論講). Debates seem to have been a common pedagogical tool in ancient Buddhist Indian universities, as well as in medieval Japan.[115] In fact, in twentieth-century Tibetan seminaries up to ten hours a day were devoted to debates.[116] The Korean seminary debates, however, are nothing like the animated performances of their Tibetan counterparts. More than actual debates, they should be understood as group preparation for the next day's class. These sessions today are rather short, usually lasting between fifteen and thirty minutes, and some seminaries have gotten rid of them altogether. Other seminaries hold such sessions only for the upper-level students.

Table 5 Basic Daily Schedule at a Monastic Seminary

Time	Student Activity
3:00 a.m.	*Toryangsŏk:* waking up the humans and spirits at the cluster by sounding the various monastic instruments
4:00 a.m.	*Yebul:* Morning chanting and bowing ritual
4:30 a.m.	*Kangyŏng:* Communal chanting of the *Diamond Sutra* or another curricular text
5:30 a.m.	Cleaning
6:00 a.m.	*Paru kongyang:* Formal four-bowl ritual meal
7:00 a.m.	*Sanggangrye:* Ritual of asking the teacher to teach
7:15 a.m.	Class (about an hour and a half)
10:00 a.m.	*Sasi Pulgong:* Midday chanting and offering ritual
11:00 a.m.	*Paru kongyang:* Formal four-bowl ritual meal
12:00–4:00 p.m.	Odd work as needed, further individual study, or communal chanting. In recent years more formal class time was added at this time.
4:00 p.m.	Cleaning
5:00 p.m.	Dinner (informal at dining hall)
6:00 p.m.	*Yebul:* Evening chanting and bowing ritual at the various halls
7:00 p.m.	*Non'gang:* Group debates/preparation for the next day's classes
8:00 p.m.	Cleaning up, preparing for bed
9:00 p.m.	Lights out

One of the teachers in Hwaŏmsa explained that they decided to do away with the debate sessions because the level of the students was too low for deep discussions without a guiding teacher, and in any case, "argumentative debates by students are usually frowned upon in Korean culture, and novices tend to have a hard time voicing their own opinions in front of their seniors." By 9 p.m., bedding is spread on the floor and lights go out in the big room. Table 5 illustrates a representative seminary daily schedule.

The 1994–1995 Reforms and Compulsory Monastic Education

Since the 1960s the Chogye Order has been attempting to systematize seminary education through a series of standardized laws. The first Chogye Education Law (*Kyoyuk-pŏp*) was promulgated in 1962. It stipulated a three-year seminary program for novices, followed by a four-year specialized system for fully ordained monks.[117] It is unclear whether this has ever been put into practice, and sure enough, several revisions ensued. It was only in the early 1980s that the traditional curricular texts were finally codified into law: seminaries were to offer a four-year program, with the first year dedicated to the *Ch'imun*, the second to the *Sajip*, the third to the *Sagyo*, and the last to the *Huayan Sutra*. More importantly, for the first time in Korean history, the law has made seminary education mandatory. All novices were now obligated to graduate from a four-year program at a monastic seminary, the Central Sangha College, or Dongguk University in order to be eligible to receive the full precepts.[118]

Laws aside, the Chogye Order did not have absolute control over the abbots and head teachers at the mountain monasteries, and although the various seminary programs were gradually unified into the same four-year traditional curricular model in the 1980s, a substantial number of novices, especially in male monasteries, was still reluctant to enter these schools. The turning point seems to have been the comprehensive Chogye Order reforms of 1994.[119] Following ongoing charges of illicit ties with the government and financial corruption of the Head of the Chogye's Main Office, Ŭihyŏn, monastic students of Dongguk University and the Central Sangha College staged large demonstrations at Chogyesa on March 28, that year.[120] Influenced by the national Korean democratization movement of the late 1980s, this new generation of monks called for a similar democratization of the Buddhist administration, the separation of the sangha from the government, and the liquidation of the Order's leading "junta." They called for the resignation of "authoritarian" Ŭihyŏn, who has been the head of the Chogye administration since 1986 and was running for office for the third straight time. But Ŭihyŏn did not go down easy. On March 29, he mobilized several hundred thugs to beat the young demonstrators out of Chogyesa. Media news images of monastic violence soon aired throughout the world, prompting Buddhist laypeople and elderly respected monastics to join the movement against Ŭihyŏn. He had no choice but to step down a month later and allow the young monks to take over.

Ŭihyŏn and eight additional monks were expelled from the Order following the 1994 ordeal, and over seventy others were punished.[121] Consequently, the entire administration has been reformed to prevent future abuse of power: central elections were broadened, abbot selection systematized, and new laws were legislated to ensure a stricter separation of powers between the administrative, judicial, and legislative bodies of the organization.[122] More significant for our discussion, however, was the creation of semi-independent Propagation and Education departments. The newly founded Education Department soon amended the Education Law with official objective criteria regarding seminary teacher qualifications in order to avoid corruption. It also attempted to give a more modernized "feel" to the seminaries by changing their name, yet again, this time to "sangha universities" (sŭngga taehak 僧伽大學). Most importantly, it began enforcing compulsory seminary education on all of its monastic novices.

The significance of this move should not go unnoticed. Scholars of Asian Buddhism have often noted that scholastic education has been pursued only by the most elite monks. Small numbers of the Thai and Tibetan sangha actually go through the seminary programs, and if any mandatory training is required for ordination at all, it is commonly short and focused on learning the ritual chants.[123] Even in contemporary Japan, where most Buddhist priests receive degrees from sectarian universities, other than short training sessions in monasteries, extensive Buddhist doctrinal education is not a mandatory precondition for ordination.[124] In Korea, for most of the twentieth century, fewer than half of the new novices are believed to have had any doctrinal education in a seminary.[125] Since the 1990s, however, instead of monastics choosing either a scholastic career in a seminary or going straight to the Chan Halls, the seminary has become a necessary step before one can receive the full precepts, become a formal Chogye-affiliated monastic, and begin his or her formal retreats. In other words, doctrinal education has become a universal precondition for formal monastic Chan practice.

Hyŏnŭng has been one of the chief engineers of this new system. He has been both a seminary teacher and the abbot of Haeinsa, and in the past several years he has been serving as the head of the Chogye Order's Education Department. In 1994, while working at the Order's headquarters, he published a seminal pioneering piece on monastic education in a Buddhist magazine. In it, he declared:

> The state of chaos in the education of the Chogye Order today arises from the confusion regarding practice and education. How are practice and education different? Education is the process of preparation for genuine practice![126]

Before we conclude this mostly historical part of the monograph and turn to discuss contemporary debates on monastic curriculums, let us briefly review the dynamics of monastic education in Korea prior to the turn of the new millennium. As we have seen, a particular historical curricular model, having its roots in the sixteenth and seventeenth centuries, was authorized in the early twentieth century as the "traditional," national, Buddhist educational program. It was gradually unified into a modern university-type four-year sequence, and was ultimately made mandatory for all novices by the Chogye Order laws. Along with this curricular canon, the daily schedules, teaching qualifications, academic calendars, and other seminary regulations were likewise systematized by the new Education Department to ensure parity and avoid corruption. Independent female monastic seminaries were established in the second half of the century, and various institutions of higher education for monastics were opened. By the 1990s, a clear-cut distinction between "traditional" education at the mountain monastic seminaries and "modern" education in Seoul's Dongguk University and the Central Sangha College was apparent. Nevertheless, this definitive division was soon blurred by novel twenty-first-century seminary reforms, to which we turn our attention in the next chapter.

3

Buddhism Simulating Buddhist Studies

Twenty-First-Century Reforms

> The actual seminary students' appreciation of the importance of sutra study is very poor. Because of traditional attitudes of contempt for study in the Chan School, which emphasizes transmittance outside of scriptures, the notion that sitting Chan is the only practice, and reading sutras is not practice at all, is widespread. As long as we do not reconsider our perceptions of the role of learning and the necessity of sutra studies for coming to terms with existential issues, the students' level of sutra understanding, analysis, and posture while reading will be nothing but sluggish.
>
> *Myŏngbŏp, a leading female monastic seminary teacher, 1998*[1]

> Monks do not believe in Buddhism. This is because monks do not know Buddhism. This may sound like a joke, but it is, in fact, the proper way to express the truth.
>
> *Tobŏm, Abbot of Silsanga, 2000*[2]

IN FEBRUARY 2000, A GROUP OF PROMINENT Chogye monastics met in Seoul for a roundtable discussion on the current state of the Order. After going through the customary cycle of formal greetings, the conversation soon heated up as one of the members broached the issue of the factional violence that erupted during the 1998 Chogye elections.[3] The participants expressed deep shock and embarrassment about these incidents (after all the fights received widespread media coverage), and debated ways to prevent such "un-Buddhist" monastic violence in the future. Haeinsa's seminary head teacher at the time, Chio, maintained that in order to avoid such inner factionalism altogether, perhaps the traditional tonsure teacher (*ŭnsa*) system should be done away with—as it may promote local allegiances—and all postulants should be under the responsibility of the central administration.[4] He added that better education was needed to prevent violence in the sangha, stating that the study of the *Dharmaguptaka Vinaya,* not formally part of the seminary curriculum, was absolutely necessary. Other participants agreed. The abbot of Silsangsa, quoted in the chapter epigraph, argued animatedly that if monks had really understood Buddhism, such violence would never have erupted in the first place. He called for a stricter system of evaluation in the seminaries to make sure all graduates who were eligible to receive the full precepts will be knowledgeable—and thus pious, ethical, and peaceful—Buddhist monks. All in all, the consensus seems to have been that the traditional curriculum and seminary system were inadequate for creating good moral monastics, and reforms were unavoidable.

This description of the roundtable critique of the traditional monastic education system makes for just one drop in a deluge of disapproval. This chapter thus begins by delineating similar attacks on the traditional curriculum articulated from within the Chogye Order in the past twenty or so years. These criticisms have recently been actualized into far-reaching curricular reforms, which, as I will argue, tend to replicate, both in form and in content, the pedagogical practices and ideals of modern Buddhist Studies. Aside from commenting on these fascinating mimetic developments, the chapter examines the widespread opposition to these pedagogical changes voiced by a number of conservative seminary teachers. It ends with a short investigation of the current clerical education systems of the other two dominant Buddhist organizations in contemporary Korea, the T'aego and Ch'ŏnt'ae Orders.

The Traditional Curriculum under Attack

Over the past twenty years or so the traditional curriculum and seminary system have been under attack. Be it in internal Chogye Order seminars, Buddhist journal articles, or online blogs, prominent monastics have frequently criticized the system for being archaic, outdated, skewed, incomprehensible, intolerably lacking, and internally incoherent—and have called for extensive reforms. As early as 1995, a monk by the name of Sŏran argued that the main problem with the education system was the backwardness of the curriculum. He claimed that it reflected certain historical Buddhist trends specific to Korea, but had very little relevance to the world today, and added that it was next to impossible to grasp Buddhism as a whole by studying it.[5] A different monastic by the name of Hyŏnsŏk similarly contended that the curriculum reflected particular Chan-focused, seventeenth-century Korean mountain Buddhism and was thus not really representative of the religion in general.[6] Others agreed that placing too much emphasis on such an ancient curriculum in today's modern information society makes Korean Buddhism seem archaic and irrelevant.[7] Tonghwasa's head teacher, Haewŏl, has been especially explicit about this. In a 2003 seminar, he stated that "it was impossible to understand Buddhism correctly through the seminary system of the day," and attempted to deconstruct the *Sajip* and *Sagyo* texts in order to show their inability to convey general Buddhist doctrine and soteriology.[8]

The context underlying these attacks seems to have been the changing conceptions regarding the fundamental objectives of monastic education. As self-perceptions of monastics in Korea gradually evolved from seeing themselves mostly as mountain Chan practitioners to placing increasing weight on their social role as propagators, seminary education began to be viewed not simply as a preparation for individual practice toward spiritual attainments, but also as a training for teaching and proselytization. Training Buddhist missionaries has, in fact, been one of the major objectives of the creation of Buddhist higher-education facilities throughout the twentieth century, yet, as we have seen, monastic mountain seminaries mostly maintained their Chan-focused traditional programs.[9] Beginning in the 1990s, however, education critics within the sangha began to call for more comprehensive seminary curricula, and programs that would be able to foster monastics skillful in explaining Buddhism to the general public.[10] In other words, reformers contended that seminary education should not focus on Chan alone, but convey an overall knowledge of Buddhism in its historical context and in relation to modern social ethics so that it could be used in future propagational and pedagogical undertakings.[11]

To be sure, this has been a controversial perspective. A considerable number of monastics maintained all along that Chan practice rather than bookish knowledge makes one a better propagator—one who is able to speak confidently from his or her own experience. Most contemporary Chogye reformers, however, follow the logic that Chan practice may allow one to know the sensation of hot and cold, but a different kind of knowledge is necessary in order to be able to explain these sensations to those who have not yet experienced them themselves.[12] One of the monks working at the Education Department, Pŏbin, stretched this rationale further, arguing that seminary education should foster a creative and initiative spirit, nurturing monastics who will not only be able to reach out and missionize among young Korean intellectuals, but who could also become social leaders on the national stage.[13] He expressed hope for Buddhist participation in Korean public discourse regarding the environmental and economic labor issues of the day. Better educated monastics would also be likely to receive greater respect in contemporary Korean society, he reasoned, and thus would be able to attract more followers.[14]

It is especially interesting to discover what it was exactly that many of these reformers viewed as the missing curricular components, which would make a more general understanding of Buddhism possible. Above all, the missing link is most frequently understood as being the Theravāda texts of the *Nikāyas,* or their counterpart, the *Āgamas*. A seminary teacher from Paegyangsa, to cite just one example, argued in a symposium in the year 2000 that although the principles of the Theravādin *Āgamas* were reflected in the Mahāyāna sutras, studying them separately would allow a better general understanding of Buddhism, and they must be added to the curriculum.[15] A special workshop on teaching the *Nikāyas* (so-called early Buddhism) was organized by the Chogye Order in 2012, with over eighty seminary teachers participating. Presentations in this meeting made clear that the way Korean Buddhism was practiced—that is, "giving students a confusing *huatou* and letting them struggle with it for a long time without knowing much about what the Buddha actually taught"—makes the understanding of Buddhism rather foggy. Instead, it was important for all monks to study the "early teachings" in order to get a clear idea of Buddhism's main structures and doctrines—the four noble truths, nirvana, the five aggregates, and the twelve-linked *pratītyasamutpāda* are explicitly cited—on which to base their practice.[16] In other words, seminary leaders stressed the need to learn the *Nikāyas* as a doctrinal basis for understanding the supposedly later Mahāyāna texts. The head of the Chogye Education Department himself, evincing adopted orientalist tendencies, stated in 2010 that one of the greatest problems with the traditional curriculum was that it was not "sticking to what the Buddha actually taught."[17] "Early Buddhism" was not part of the historical curriculum due to lack of sources, he argued, but with the increasing availability of Korean translations, studying the *Nikāyas* would be beneficial for developing a systematic understanding of Buddhism.

Now this is quite significant. It is true that in general East Asian Mahāyāna Buddhists historically did not disregard the texts of the Small Vehicle altogether, but often portrayed them simply as shallower (*ch'ŏn* 淺) teachings in their classification-of-doctrines schemas.[18] We have also seen, in the previous chapter, how Indian Buddhism has gradually become more important to Buddhist reformers in Mahāyāna regions throughout the twentieth century. Today, these Protestant-like tendencies are echoed by some of the Korean curriculum reformers who lament that the "words of the (Chan) patriarchs" are studied in seminaries instead of the real "word of the Buddha" as found in the Pāli Canon.[19] The Indian emphasis on the four noble truths and the twelve-link chain of causation, rarely mentioned in earlier Korean Buddhist curricula, are now seen as the most fundamental Buddhist teachings through which the more sophisticated Mahāyāna and Chan texts should be perceived and understood. In fact, mirroring the early-modern propensities of Rhys Davids and his fellow orientalists to search for authentic Buddhism in the ancient texts—instead of in living practices—Koreans established their very own Pāli Text Society in

1996, and began publishing vernacular translations of the *Nikāyas,* the *Visuddhimagga,* and similar works in the 2000s.[20]

The Indian sutras were not the only component missing from the traditional curriculum according to recent Chogye education reformers. The absence of the Indian Vinaya has also become rather conspicuous. A Dongguk University adjunct monk-professor and a former Chogye Education Department member, T'oehyu, argued in a recent seminar that the admonitions literature traditionally studied in seminaries—as well as the Pure Rules and bodhisattva precepts—have been "polluted" by Chinese Confucian ethics, and only the *Dharmaguptaka Vinaya* could really teach novices how to behave like Buddhist monks.[21] The "practical Vinayas" of East Asian Buddhism were no longer adequate, and a return to the Indian Vinayas encouraged instead. One of Haeinsa's seminary teachers, Chongmuk, explained rather reasonably that although some of the precepts in the Indian Vinayas were irrelevant to today's world and could not be followed, these rules should not be discarded altogether but rather studied historically in order to understand the original purpose of the Buddha and to promote faith.[22] Since the early 2000s, the Education Department has been planning to rectify this dearth in Vinaya study by installing a Vinaya Master in each and every seminary.[23] More importantly, as will be discussed below, introductory courses to the various Indian Vinayas have by now become a mandatory part of the new, unified Korean curriculum.

It is rather surprising to discover that even the Mahāyāna and Chan texts of the traditional curriculum have recently been attacked and deemed unsatisfactory. Contemporary critics deemphasize the importance of learning the historically more popular scriptures of the *Śūraṃgama* and the *Sutra of Perfect Enlightenment,* while some would like to add the *Lotus* and *Vimalakīrti* sutras to the curriculum instead.[24] In 2006, the Chogye Education Department recommended teaching only Dahui's *Letters* supplemented by the *Platform Sutra* instead of the full *Sajip* texts.[25] Soon afterward, a Dongguk University monk-professor argued in a Chogye conference that the *Sajip* treatises were not the best texts available for understanding Kanhua Chan, and recommended studying the more internationally well-known *Gateless Barrier* (*Wumenguan* 無門關) instead.[26] Another Dongguk professor contended in a different Chogye seminar that it was impossible to understand the *Awakening of Faith* without basic knowledge of the four noble truths, and that it was impossible to understand the Chan treatises of the *Sajip* without a preliminary study of the *Platform Sutra* and the essays of Bodhidharma.[27]

These proposals, which as we shall soon see have made actual impact on the contemporary monastic curriculum, illustrate the current shift of Buddhism on the peninsula away from its particular indigenous orthodoxy and closer to that of modern Buddhist Studies. The *Lotus, Platform, Vimalakīrti,* and *gongan* collections such as the *Gateless Barrier,* have been placed in a central position in modern Buddhist Studies textbooks and courses in the West and in Japan, while the *Śūraṃgama, Sutra of Perfect Enlightenment,* Dahui's *Letters,* Gaofeng's *Chan Essentials,* and other Korean traditional curricular texts have received comparatively little attention. The hegemony of modern Buddhist Studies, owing a great deal to historical Western contacts with particular Japanese sectarian Buddhist scholars, is now swaying traditional Korean Buddhist seminary education in its direction.

Another source of critique of the traditional curriculum has been its perceived internal and external incoherence. Internally, it has been repeatedly argued that the inconsistency between the sudden-enlightenment-followed-by-gradual-cultivation ideal of Zongmi's *Preface* and Chinul's *Excerpts* and the more sudden and complete subitist ideal found in Gaofeng's *Chan Essentials* was too confusing for monastic novices.[28] Others have noted that the traditional curriculum began with Chan treatises and then proceeded to Mahāyāna sutras and argued that this was (externally) incoherent with the identity of the Chogye Order as fundamentally a Chan tradition. For that reason, Haeinsa's teacher, Chongmuk, decided to move the Chan *Sajip* texts (with the addition of the *Platform Sutra*) to the end of the curriculum, creating a different flow that begins with admonitions, then moves to the Mahāyāna *Sagyo* and *Huayan,* and culminates with Chan.[29] Chongmuk believed that this structure better fitted the ideal of "discarding the teachings and entering Chan" (*sagyo ipsŏn* 捨教入禪), often attributed to the sixteenth-century Korean Chan Master, Hyujŏng.

The large seminary of Haeinsa followed Chongmuk's program for several years in the first decade of the twenty-first century. However, this move has not been widely accepted, and a number of seminary teachers told me in private conversations that they believed it was wrong to regard the *Sajip* as Chan and the *Sagyo* and *Huayan* as Mahāyāna, as all curricular texts should be read with a Chan perspective, and in fact they were all read traditionally accompanied by commentaries written by Chan masters. This controversy aside, other, more nationalistic reformers, have claimed that the curriculum was simply not sufficiently "Korean." Some lamented the fact that although the Chogye Order constitution lists the Korean monks Toŭi (道義, 783–821) and T'aego Pou (普愚, 1301–1382) as the patriarchs of the school, their works are not studied in seminaries. Chimun argued for the need to add materials by the Silla monastics Wŏnhyo and Ŭisang to the programs as well.[30]

The content of seminary education has not been the only thing disparaged in recent decades; its form has been censured too. Principally, critics pointed out that seminaries tended to focus on labor and rituals, whereas actual textual study has been peripheral and inadequate. Some have noted that an hour or two of classes five or six times a week was insufficient, and proposals have been made to extend daily class schedules to four to six hours a day.[31] Not to mention that seminary classes were often canceled due to a whole variety of temple rituals and events, for which students are expected to do most of the preparatory work. During my stay in Pŏmŏsa, for example, most classes were canceled for a week due to preparations for an elderly monk's birthday, and when I visited Pŏpchusa, classes were canceled because students had to clean the monastery prior to a lay precepts ceremony. Contemporary reformers often voice critiques of this prioritization of labor over education in the seminaries, and call for a stronger emphasis on actual classroom study.

In a 1998 Chogye forum, one seminary teacher went so far as to argue that the entire system of communal living in one "big room"—usually seen as crucial for molding novices into monks—was prohibitive of quiet study and should be abandoned.[32] Several reformers stressed the importance of creating a stricter unified evaluation and grading system of exams and reports in the seminaries in order to foster sturdier bookish attitudes among the students.[33] A humorous seminary teacher from Haeinsa told me rather sarcastically in a recent visit that soon they might also decide to allow the seminary students to skip the morning rituals in order to get a healthier night sleep for optimal learning. I should probably report that reform proposals have not gone that far yet.

Finally, reformers have tended to criticize the passive, rote repetition and the exegetical focus in seminary classrooms, in what is often called the "Confucian school style" (see chapter two). Some have called for textual study focused on more active critique, analysis, and discussion, as well as for the use of simple, modern doctrinal introductions and textbooks instead of abstruse texts as the basis for such debates.[34] The Chogye Order has organized several seminars in recent years in order to train seminary teachers in using PowerPoint presentations, internet resources, writing assignments, and class discussions.[35]

At the center of the reform suggestions stands the debate over the "*Hangŭlization*" (*Hangŭl-hwa*) of the curriculum.[36] The texts of the traditional curriculum are all written in Classical Chinese (*Hanmun*), and reading through them has become increasingly difficult for new novices in recent years as Korea has almost completely eradicated the use of these characters in the media and their study in public schools. Critics thus claim that continuing to read the curricular texts in *Hanmun* simply takes too much time, and most effort is given to merely deciphering the characters rather than going deeper into the meaning of the texts. Desperate students have often ended up photocopying the notes of their seniors and/or purchasing modern Korean (*Hangŭl*) translations on their own. Accordingly, the head of the Chogye Education Department contended in 2010 that just as East Asians studied the Sanskrit sutras in Chinese translations, and as Korean Christians read the Bible in Korean rather than in Hebrew or Greek, Korean Buddhists should begin learning the texts in the vernacular. Of course, mastering these works in their original languages was still valuable, he added, but it should be relegated to specialized institutions rather than be the focus of the basic education of all monastics.[37] As we shall see, such suggestions to *Hangŭlize* the curriculum have met strong opposition from the majority of today's seminary teachers.

The New Curriculum

The critiques and reform proposals soon turned into actual modifications on the ground. The first came in the early 2000s, as the Chogye Education Department came up with a new recommended syllabus for all seminaries. Structured in a new way based on the Tripitaka-style classification of texts into Sutras, Vinaya, and Treatises, the Chogye attempted to supplement the traditional curriculum with more canonical Vinaya as well as with modern vernacular histories and introductions to multiple Buddhist themes. The study of computers and foreign languages was also encouraged in this new syllabus, as well as the practices of rituals, work, chanting, and even meditation for the students. The *Lotus, Vimalakīrti,* and *Platform* sutras—popular in Buddhist Studies today—as well as the *Āgamas*, were added to the program. This curricular model is presented in table 6.

Some of the larger seminaries restructured their classes according to this new Chogye recommended program, at least partially. Songgwangsa, for example, added lectures on a few treatises by Chinul and Wŏnhyo, on the *Platform* and the *Brahma Net* sutras, on Yogācāra thought, and on basic Buddhist history.[38] Most seminaries have attempted to supplement their syllabi with Buddhist history and Indian texts. Yet, all seminaries have maintained the traditional curricular texts as the basis of their programs. This began to change only in 2010 as the Chogye promulgated a new, unified curriculum mandatory for all of its affiliated seminaries. This is now the sole official required curriculum of the Chogye Order, and it paints a picture of Buddhism that is quite different from its older counterpart. It is detailed in table 7.

The first thing noticeable about this new curriculum is the change of focus from studying *Hanmun* classical texts to going through various vernacular-based thematic overviews and introductions. As we have seen, before 2010, seminary curricula were based on readings of the Classical Chinese traditional curricular texts, only marginally supplemented by general histories. Now, however, only one class per semester—less than one-fourth of the entire curriculum—is dedicated to such readings of classical texts, while the rest of the study is done with general textbooks. This makes for a great hermeneutic shift in the way textual study is done in monastic settings in Korea. Seminary teachers often regard the traditional exegetical style of reading and decoding classical texts in their original languages—in this case Classical Chinese—as a form of Buddhist practice in itself, while reading summaries and histories as a more secular pedagogical form, which involves gaining knowledge about a topic. The difference is principally between viewing study as a form of

Table 6 Chogye Order Curricular Plans in the Early 2000s

	Sutra	Vinaya	Treatise	Electives	Practice
Ch'imun Course (緇門)	*Admonitions to the Gray-Robed Monks*	Introduction to Vinaya	1. History of Indian Buddhism 2. Introduction to Religious Studies 3. History of Buddhist Doctrine	1. Computers 2. Rituals 3. Foreign languages 4. *Āgamas* 5. Mādhyamika and Yogācāra 6. *Lotus Sutra* 7. *Vimalakīrti Sutra* 8. *Platform Sutra*	Morning rituals, communal work, meditation, and chanting
Fourfold Collection Course (四集)	1. Zongmi's *Preface* 2. Dahui's *Letters* 3. Chinul's *Excerpts* 4. Gaofeng's *Chan Essentials*	The Novice Precepts	1. History of Chinese Buddhism 2. Introduction to the Sutras 3. Introduction to Chan Texts		
Four Sutras Course (四敎)	1. *Śūraṃgama Sutra* 2. *Awakening of Faith* 3. *Diamond Sutra* 4. *Sutra of Perfect Enlightenment*	Daoxuan's *Jingxin jieguan fa* (淨心戒觀法)	1. History of Korean Buddhism 2. Introduction to Mahāyāna Buddhism 3. Comparative Religion		
High Teachings Course (大敎)	*Huayan Sutra*	*Brahma Net Sutra*	1. History of Chan Thought 2. History of the Chogye Order 3. Propagation Methods		

Source: I put this table together by combining two Chogye Order proposals that were put forth in 1999 and 2007. See: Taehan Pulgyo Chogyejong Kyoyugwŏn, "(Untitled Report)," 1999, 75–76; and Taehan Pulgyo Chogyejong Kyoyugwŏn, "Sŭngga kyoyuk kwajong mit kyoyuk kigwan annae."

Table 7 The New Compulsory Unified Chogye Order Seminary Curriculum

Year	First Semester	Second Semester
First year	1. Reading Chinese Buddhist Texts 1 2. Introduction to Buddhism 3. Introduction to Vinaya 4. History of World Buddhism (video lectures) 5. Elective	1. Reading Chinese Buddhist Texts 2 2. Understanding Early Buddhism 3. Introduction to Chan 4. History of Korean Buddhism 5. Elective
Second year	1. Reading Chinese Buddhist Texts 3 2. Early Buddhist Texts 1 3. Buddhist Rituals 1 4. Beginner Buddhist English 1 5. Understanding Buddhist Cultural Heritage (video lectures)	1. Reading Chinese Buddhist Texts 4 2. Beginner Buddhist English 2 3. Prajñā and Mādhyamika Thought (video lectures) 4. Buddhist Rituals 2 5. Elective
Third year	1. Reading Chinese Buddhist Texts 5 (*Diamond Sutra*) 2. Readings in Chan Anthologies 3. Propagation Methods (video lectures) 4. The Vinaya and Buddhist Ethics (video lectures) 5. Elective	1. Reading Chinese Buddhist Texts 6 2. Understanding Kanhua Chan 3. Yogācāra and Tathāgatagarbha Thought 4. Pure Land Thought 5. Elective
Fourth year	1. Reading Chinese Buddhist Texts 7 2. Huayan Thought 3. Elective	1. Reading Chinese Buddhist Texts 8 2. Buddhism and Society (video lectures) 3. Elective 4. Thesis Writing

Source: Taehan Pulgyo Chogyejong Kyoyugwŏn, "2014 yŏndo sŭngga taehak p'yojun kyoyuk kwajŏng annae."

contemplative practice in itself, and seeing it as preparation for practice. Soon we shall see how this aspect of the new curriculum is almost universally disputed by seminary teachers today.

For now, we may note that, aside from the *Diamond Sutra*—which remains mandatory reading in the third year—seminary teachers may select the texts they wish to teach in the Reading Chinese Buddhist Texts courses. Most choose, time permitting, to continue to teach some of the texts of the traditional curriculum. Almost all continue to read at least a part of the *Ch'imun* in the first year and several chapters from the *Huayan* in the last.[39] However, due to lack of class time, much of the *Sajip* and *Sagyo* texts have had to be set aside. The *Sajip* texts have suffered the most from these reforms. Most seminaries elect to read Dahui's *Letters*, but only a few teachers also go through Gaofeng's *Chan*

Essentials or Zongmi's *Preface*. Chinul's *Excerpts* has been deleted from the schedules of all seminaries today, even at his home temple of Songgwangsa.[40] The *Śūraṃgama* has not fared much better, and most seminaries today only read through the first chapters of the *Awakening of Faith* (and perhaps some of the *Sutra of Perfect Enlightenment*) in their third year Chinese Buddhist Texts courses.[41]

Instead of *Sajip* and *Sagyo* readings, and as a response to the critiques of the traditional curriculum discussed above, the new program involves three required courses that deal exclusively with Pāli Buddhism (Introduction to Buddhism,[42] Understanding Early Buddhism, and Early Buddhist Texts 1); four required new Vinaya-related courses (Introduction to Vinaya, The Vinaya and Buddhist Ethics, and Buddhist Rituals 1 and 2); four general overviews of various Mahāyāna doctrines (Prajñā and Mādhyamika Thought, Yogācāra and Tathāgatagarbha Thought, Pure Land Thought, and Huayan Thought); three new Chan introductions (Introduction to Chan, Reading Chan Anthologies, and Understanding Kanhua Chan); and five required classes on Buddhist history, culture, and propagation (History of World Buddhism, History of Korean Buddhism, Propagation Methods, Understanding Buddhist Cultural Heritage, and Buddhism and Society). The only required language classes on the curricula are English rather than Pāli, Sanskrit, or Chinese. Two "Buddhist English" classes are now mandatory courses in the second year, and the Chogye Order has recently published two Buddhist English textbooks to be used in these classes.[43] As will be discussed further in the next chapter, the purpose of studying English in monasteries is primarily international propagation, and the textbooks thus focus on useful expressions for welcoming foreign visitors to the temples and for guiding Temple Stay participants.[44]

Seminary teachers tend to emphasize that "students are like trees that have been replanted somewhere else and thus can easily be disturbed from the outside, so they must be strictly isolated."[45] As the various admonitions similarly illustrate, the less monastic novices associate with the laity, the better. Consequently, lay involvement with the seminaries has been frowned upon and often strictly forbidden. Nevertheless, due to the sheer amount of new specialized courses to be taught in the new program, many of the monasteries today simply had to resort to inviting lay academic specialists or language teachers to come to the monasteries and teach once or twice a week.[46] In addition, some have opened their gates and begun sending their novices to attend classes in nearby secular universities for credit. Both Hwaŏmsa and Paegyangsa are examples of temples that have established connections with nearby universities and regularly dispatch their novices to classes on social welfare outside the monastery proper.[47] To remedy the lack of specialist teachers in the seminaries, the Chogye Order has recently prepared a variety of video lectures for the new courses on the curriculum.

The new program includes seven elective courses throughout the four years. The formal list of authorized electives illustrates the same tendency to add courses on Indian Buddhism, general Mahāyāna, and contemporary issues related to Buddhist culture and society. The list consists of Early Buddhist Texts 2, Understanding the Abhidharma, Introduction to Mahāyāna, Tiantai Thought, Esoteric Buddhism, Mahāyāna in Practice, Reading Chan Anthologies 2, Chan Practice, Guiding Chan Meditation, Computers, Buddhism and Eastern/Western Philosophy (video lectures available), Buddhist Biology, Buddhism and Social Welfare, Buddhism and Women, Understanding World Religions (video lectures available), Buddhism and Science, Buddhist Psychological Counseling, Essay Writing, Buddhist English (Intermediate and High), Chinese, Japanese, Tibetan, Sanskrit (video lectures available), and Pāli (video lectures available). Nevertheless, my fieldwork in seminaries in 2014–2015 showed that no teachers had yet dared to venture into teaching such classes as Buddhism and psychology, science, biology, and so forth, and most either used video lectures for their electives or kept to the more conventional Mahāyāna and Chan electives.

Attempting to provide proper class time for the numerous new required courses on the reformed curriculum, some (though certainly not all) seminaries have added an additional hour or two of formal classes in the afternoons.[48] Final exams at the end of semesters have also been gradually becoming the norm, though no actual grades are usually given. Students often explain that these exams do not really matter, and failure to pass is not likely to create problems in graduating. Some teachers give out writing assignments as well, adding a whole new dimension to the kind of knowledge expected of Buddhist monks in Korea. In Songgwangsa, for instance, all novices write a twelve-page graduation thesis in their final year. New modern classrooms with desks and chairs have replaced the traditional form of having classes in the "big rooms" in some of the schools. Group graduation trips, most commonly to the Buddhist sites of India and sometimes to famous mountains in China or Japan, have also become customary. I provide the current schedules of T'ongdosa's seminary in table 8, as an example of the way the new syllabus has been adopted in one particular location.

Buddhism Simulating Buddhist Studies

Oliver Freiberger wrote in 2004 that "the discipline of Buddhist Studies has created its own teaching canon: a secondary canon, as it were, extracted from the primary one."[49] More recently, Stephen Berkwitz surveyed the genre of "textbook Buddhism," which, he convincingly argues, is a largely coherent form of the religion as imagined by modern scholars in an attempt to summarize this multidimensional tradition across time and place, focusing on Indian history,

Table 8 The 2013 Seminary Class Schedules of T'ongdosa

<table>
<tr><th colspan="2">First Semester</th><th>Mon</th><th>Tue</th><th>Wed</th><th>Thurs</th><th>Fri</th><th>Sat</th></tr>
<tr><td rowspan="3">First year</td><td>7:00–8:15</td><td colspan="5">Chinese Buddhist Texts (Guishan's Admonitions from the Ch'imun)</td><td>Understanding Early Buddhism (video lecture)</td></tr>
<tr><td>8:15–9:30</td><td colspan="3">Introduction to Buddhism, History of Korean Buddhism</td><td colspan="2">Early Buddhist texts (Suttanipada)</td><td></td></tr>
<tr><td>afternoon</td><td></td><td></td><td></td><td></td><td></td><td></td></tr>
<tr><td rowspan="3">Second year</td><td>7:00–8:15</td><td colspan="3">Chinese Buddhist Texts (Diamond Sutra)</td><td></td><td rowspan="2">Understanding Abhidharma</td><td>Understanding Buddhist Cultural Heritage (video lecture)</td></tr>
<tr><td>8:15–9:30</td><td colspan="3">Chinese Language, The Order and Modern Ethics</td><td></td><td></td></tr>
<tr><td>afternoon</td><td></td><td></td><td></td><td></td><td></td><td></td></tr>
<tr><td rowspan="3">Third year</td><td>7:00–8:15</td><td colspan="3">Chinese Buddhist Texts (Diamond Sutra)</td><td rowspan="2">Chinese language</td><td></td><td>Propagation Methods (video lecture)</td></tr>
<tr><td>8:15–9:30</td><td colspan="3">Chinese Buddhist Texts (Awakening of Faith)</td><td></td><td></td></tr>
<tr><td>afternoon</td><td></td><td></td><td></td><td>Chanting rituals</td><td></td><td></td></tr>
<tr><td rowspan="3">Fourth year</td><td>7:00–8:15</td><td colspan="3" rowspan="2">Chinese Buddhist Texts (Huayan Sutra)</td><td rowspan="2">Special lecture</td><td colspan="2" rowspan="2">Chinese Buddhist Texts (Huayan Sutra)</td></tr>
<tr><td>8:15–9:30</td></tr>
<tr><td>afternoon</td><td></td><td></td><td></td><td></td><td></td><td></td></tr>
</table>

Second Semester		Mon	Tue	Wed	Thurs	Fri	Sat
First year	7:00–8:15	Chinese Buddhist Texts (The *42-Sections Sutra* and the *Bequeathed Teachings Sutra*)		Understanding World Buddhism (video lecture)	Chinese Buddhist Texts (The *42-Sections Sutra* and the *Bequeathed Teachings Sutra*)		
	8:15–9:30	Early Buddhist Texts, Introduction to the Vinaya, Mahāyāna Precepts			Introduction to Chan		
Second year	7:00–8:15	Chinese-character Buddhist Texts (*Mirror of Sŏn*)		Introduction to Mahāyāna	Chinese-character Buddhist Texts (*Mirror of Sŏn*)		Prajñā and Mādhyamika Thought (video lecture)
	8:15–9:30	History of World Buddhism (video lecture)			Chinese language		
	afternoon		Chanting rituals				
Third year	7:00–8:15	Chinese Buddhist Texts (*Śūraṃgama Sutra*)					Buddhism and Society (video lecture)
	8:15–9:30	Understanding Kanhua Chan, Yogācāra and Tathāgatagarbha Thought			Chan Anthologies (Chinul's *Secret of Cultivating the Mind, Susim kyŏl* 修心訣)		
Fourth year	7:00–8:15	Chinese Buddhist Texts (*Huayan Sutra*)		Pure Land Thought	Chinese Buddhist Texts (*Huayan Sutra*)		
	8:15–9:30						

Source: Data collected during a visit in October 2013.

karma, rebirth, and the four noble truths.[50] The discipline of Buddhist Studies has certainly been reframing Buddhism by canonizing these particular foci into its "sacred" textbooks. This new canon was selectively extracted out of the "primary" Asian canons, yet, in many ways it has by now replaced them, making it increasingly unclear whether it is the scholars who study the Buddhists or the Buddhists who study the scholars. Indeed, instead of scholars looking into the living curricula of Asian monasteries in order to find out what Buddhism is all about and what texts they are supposed to be studying, it seems more common for monastics to be the ones who look for Buddhism outside their own monasteries—in secular university halls, libraries, and English introductory textbooks.

In his introduction to Baudrillard's *The Gulf War Did Not Take Place,* Patton recalls a fascinating occurrence from the first Gulf War when "the CNN cameras crossed live to a group of reporters assembled somewhere in the Gulf, only to have them confess that they were also sitting around watching CNN in order to find out what was happening."[51] Reporters watching the news in order to find out what they are supposed to be reporting seems to some extent comparable to Asian Buddhist monastics looking outside their clusters to the canons of modern Buddhist Studies in order to find out what they are supposed to be doing in their monasteries.

Encounters between peoples and cultures often ignite the mimetic syndrome, in which one culture emulates another in the hope that some of the power of the "other" will rub off on to themselves. Panamanian Cuna Indians replaced their idols with figurines of white conquistadores and Meiji Japanese businessmen exchanged their robes for suits and ties in order to partake in the power of the hegemonic "other."[52] In a similar way, Michael Lambert has highlighted the mimetic dimensions of the Tibetan School for Buddhist Dialectics in Dharamsala, which in recent years has become more feminist, individualistic, and democratic in order to foster strategic alliances with the liberal West for the support of the Tibetan nationalist project.[53] Unlike the exiled Tibetans, Korean monastic reformers certainly do not embrace such explicit political motivations, yet, by mimicking the practices of Buddhist Studies, they do expect that some of its modern, rational, educated "aura" will rub off and enable them to project a more powerful image, expedient for the propagation of their faith.

One interesting piece of evidence for this contagion might be found in the *Teacher Guides* the Chogye Order published in 2012. These teachers' textbooks were distributed to all seminaries, and although not yet widely used to date,[54] they represent the official authorized direction the Order wishes to take. The Education Department put together seven such books, each on a different theme—Early Buddhism, Mahāyāna, Chan, Chinese Texts, Applied Buddhism, Buddhist History, and Vinaya and Ethics—overall containing forty-one separate course syllabi.[55] Remarkably, the reading lists for these syllabi include

Korean translations of thirty of the most canonical works in Western languages in Buddhist Studies. Étienne Lamotte's tome on Indian Buddhism is there, as is Walpola Rahula's *What the Buddha Taught,* which has perhaps become *the* canonical text of Buddhist Studies taught in numerous university Introduction to Buddhism courses.[56] Frederick Streng's book on Nagarjuna is also now part of the official Chogye syllabi, along with Francis Cook's introduction to Huayan thought, Christopher Queen and Rick Fields' treatment of modern Buddhism, as well as publications on comparative religion by Ninian Smart, Joachim Wach, Eric Sharpe, and others. Two books by Paul Williams on Mahāyāna Buddhism are also recommended for seminary learning, perhaps indicating that Korean monastics are unaware of his famous refutation of Buddhism and conversion to Catholicism.[57] Mel Gibson's *The Passion of Christ,* along with the 1993 film *The Little Buddha,* are also recommended on the Comparative Religions syllabus. Aside from Korean books and translations of English books, the syllabi also include forty-eight translations of Japanese academic sources.

It is also interesting to discover that the seven syllabi offered in the *Teacher Guide* for the Chinese Text Reading courses do not include course plans for classes on the *Sajip* texts or the *Śūraṃgama Sutra*. Instead, they offer programs of study of the *Platform Sutra* and two native Korean texts: the thirteenth-century mythological-historical collection of the *Samguk yusa* (三國遺事, Memorabilia of the Three Kingdoms), and the sixteenth-century *Mirror of Sŏn*.[58] If we view these syllabi as the proposed new canon of the Chogye Order—and I do believe we should view them this way—then the trend is clear: they represent a move away from the texts that traditionally informed Korean Buddhism and into different kinds of texts and foci, those of modern Buddhist Studies.

To be sure, this re-importation of Buddhism is by no means strictly a local Korean phenomenon. Scholars have long noticed similar "reverse-orientalism" and "pizza-effects," in which just as pizzas have been re-imported from America to Italy to form the contemporary style of the food, modern Western-influenced types of Buddhism have often become popular in East Asia, replacing traditional forms of the religion.[59] Some well-known examples of this are Henry Steel Olcott's 1881 *Buddhist Catechism,* which has been studied by monastics in Ceylon; Paul Carus's *The Gospel of Buddhism,* which has been studied by Pure Land priests in Japan; and the Thai monastic textbooks written by King Chulalongkorn and Prince Wachirayan that have covered materials drawn from Rhys Davids and the Pāli Text Society.[60] Other examples include the (New Age) writings of Osho Rajneesh on Zen, which have reportedly been read in Japanese monasteries; Jeffrey Hopkins' English commentaries on certain sutras, which have been read by exiled Tibetan monks during the Kalachakra initiation; and Joseph Goldstein's books on Insight Meditation, which are occasionally studied by Burmese monks.[61] John Nelson reported of a

Japanese Rinzai Zen monk, Rev. Kawakami, who returned to Japan after studying religion in an American university and decided to propagate and focus his teaching on the Dhammapada—usually understood as Theravādin.[62] Some of the contemporary Chogye Order reformers were certainly likewise influenced by this modern academic canon directly, while studying in foreign universities. A former Haeinsa seminary teacher who has been one of the leaders of the current reforms, for example, graduated from Columbia University. Most Chogye monastic reformers, however, have come to rely on the canon of Buddhist Studies through the curricula of their very own Dongguk University.

In his *Curators of the Buddha,* Donald Lopez seems to have prophesized the current reforms in making the argument that Western scholars of Buddhism created an authentic Buddhism through which "all the Buddhisms of the modern Orient were to be judged, and to be found lacking."[63] Contemporary Chogye Order reformers have been doing just that—judging and reinterpreting their traditional curriculum through the lens of the canon of Buddhist Studies, and finding it inadequate. Nevertheless, prudent readers may have noticed that I have been careful thus far not to identify this canon of Buddhist Studies as "Western." I do believe that it was formed mainly in the affluent universities of North America, Europe, and, to some extent, Japan, and these prominent institutions imbue the emerging canon of Buddhist Studies with legitimacy in the eyes of many Asian Buddhists. Nevertheless, it is not only Westerners—whatever that category may still mean today—who are involved in the creation of this new canon, but academics from a plethora of national and ethnic backgrounds, many of whom are practicing Buddhists themselves, and a minority of whom are ordained monastics. In fact, certain scholars have been calling for the need to bridge the gap between Buddhist theology (with insider perspectives and goals) and religious studies (with outsider perspectives) in Western academia, and pioneering programs in "Buddhist Ministry" have been recently established at Harvard and at Boston University.[64]

The canon of Buddhist Studies focuses mainly on the Pāli sutras and on several oft-translated and studied Mahāyāna works. The Japanese influence on the Chan (or Zen) part of this canon is palpable, as most scholars of Zen (as well as many Western practitioners) focus their research on Japan. This Japanese impact on the Buddhist Studies canon can be traced back to early-twentieth-century Japanese teachers who taught in the West, and has been sustained to this day through established institutional and financial connections between North American and Japanese universities, which enable students to pursue the study of Japanese Buddhism with relative ease. Countless Buddhist Studies scholars, even those not specializing in Japanese Buddhism, are trained in the Japanese language in order to read secondary research originating in Japan, a trend that must contribute to the bias.[65]

The Buddhist Studies canon consequently tends to focus on the key texts emphasized by Japanese Zen masters, on the *Platform* and the *Vimalakīrti* sutras, the *Gateless Barrier* and other kōan collections studied in Japanese Zen monasteries, as well as on the writings of Dōgen and other prominent Japanese teachers.[66] Although the fallacy of categorizing Buddhist history through the sectarian eyes of modern Japanese scholarship has been increasingly acknowledged by recent research,[67] these categories have nonetheless by now become the elementary "common sense" of the discipline. As we have seen in chapter one, most works found on the Korean traditional curriculum only receive marginal attention in the canon of Buddhist Studies. Yet, the new reforms bring the Chogye Order's pedagogical program closer to the curricula of Buddhist Studies, and subsequently bring Korean *Sŏn* closer to Japanese Zen. Many of the seminary teachers, however, have been unhappy with these changes, often viewing them as the "secularization" of their traditional monastic lifestyle.

The Education Department versus Seminary Teachers

A Chogye survey conducted in the year 2000 among 30 seminary teachers and close to 700 students revealed that only 56 percent supported curricular modifications.[68] Almost all of these reform supporters, however, thought it would be best to simply supplement the traditional program with some general courses in religious studies, Buddhist history, and English (as many as 54 percent wanted English classes). Only 25 percent thought the *Ch'imun* and *Sajip* should be substituted by modern subjects, and over 85 percent did not wish to extend the daily class time beyond three hours a day.[69] A more general 2009 survey among over a thousand Chogye Order monastics who were not necessarily associated with seminaries illustrated more favorable attitudes toward curricular reforms. Seventy-four percent of the respondents in that survey contended that the traditional curriculum must be modernized.[70]

Nonetheless, many of the more conservative seminary teachers strongly opposed the rearrangement plans, some bluntly shunning the seminary reform colloquia organized by the Order. H. M. Vos has likened canonization to putting on a straitjacket, fixing a particular tradition in such a way that dismantling it may release madness and chaos.[71] The particular canon of texts that has been fixed as the traditional curriculum of Korean Buddhist monasticism has likewise come to encapsulate notions of stability, authority, and identity, and its de-canonization has thus been seen as precarious. Hence, it is perhaps unsurprising to find that most seminary teachers I have met in monasteries in recent years, while grudgingly altering their syllabi, continue to voice objections to the new curriculum. Change could not have happened without a fight.

Haeinsa, perhaps the most politically oriented monastery in Korea, with close connections to the Chogye administration, was the first to transform its curriculum in 2010–2011 in line with the new Chogye plans.[72] Soon afterward, some of the smaller seminaries, such as Sudŏksa and Hwaŏmsa, which have been more favorable to the changes, began transforming, as did the female seminaries that generally tend to be less disputatious with the central authorities. In 2012, the seminary of Songgwangsa also began to reform its curriculum. Many of the teachers I have talked with have said that this surprised everyone, because Songgwangsa was generally known to be highly conservative, and a Study Supervisor (*Hakkam*) from one of the nunneries whispered in my ear that "they were simply bribed to change." One of the lay workers in the Chogye administration confirmed that seminaries that resist directives have sometimes received economic incentives to reform.

Yet, persistent opposition remained in T'ongdosa, Korea's largest male Buddhist seminary today, as well as in some smaller monasteries, such as Pŏmŏsa and Ssanggyesa. The dispute between T'ongdosa and the headquarters was so tense at one point, in fact, that the monastery boycotted the annual joint seminary sporting event organized by the Order in 2012. In 2013, the Education Department finally decided to put an end to this conflict and threatened that novices who were not taught according to the new program will not be able to receive the full precepts after graduation and become official Chogye-affiliated monastics. This made all open opposition disappear. Today, all seminaries officially claim to follow the new curriculum.

The main grievance of teachers who resist the new curriculum is that it converts their monasteries into secular universities. As early as 1995, a traditionalist monk by the name of Sŏran argued vehemently that "converting practice places to universities is like giving up the original attitude of the sangha," and that trying to mix monasticism with modern universities is as ridiculous as "wearing a Confucian hat along with a Western-style suit and tie."[73] His passionate opposition to the reforms was tangible as he hyperbolized, arguing that converting seminaries to universities was equal to "killing the Buddhists and the Buddha Dharma, and returning monks to secular life."[74]

One thoughtful Ssangyesa seminary teacher had a more romantic criticism for such reforms. He explained that when regular people get sick they eat (medicine) in order to get better, but monks fast and rest the body to get better. Similarly, he stated, secular universities teach by filling the mind with knowledge and seminaries teach in order to rest the mind.[75] He added that the teaching method of simple memorization of short passages every day is a great way to rest and clear the mind, much more fruitful for monastics than stuffing the brain with a great deal of knowledge.[76]

This sort of reasoning seems to be echoed in Paul Griffiths' distinction between "religious reading" and "consumerist reading."[77] "Religious reading" involves deep engagement with particular texts—savoring, vocalizing, copying, and commenting on them "in the service of creation, maintenance, and development of religious accounts."[78] "Consumerist reading," in contrast, is what academics do—reading a mass of multiple texts in a disengaged, detached manner. The bibliography of this very book demonstrates the reality of these claims. Not only does Griffiths agree with some of the seminary teachers that such "religious reading" is more fitting for religious settings, he goes further, arguing that "consumerist reading" may not even be the best way for university scholars to study religion, as it distances them from their object of study.

A Pŏmŏsa teacher expressed what might be the most pessimistic critique of modernizing the seminaries:

> As the sangha educational environment gets contaminated by materialistic culture under the "pretty name" of modernization, its autonomous nature is gradually lost. Great material facilities rather become causes for the obstruction of practice, making the minds of the monastic students scattered and generally without interest in study. Many students do not know why they came to the seminaries and what they have to do there, feel no interest in the courses studied, and gradually lose confidence in their way. They therefore become interested in things that are unrelated to practice, and the only purpose of their stay [in the seminary] is receiving the full bhikṣu precepts at the end [of their course].[79]

Many seminary teachers express similar concerns regarding the compatibility of their novices with this new, academically oriented curriculum. A teacher from Pŏpchusa told me that most of his students were not interested in study and were simply waiting to graduate in order to join a Chan Hall. Others have pointed out that many of their students were older—in 2012 only 27 percent of new Chogye novices were under the age of 30, 36 percent being over 40[80]—and were thus not very attracted to study. Some of them supposedly had "complexes" about school study as they were not very good in that field before leaving home. In fact, only approximately 30 percent of new monastic novices in Korea graduated from a university before leaving home, which is only about half of the overall ratio of university graduates in the country.[81]

A female novice from Unmunsa told me rather poignantly that if she wanted a textbook education she would not have left home, and is very disappointed to have to go through such an academic curriculum in the mountains. Many new monastics leave home in order to get away from such secular activities, and are similarly disappointed to have to go through the new seminary program, which resembles to a large extent the system they were eager to leave behind. Nevertheless, not all novices are disappointed and more than a few do enjoy their scholarly pursuits in the seminaries. Some argue that making the seminary a mandatory condition for full ordination is problematic, as those who are not interested in book learning must study together with those who are, a situation that damages the overall classroom environment and performance.[82]

Virtually every seminary teacher I have met expressed his or her opposition to the *Hangŭlization* of the curriculum. The vernacularization of Buddhism in Korea began as soon as the new alphabet was invented in the fifteenth century, accelerated in the twentieth century with numerous sutra translation projects led by individuals such as Yongsŏng and institutions such as Pongsŏnsa, and culminated with the initiation of the translation project of the entire Buddhist canon into Korean in 2007.[83] In recent years, some of the liturgical chants—most conspicuously the *Heart Sutra*—are also regularly recited in their modern Korean translation, a fact that may contribute to the general understanding of the sutra, but nonetheless simply does not sit well on the beat of the *mokt'ak*, the small wooden fish instrument used in rituals. The main complaint of the seminary teachers about the *Hangŭlization* of the curriculum, however, is not concerned with the correct chanting rhythms, but with the perceived loss of the special "taste" of the Chinese characters in translations and overviews. Studying a large number of introductory courses is often understood as making seminary study more superficial, and the study of the Chinese texts—with the various possible crisscrossing connotations of each character—as deeper and more satisfying. In fact, it has been reported that the traditional characters are used in place of the new simplified ones in religious settings even on the Chinese mainland, as they are believed to better embody authoritative pasts and to inspire more profound comprehensions.[84]

One of the leaders of the opposition to the new Chogye program and to the *Hangŭlization* of the curriculum is the current head teacher of T'ongdosa, Hyŏnjin. Hyŏnjin is admired by his students and seems to be very well respected, not only in the T'ongdosa community, but among other monastics in the Order as well. He turned out to be a great host, too. When I visited T'ongdosa's seminary in 2014, he greeted me with a bright smile, showed me his several-hundred-years-old edition of the *Huayan Sutra,* and prepared his best tea leaves for our conversation. He said he believed that a deep engagement with a single passage, tasting and chewing it over and over, and going deeper into its meaning, was a much more significant practice for monks than learning a mass of texts.[85] He emphasized that this type of study was better in *Hanmun,* not simply because he liked the Chinese characters, but because a lot of the complex meaning of the characters was simply lost in translation. Echoing what seems to be a prevalent understanding among seminary teachers, he explained that there was no need to study early Buddhism separately, as Mahāyāna encapsulated the early teachings completely. In fact, Hyŏnjin claimed that if studied properly—with commentaries and a good teacher—the *Huayan Sutra* encapsulated the entire teachings of Buddhism and no other textual study was necessary for monastics. He is a charismatic speaker, and when I left his room I found myself strangely convinced.

To be sure, more reform-minded monastics tend to caricature the seminary teachers' attachment to the Chinese characters. They seem to have a point in claiming that teachers resist *Hangŭlization* in order to maintain the social prestige they earned as experts in the texts of the traditional curriculum. Their skill in Classical Chinese could be considered to be their monastic "social capital" that ensures their perpetual retention of positions of power in the Order, and some may fear losing this special status. A blogger, probably a Chogye monastic, who calls himself Magnolia (*Hubak namu*), has ridiculed seminary teachers for clinging to the Chinese texts as the "original" despite the fact that the texts are themselves understood to be translations of Sanskrit. He added that many teachers have simply become too comfortable in their chairs and too lazy to start preparing for new courses.[86] Other reformers argue, somewhat sarcastically, that teachers tend to resist allocating more study time as they need the students for a variety of other sundry tasks at the monastery. A Tonghwasa teacher told me with a dose of ambivalent humor that if novices were to actually spend so much time studying, "who will ring the bells, chant, and clean the monastery?"

Some seminary teachers who were in favor of curricular reforms in the early 2000s now lament that they may have gone too far. One monastic teacher calculated that several years ago the *Huayan Sutra* was studied for a total of 336 hours in the seminaries, but was now reduced to a mere unproductive 28-hour course called Huayan Thought.[87] Even the teachers at Haeinsa, the seminary that led the reforms, now express objections to the new system. One of them told me explicitly that the new program is "Buddhist Studies, not Buddhism," and he does not want to be a part of it. Chungmok, an elderly Haeinsa teacher who has been active in the Chogye reforms debate told me that there are simply too many classes in the new program. He believes that the best thing would be to have a 1:1 ratio between traditional and modern classes. When I asked him why, if so many teachers object to the new program, the Education Department continues to insist on it? He calmly explained that he was working with several other seminary teachers on an orderly report regarding the application of the new curriculum and the need for another reform. He plans to present this report to the Chogye administration in the near future, and only time will tell whether the new program will be restructured yet again, soon.

The Seminaries of the T'aego and Ch'ŏnt'ae Orders

The T'aego Order (太古宗) is undoubtedly the second most dominant Buddhist institution in Korea, embracing over three thousand affiliated temples and almost nine thousand clergy members as of 2013.[88] It parted ways with the Chogye Order in 1970 after a long and violent so-called Purification Movement.[89] The separation between the Chogye and the T'aego is not doctrinal but disciplinary: T'aego clergy members are allowed to eat meat and marry openly while Chogye monastics are not supposed to. Nevertheless, many of the T'aego clergy I have met made it a point to emphasize that not all of them get married, and I did get the impression that a large ratio of the female members, in particular, lead an abstinent life. The T'aego actually maintains a slightly larger number of temples than the Chogye, but the majority of them are small, family-run, urban shrines.

Seminary education is not a mandatory requirement for ordination in this Buddhist organization and very few actually go through it, though the clergy working at the headquarters assured me that they were planning a reform to make education obligatory for ordination, just as it is in the Chogye Order. In fact, a small number of ambitious T'aego Order monks end up studying in Chogye seminaries.[90] The only currently operating T'aego Order mountain monastic seminary, housed in beautiful Sŏnamsa, has had only about three hundred graduates since it was established in 1975.[91] It is a mixed-gender monastery that housed eighteen male and seven female T'aego clergy students when I visited in 2014. Only two teachers taught at this small school at the time. The monastery also houses perhaps the sole T'aego Order Chan Hall—although only four to five clerics sit there in each retreat—and they also have plans to establish a Vinaya School.

Ironically, the T'aego, often stigmatized as a modern, impure Buddhist institution, operates the only seminary in Korea today that still follows the entire "pure" traditional curriculum. Nevertheless, just as in the Chogye Order, the T'aego main offices have recently been busy making plans to supplement and broaden this syllabus. The proposed program (shown to me at the headquarters) intends to supplement the traditional curriculum with courses on Indian Buddhism, Buddhist psychology and science, BBC documentaries on Buddhism, Thich Nhat Hanh's books on Vipassanā, video talks by the Dalai Lama, the *Laozi*, the *Book of Changes*, the *Analects*, classes on Tibetan Buddhism, translations of the writings of the eccentric New Age writer Ken Wilber (!), and even translations from the writings of Indian hippie gurus Maharishi and Osho Rajneesh. This curriculum plan is so broad one may very well ask if Buddhism is still its central focus.

Yet, my visit to Sŏnamsa proved that, central plans aside, life goes on as usual in the mountains. The texts of the traditional curriculum were still studied at the seminary in *Hanmun* for an hour every morning, five days a week. For students of the first two years the morning classes were supplemented by ritual classes in the afternoons. These days they also hold an hour a week of "Early Buddhism" lectures for the first two years, and *Abhidharmakośa* classes for the latter two. Once a week, they sit together for a communal fifty-minute Vipassanā meditation session (not Kanhua Chan but Vipassanā), as well as hold a calligraphy class. When I asked the friendly fifty-something-year-old students who showed me around the seminary about the books by Osho, Wilber, and the Dalai Lama noted above, they told me that they are in fact available in the seminary's library and recommended for reading, but there are no classes actually dedicated to them to date.

As most T'aego clerics operate small temples and are unable to leave for a monastic seminary in the mountains, a different kind of school was established for them in 1983: the Tongbang Buddhist School. It sits in an alley behind Yonsei University in Seoul, not far from the large T'aego temple of Pongwŏnsa. It is housed in a rather indistinct and somewhat rundown, four-story building, which hides the fact that it is essentially the main school of the Buddhist T'aego Order, now boasting over 1,500 alumni. It offers two-year courses in five different departments: Buddhist Studies, Buddhist Dance, Buddhist Arts, Sangha Studies, and Sutra Translation. What is most distinct about this school, though, is that all classes are filmed and students are able to stay in their temples and attend online. I audited classes in the Sangha Studies Department at this school in 2013–2014, and twenty-nine out of the thirty-three students enrolled at the time took classes online and did not show up to class. In one case, I was the only student actually sitting in class! Others commuted, and there was also a small dormitory on-site that housed a few students. The school is open to both men and women, ordained and lay, but virtually all lay students I talked to were planning to ordain in the near future. Lay students usually wore traditional Korean clothes (*hanbok*) to class, and I gathered that many of them were children of an ordained parent. Interestingly, a significant number of ordained students did not belong to the T'aego Order but to other small Buddhist-affiliated New Religious Movements.

The Sangha Studies Department, established in 2004, essentially offers a shortened version of the traditional curriculum. The *Ch'imun* is studied in the first year, the *Chan Essentials* and the *Awakening of Faith* in the second, and these are supplemented by an Introduction to Sangha Studies, as well as by the required courses for all departments in Mahāyāna Thought, History of the T'aego Order, Rituals, *Abhidharmakośa,* Buddhist Social Welfare, and Propagation. When I attended in 2013, the *Ch'imun* was taught once a week for an hour and a half by a lay Buddhist professor specializing in Classical Chinese. Classes focused on rigorous analysis of the grammatical structures used in the text. My classmates and I—as well as perhaps most online viewers—certainly had a hard time following. The Introduction to Sangha Studies was taught by an elder T'aego cleric and one of the headmasters of the school, Suam. Classes began and ended with a bow accompanied by the *mokt'ak* instrument in an attempt to give the lecture a more monastic Buddhist feel. Much of the class contents dealt with explaining the concept of "sangha," and Suam often began his sentences with "although we in the T'aego Order do not follow this," the sangha was traditionally supposed to do such and such. In fact, the apparent complexities of trying to maintain an ordained status while living a family life often popped up during lectures at this school.

Another T'aego school opened quite recently in a suburb of Seoul, allowing clergy and laypeople to commute for classes in ritual (*pŏmp'ae*) or in another shorter version of the traditional curriculum. This school is called the Anjŏng Buddhist University, and it was opened in 2012 in Anyang (fig. 2). It is still rather small, with fewer than twenty students enrolled, almost half of whom are laypeople preparing for their ordination. The "traditional seminary course" here offers a four-year program beginning with the *Ch'imun* in the first, the *Sajip* in the second, the *Śūraṃgama* and the *Awakening of Faith* in the third, and the *Sutra of Perfect Enlightenment* and the *Diamond Sutra* in the fourth. Apart from the *Huayan Sutra,* which has been dropped from this program, it corresponds completely to the traditional curriculum. This is a new initiative and it is still unclear how successful and popular it is going to be.

The Korean Ch'ŏnt'ae Order (Ch. Tiantai; J. Tendai, 天台), which encompasses 350 temples and over 400 monastics, is the only other Buddhist organization in Korea that runs its own monastic seminary.[92] The Order was established in 1966, with the clear intention to link it to the tradition of Mt. Tiantai, though I believe it should perhaps be viewed as a Buddhist-affiliated New Religious Movement. Priests were at first allowed to remain married, though today this has been banned. Female monastics do not shave their

FIG. 2. Class time at the T'aego Order's Anjŏng Buddhist University.

heads but wear it back with two pins, and all must live in the main temple of Kuinsa. Only male monastics are allowed to head branch temples. Interestingly, monastics at this institution still do not take the full precepts, which they view as Hīnayāna. Their main practices are the chanting of *Kwanseŭm posal* (觀世音菩薩, Avalokiteśvara Bodhisattva), and diminishing sleep. New postulants are not supposed to lie down at all for the first six months, and monastics claim to only sleep about three to four hours a night and spent the rest of the dark hours chanting.[93] Numerous laypeople go to Kuinsa and other affiliated temples and participate in all-night chanting vigils. Monastics are expected to join at least two monthly retreats a year, where instead of standard meditation, chanting *Kwanseŭm posal* is practiced for long hours throughout the day.

Kuinsa, the head temple of the Ch'ŏnt'ae Order, is probably the largest monastery on the peninsula. It feels more like a small village than a temple, full of commotion and sound, buses of laypeople coming and going, and chanting constantly heard from the huge halls. A rudimentary seminary was established there in 1982, but only in 2005 did it institute a systematized, mandatory three-year education program for all postulants.[94] When I visited in 2014, the head teacher explained that there were now eleven teachers at the school, most of whom were laymen, and that male and female students held classes together, but practiced separately. He emphasized that practice, rather than classroom study, was the focus of the seminary, explaining that postulants worked all day in the fields or in the kitchen and only attended short evening classes between 8 and 10 p.m.[95] In fact, during the first two years, classes were held only three times a week. The curriculum was a mix of texts from the Korean traditional curriculum along with selected works from the Tiantai tradition. Zhiyi's *Lesser Calming and Contemplation* (*Xiaozhiguan* 小止觀) was studied in the first two years, along with the Korean *Ch'obalsim* admonitions, the *Novice Precepts and Decorum,* and Chegwan's *Tiantai Outline of the Fourfold Teachings* (*Ch'ŏnt'ae sagyoŭi* 天台四教儀). The third and last seminary year was more classroom-oriented, with lessons six times a week on the *Ch'imun, Diamond Sutra, Awakening of Faith,* and *Lotus Sutra,* as well as general introductions to early Buddhism and to Mādhyamika and Yogācāra. Almost all study was done in the vernacular Korean rather than in *Hanmun,* and, instead of homework, students were encouraged to stay up late chanting. Interestingly, it seems that the traditional Korean Buddhist curriculum, even if not adhered to completely, remained the central prototype of textual education that all major Buddhist organizations on the peninsula today continue to grapple with.

4

Toward Buddhist Pluralism

Monastic Graduate Schools and Internationalization

SCHOLARS HAVE TENDED TO CHARACTERIZE KOREAN BUDDHISM as "syncretic" and "all-encompassing" (*t'ongbulgyo* 通佛教). Eun-su Cho has traced the origins of this discourse to the early-modern scholar Ch'oe Namsŏn, who, while attempting to identify what was unique about Korean Buddhism, raised the seventh-century figure, Wŏnhyo, from near oblivion and made him and his supposed syncretic vision the central prototype of the religion on the peninsula.[1] Nevertheless, as we have seen, the traditional curriculum was anything but all-encompassing. It reflected a very specific and limited lineage-based form of textual Kanhua Chan. Still, it seems that prophecies do have a tendency to fulfill themselves, and, with the new curricular program, the Chogye Order is becoming one of the most diversified and pluralistic Buddhist institutions in the world today. A far cry from Dahui's concentration on one single "critical phrase," Korean monks today should all possess multifaceted knowledge of Sri Lankan Buddhist texts, the various Indian and Chinese Mahāyāna schools, the different Vinayas, the histories of the creed in India, Tibet, China, Korea, and Japan, Chan literature, as well as modern interpretations of Buddhism, before they are allowed to ordain. Clearly, then, the new curriculum carries Korean Buddhism closer to the *t'ongbulgyo* ideal.

In her renowned 2005 book, *The Invention of World Religions,* Tomoko Masuzawa argued that, prior to the nineteenth century, "neither European observers nor, for the most part, native 'practitioners' of those various devotional, contemplative, divinatory, funereal, and other ordinary and extraordinary cults that are now roundly called Buddhist had thought of these divergent rites and widely scattered institutions as constituting a single religion."[2] This claim is somewhat questionable. Urs App has demonstrated, for instance, that not long after arriving in Asia, European missionaries in the seventeenth century were already able to connect the dots and figure out that various cults from Siam to Japan all centered on the same figure of the Buddha.[3] Asian Buddhists themselves were certainly aware all along that their tradition was not a local one but had spread out from India across East Asia. Masuzawa may have overstated her case regarding the lack of awareness of the existence of a broad, multi-locale, Buddha-related tradition before modern times, but her analysis of the re-contextualization of Buddhism as a "world religion" during the late nineteenth and early twentieth centuries is certainly insightful and instructive. The general inclination of East Asian Buddhists for at least a millennium has been to narrow the perspective and focus on the teachings and practices of particular lineages. This tendency has been reversed in modern times, and local Buddhists gradually attempt to participate in and contribute to a new, unified, all-encompassing world religion.

As discussed in the previous chapter, the new Chogye curriculum has been revolutionary in both form and content. It embodies such crucial focal shifts as learning vernacular Korean textbooks instead of interpreting Chinese texts, reading for knowledge instead of reading as practice, and perhaps most importantly, presenting a universal program inspired by modern Buddhist Studies that attempts to encapsulate various forms of Buddhism in place of the textually based Huayan-Chan local tradition.[4] This chapter continues to examine the drift of contemporary Korean Buddhism toward a broader Buddhist pluralism by examining two additional interrelated tendencies: the construction of diverse new monastic graduate schools and the increasing participation of international members in the Chogye Order community.

Pluralism and diversity have become such central sociopolitical values in the developed world at the turn of the twenty-first century, that scholars have begun referring to it as the "participatory turn."[5] Increased individualism and globalization have made uniformity seem rather old-fashioned, and shared participation of distinct societies and diverse traditions under one roof has become increasingly encouraged.[6] The Chogye Order has responded to this general zeitgeist by establishing diverse educational institutions aiming to foster specialists in multiple new, sometimes foreign, forms of Buddhism. Specialized graduate schools have recently been opened to train Korean monastics in the canonical Vinayas, Pāli Buddhism, Indo-Tibetan Mādhyamika, esoteric rituals, various forms of meditation, as well as in the English of "global folk Buddhism." In fact, it is not only the dharma of the Chogye Order that has been recently pluralized, but also the sangha. A growing number of foreigners regularly participates in the community of the "Korean Chogye Order," either as ordained monastics or as lay practitioners, both inside and outside of Korea. Buddhist pluralism on the peninsula is thus manifest in the increased operation of various forms of Buddhism under the umbrella of the Chogye Order, via diversified curricular subjects, educational institutions, doctrines, languages, contemplative practices, specialists, and nationalities.

Transforming Seminaries into Monastic Graduate Schools

Everyone in the Chogye Order today seems to be concerned about the diminishing numbers of new matriculants. Certainly, it does appear that there is good reason for some distress. Statistics show that while approximately four hundred new novices were ordained with the Order each year in the 1990s, these numbers gradually fell in the 2000s, to the point that these days only about two hundred male and female Koreans annually leave home to join the Chogye Order.[7] Some relate the higher numbers of new monastics in the late 1990s to the financial crisis in the country at the time, and believe that with economic betterment fewer people choose to leave for the mountains. Others relate this decline to more general secularizing tendencies in modern society, or to losing much of the religious population to Christianity.

Whatever the reasons for this drop in numbers may be, the Chogye Order has been trying to address this problem by devising interesting new propagation strategies. A unique, new Buddhist education system for the laity has been proliferating in the twenty-first century, already involving over five hundred temples and a half a million students, while the touristic Temple Stay program nowadays attracts over two hundred thousand participants to monasteries every year.[8] The Order has developed several smartphone propagation apps—including games for both children and adults—and some of its monastics make regular appearances in the popular media. When all this activity failed to make a substantial impact on actual ordination numbers, the Chogye decided in 2014 to begin accepting ordinations of minors—for those between the ages of thirteen and nineteen, with parental consent—promising full scholarships to Dongguk University upon their graduation from high school. Inspired by similar practices in Southeast Asia, it also initiated a new system of temporary trial ordinations for periods of thirty, sixty, and ninety days, or one to three years, in the hope that some of the participants would make this temporary experience permanent.[9] According to the monks in charge of the program at Wŏlchŏngsa, the temple that leads the project, a significant number of temporary monastics did end up ultimately ordaining with the Order. In addition, in 2016, the Order initiated an all-out national advertising campaign for joining the sangha, hanging posters in university campuses depicting smiling monks and nuns with slogans such as “Happy Travels, Happy Home-leaving” and “Freedom, Journey” (fig. 3).

What is more pertinent to our discussion, however, is the fact that, along with the diminishing numbers of new novices, many of the seminaries

FIG. 3. Advertising posters for joining the Chogye Order's sangha.

have recently found themselves with very small student bodies. Twelve out of the nineteen seminaries operating in 2003 housed over thirty students, yet only six seminaries had such enrollment numbers in 2013 (see table 9 for monastic schools' student numbers throughout the ages). As the overall number of seminary students in Korea dropped by almost half in the last ten years—from 1,106 to 566—some Chogye Order reformers suggest that there is simply no need for so many seminaries any longer. They propose that the Central Sangha College would be sufficient to house all Chogye novices and can serve as the sole required institution, and it would be better if all seminaries would simply transform into specialized graduate schools for those wishing to continue research, and for fostering teachers and specialists in diverse Buddhist fields.[10] Monasteries that house seminaries and wish to maintain their prestige have been resisting this move, some claiming that it is in fact the seminaries that should remain as the basic institutions and the Central Sangha College that should transform into a specialized graduate school.[11] Nevertheless, the process of converting temple seminaries into graduate schools is already under way.

In twentieth-century Korea, monastics wishing to continue pursuing advanced study and research after graduating from a seminary did have some options. Two monastic teacher-training academies, the Hwaŏm Academy and Hwangak Buddhist Academy, were operating in the 1980s, offering advanced study of the traditional curricular texts.[12] More importantly, several specialized Vinaya Schools (*yulwŏn* 律院), centering on the research of the Indian

Table 9 Monastic Seminary Enrollments

	Institution	Students in 1918[a]	Students in 1937[b]	Students in 1976[c]	Students in 1982[d]	Students in 1995[e]	Students in 1998[f]	Students in 2003[g]	Students in 2013/14[h]
Male seminaries	Paegyangsa	19	24	15	–	15	7	5	Closed in 2013
	Pŏmŏsa (re-opened in 1962)	32	66	41	–	13	26	47	31
	Pŏpchusa (re-opened in 1971)	29	11	45	45	17	30	44	20
	Pulguksa (since 1975)	–	–	35	32	17	15	16	23
	Songgwangsa (re-opened in 1983)	47	27	–	–	35	76	72	30
	Sudŏksa (since 1996)	–	–	40[i]	–	–	10	16	19
	Ssanggyesa (re-opened in 1988)	–	10	–	–	20	–	34	15
	Chikchisa (since 1981)	–	–	–	–	5	19	17	10 (closed in 2013)
	T'ongdosa	93	?	27	58	48	54	65	55
	Haeinsa	20	37	77	112	116	89	82	54
	Tonghwasa (re-opened in 2000)	55	49	28	–	–	–	36	18
	Hwaŏmsa (since 1969)	–	–	20	–	12	16	23	19
	P'agyesa	–	14	–	–	–	–	10	Closed
	Sŏnunsa (since 2003)	–	–	30	–	–	–	10	Closed in 2012
	Total male enrollment			**409**[j]	**247**	**309**	**352**	**487**	**284**

Female seminaries	Tonghaksa (since 1956)	–	–	–	75	123	151	133	55
	Pongnyŏngsa (since 1975)	–	–	30	72	138	107	99	40
	Samsŏn (since 1979)	–	–	–	–	35	36	39	Closed in 2014
	Unmunsa (since 1958)	–	–	116	147	218	235	232	132
	Ch'ŏngamsa (since 1987)	–	–	–	–	88	103	116	55
	Total female enrollment	–	–	**313**[k]	**352**[l]	**602**	**632**	**619**	**282**
Total seminaries' enrollment		**764**	**718**[m]	**722**	**599**	**911**	**984**	**1,106**	**566**
Central Sangha College						–	320	224	155
Dongguk University (Seoul)						–	71	55	58
Dongguk University (Kyŏngju)						–	78	89	52
The Elementary Chan Hall (male)						–	72	241	50
The Elementary Chan Hall (female)						–	–	67	12
Total basic institutions enrollment						–	**1,525**	**1,782**	**893**
Monastic Graduate Schools	Central Sangha Graduate School					–	12	7	56
	Unmunsa Chinese Texts Graduate School (since 2013)					–	6	2	10
	Tonghaksa Huayan Graduate School (since 2008)					–	11	12	10
	Silsangsa Huayan Graduate School (since 1995)					–	–	–	Closed in 2012
	Pongsŏnsa *Śūraṃgama* Graduate School (since 1994)					–	7	5	10

(continued)

Table 9 Monastic Seminary Enrollments (*continued*)

	Institution	Students in 1918[a]	Students in 1937[b]	Students in 1976[c]	Students in 1982[d]	Students in 1995[e]	Students in 1998[f]	Students in 2003[g]	Students in 2013/148[h]
Monastic Graduate Schools (continued)	Tonghwasa Chinese Texts Graduate School (since 2011)					–	–	–	28
	Chikchisa Chinese Texts Graduate School (transformed in 2014)					–	–	–	4
	Samsŏn Chinese Texts Graduate School (transformed in 2014)					–	–	–	24
	T'ongdosa Vinaya School (re-opened in 2005)					–	–	–	21
	Haeinsa Vinaya School (since 1968)					–	6	9	11
	Songgwangsa Vinaya School (since 1988)					–	–	10	3
	Paegyangsa Vinaya School (since 2006)					–	–	–	4
	Ch'ŏngamsa Vinaya School (since 2008)					–	–	–	20
	Pongnyŏngsa Vinaya School (since 1999)					–	–	5	16
	Unmunsa Vinaya School (since 2008)					–	–	–	10
	Pŏmŏsa Vinaya School (since 2013)					–	–	–	8
	Tonghwasa Vinaya School (since 2011)					–	–	–	20
	P'agyesa Vinaya School (since 1997)					–	5	4	?
	Ŏsan Ritual School (since 1997)					–	18	8	36
	Korean Buddhism Traditional Ceremony Academy (since 2012)					–	–	–	17
	Yumasa Chan Graduate School (transformed in 2012)					–	–	–	15

	Paegyangsa Mādhyamika and Yogācāra Graduate School (transformed in 2013)	–	–	–	12
	Sŏnunsa Early Buddhism Graduate School (transformed in 2012)	–	–	–	16
	International Buddhist Graduate School (since 2012)	–	–	–	14
Total Graduate Schools enrollment		–	**65**	**62**	**365**

a Anonymous, "Chosŏn Pulgyo ch'ongbo."
b Information collected from Nam, "Han'guk Pulgyo chŏnsŏ rŭl chungsimŭro pon Chosŏn sidae sawŏn kyoyuk."
c Chŏng, "Han'guk Pulgyo ŭi hyŏnhwang kwa munjejŏm," 200–201.
d Ibid., 202. This seems to include only partial numbers for select seminaries.
e Statistics received from the Chogye Order.
f Statistics received from the Chogye Order.
g Statistics received from the Chogye Order.
h According to my own fieldwork in institutions throughout the country.
i At the time there were only forty female students.
j This number includes student numbers of several seminaries not found on the list as they closed before the 1990s: Sinhŭngsa (seven), Wŏlchŏngsa (ten), Kŭmsansa (fifteen), Taehŭngsa (eight), and Pongsŏnsa (twelve).
k This number includes female students in other seminaries operating at the time such as: Hwaunsa (forty), Magoksa (forty-two), Taewŏnsa (twenty), and Sŏngnamsa (twenty-five).
l This number includes female seminaries that closed long ago, such as Hwaunsa (thirty-four) and Hŭngguksa (twenty-four).
m This is a minimum number. Apart from the temples listed above other seminaries were relatively large at the time: Kŏnbongsa and Sŏkwangsa hosted forty-one students each, Kounsa thirty, Kimyongsa twenty-eight, and Kaeunsa twenty-six.

Dharmaguptaka Vinaya, began operating in the mid-twentieth century. The first is said to have been established in T'ongdosa in the 1950s, another was erected in Haeinsa in 1977, while Songgwangsa opened its own Vinaya institution in the late 1980s.[13] Such specialized monastic Vinaya Schools are quite unique to Korea, as they involve textual study of Vinaya literature rather than ritual training in preparation for ordination, which has been the role of similar institutions elsewhere.[14] As we have seen in the previous chapter, much critique has been voiced within the Order about the lack of study and knowledge of the canonical Vinayas, and, in order to remedy this, as many as seven new monastic graduate Vinaya Schools were established on the peninsula since the turn of the new millennium.[15] These include the first female Vinaya School, opened in Pongnyŏngsa in 1999, followed by the foundation of similar institutions in both Unmunsa and Ch'ŏngamsa in 2008.

The curricula of these graduate schools today often include not only readings from the *Dharmaguptaka Vinaya,* but also classes on Chinese Pure Rules literature, the *Brahma Net Sutra,* comparative Vinayas, modern law and ethics, and ritual practice. Resembling the structure of modern secular graduate schools, the programs involve two years of basic courses equal to a monastic MA, followed by an optional three additional years of research. Students at these institutions are encouraged not to suffice with simple knowledge of the historical literature, but to utilize it and develop new regulations and rituals fitting modern times for the Order as a whole.[16] In fact, in recent years Vinaya school students were involved with the formulation of new liturgies for ordinations and with the compilation of a new, modern Chogye Order Pure Rules code.[17] The number of scholars studying in these schools is relatively small, and as they are not novices any longer but fully ordained monastics, schedules tend to be looser. When it comes to the Vinaya rules, however, they are often quite strict, and I—as a layperson—was not allowed to actually enter their classrooms or examine their textbooks, since, according to the *Dharmaguptaka,* laypeople are prohibited from studying the Vinaya.

Apart from these Vinaya graduate schools, the Chogye Order has been encouraging the opening of a variety of other specialized monastic schools. In the early 2000s, it was decided at the headquarters that the licenses of seminaries housing fewer than forty to fifty students should be revoked.[18] Due to strong resistance from the seminaries, this minimum number dropped to twenty in 2009. Yet, only four of the male seminaries today are able to meet this requirement. In recent years, therefore, several smaller seminaries that were unable to withstand the pressure from the Order have closed down, some converting their facilities into specialized graduate schools. In 2012, P'agyesa's seminary closed down, Yumasa's seminary transformed into a Chan Graduate School, and Sŏnunsa's school was converted into an Early Buddhism Graduate School. A year later, Paegyangsa's seminary closed down and the Mādhyamika Graduate School was erected instead, while Chikchisa's school transformed into a Chinese Texts Monastic Graduate School. More recently, the Samsŏn female seminary in Seoul was forced to close down as well, as it did not meet the new criterion in which all seminary students must live together in the monastery; it has been transformed into yet another Chinese Texts Graduate School.[19] The Buddhist media reported that, in the near future, the Chogye Order intends to be firmer in enforcing the minimum quotas and closing down seminaries in order to create a more stable, unified, and financially solvent system of basic monastic education for all novices.[20] To avoid closure, some seminaries today attempt to lure prospective novices by offering larger stipends and even new iPads to new students, but with the decrease in new monastic numbers it is unlikely that the smaller seminaries will be able to survive for long.

Before the mid-1990s, only four or five specialized advanced study institutions were available for Chogye monastics. Now there are twenty-four. Although seminary student bodies are becoming smaller, the number of monastic graduate students actually jumped six times in the last decade. These new institutions illustrate yet again the tendency of the Chogye today to broaden its Buddhist interests and encourage learning of more pluralistic Buddhist curricula. Apart from the ten Vinaya Schools and the seven graduate schools focusing on Chinese textual programs that resemble, to an extent, the traditional curriculum, the Early Buddhism Graduate School at Sŏnunsa, for example, offers both textual analysis and chanting in the Pāli language six days a week, led by Chogye monastic teachers who have studied in Sri Lanka, India, and Thailand. Its syllabus includes readings from the *Jātaka* tales, the *Nikāyas,* the *Dhammapada,* and from extra-canonical Pāli texts, such as the *Milindapanha,* which has been dominant in the "textbook Buddhism" of Buddhist Studies.

Another example is the new Mādhyamika Graduate School operating at the monastery of Paegyangsa. It offers Sanskrit language classes and readings from the works of Nāgārjuna, Candrakīrti, Aryadeva, and Śāntideva—figures who were particularly dominant in the formation of Tibetan Buddhism and most of whose works were virtually unknown in Korean Buddhist circles prior to the late twentieth century. One of the teachers at the institution told me that first-year graduate students study the "Introduction to Mādhyamika" using translations of Paul Williams' books. Study here is still quite rudimentary, and classes only take place twice a week for a small group of monastics who commute to the monastery. Students confess that they are still having difficulty reading the texts in Sanskrit, yet the school is young, and it is not impossible that part of the Korean Chogye sangha will soon become specialists in Sanskrit and in Tibetan-centered Mādhyamika Buddhism.

Mention must also be made of the Chogye Order's plans to establish monastic graduate schools centering on Yogācāra and on Pure Land thought in the near future. As in the Mādhyamika Graduate School, Sanskrit study is scheduled at the Yogācāra institution, while the focus of the Pure Land Monastic Graduate School is intended to be on learning the Japanese language, along with readings of Chinese, Korean, and Japanese (Shinran) Pure Land works. The official recommended Chogye Order curricula for the various monastic graduate schools are presented in Appendix A.

Two specialized (so-called esoteric) ritual chanting schools were also established in recent years: the Ŏsan Ritual School (Ŏsan chakpŏp hakkyo; see fig. 4), established in Seoul in 1997, and the Traditional Korean Buddhist Ritual Academy (Han'guk Pulgyo chŏnt'ong ŭiye chŏnsŭngwŏn), established in Kimpo in 2012. These institutions do not teach the basic daily rituals all Chogye monastics are familiar with, but rather the more complex chanting and dancing involved in funerary, memorial, and healing rites, which are commonly called *pŏmp'ae* (梵唄).[21] In late-twentieth-century Korea, the T'aego Order was considered to be the Buddhist organization that specialized in ritual, and the founding teachers of both new Chogye Order institutions initially studied *pŏmp'ae* in a T'aego school at Pongwŏnsa. Both are also recognized by the Korean government as Masters of Intangible Cultural Heritage for their expertise in these traditional rituals, and their schools are thus partially funded by the national government.

The rationale behind opening these institutions has been the unification of the various styles of ceremonial chanting performed within the Order, as well as the fostering of a group of Chogye-affiliated ritual specialists able to perform on special occasions.[22] I was allowed to join several classes in these schools, where the format reminded me of the preparation for my own Bar

FIG. 4. Students examined on their ritual performance at the Ŏsan Ritual School.

Mitzvah. The teacher performed the chants using the "correct" tones, and the students—males and females together—repeated after him, and used their iPhones to record the lesson in order to review it later at their home temples. Chants were accompanied by training in playing the drums, bells, and cymbals used in the ceremonies. Interestingly, the establishment of these schools seems to have revived old Buddhist institutional rivalries, and I recently encountered a short opinion piece in a T'aego Order newspaper lamenting the fact that the Chogye is now surpassing it even in its own field of specialty, that of rituals.

English-Speaking Buddhism

Perhaps the most striking new Chogye Order specialized monastic institution is the International Buddhist Graduate School (Kukche Pulgyo taehak), which was founded in Hwaunsa in 2012. All classes at the school are conducted in English with the intention of fostering monastics who will be able to propagate (Korean) Buddhism abroad and lead Temple Stay programs for foreigners. It has been reported that in some Southeast Asian localities English was still regarded as "animal science," and its teaching in monasteries banned.[23] The Korean Chogye Order, however, accepted the global hegemony of English and is striving to participate in its symbolic power and social prestige.

There is little doubt that in the twentieth century English became the universal language used for conveying knowledge. Minae Mizumura mused that perhaps the ultimate victory of English occurred in the 1980s, when Racine was utterly forgotten and Shakespeare became the world's most celebrated poet, and when "air mail" fully replaced "*par avion*" in the parlance of international mail.[24] In Korea, the first English schools were established in the 1880s, and it was during the Japanese colonial period that English became a required subject in all secondary schools.[25] Since the second half of the twentieth century, the Korean government has invested great resources in English language education for the international competitiveness of Korean firms, and fluency in the language has come to replace knowledge of Classical Chinese as the key marker of educational distinction and social stature.[26] Koreans today often resort to far-reaching measures in order to join this privileged class of English speakers, perhaps spending more than any other nation on private English lessons, sending their kids—sometimes by themselves—to live in English-speaking countries for several years, and even, in extreme cases, undergoing "linguistic operations" (frenectomies) to surgically enlarge their tongues to allow better English pronunciation.[27]

It has been mentioned in previous chapters that some monastic seminaries supplemented their curricula with English classes in the 1980s, and that the Chogye Order has been publishing its own Buddhist English textbooks in recent years. The new twenty-first-century monastic curriculum devotes less time to the reading of Classical Chinese texts and places greater stress on English study, a turn that reflects—if a tad late—secular trends in Korean society. What we must pay attention to, however, is that English, like any other language, is loaded with sociohistorical baggage, and that learning it necessarily involves an indoctrination of sorts in the cultures of English-speaking nations. Commentators have noted, for example, that English study in contemporary Korea facilitates change toward more liberal and progressive worldviews.[28] In a similar way, Buddhism learned in English and via English materials certainly carries Korean monasticism in the direction of what David McMahan has labeled "global folk Buddhism":

> What is unique to the postmodern situation is that the local vernaculars, customs, dialects, and practices of global folk Buddhism are not local—they are instead bound up with global systems of media, commerce, and international popular cultures. Their venues are the popular book, lecture tour, concert stage, website and CD.[29]

Indeed, one thing that seems clear about the global Buddhism of today is that it is pluralistic. In fact, perhaps it should be further stressed that it is pluralistic rather than ecumenical. Though the difference may be slight it is rather telling, as ecumenism principally denotes the incorporation and unification of various ideas into one whole, while pluralism is a system that accentuates the sustaining of diversity without submergence. In other words, if ecumenism is a smoothie, pluralism would be a salad. Still, McMahan may not have paid sufficient attention to the fact that this global Buddhist pluralism—despite involving numerous dialects—primarily takes place in one particular language. The prophets of our global folk Buddhism—be it the Dalai Lama, Thich Nhat Hanh, or the international scholars at Harvard, Berkeley, and Cambridge—publish their work primarily in English. And it is their work—either in English directly or in vernacular translations that carry the spirit of the English language—that is entering local monasteries in Korea and around the world.

The fourteen, all-female, monastic graduate students of Hwaunsa's International Buddhist Graduate School attend regular English classes every morning taught by two young American teachers. One of the two told me he often makes use of YouTube videos of Dharma talks by ("global folk") American Zen teachers in his class. The headmaster and founder of the school, Chijŏng, is a gentle yet outspoken nun who is highly critical of the "traditionalist" formalities of the Chogye Order. She teaches the afternoon classes, which focus on reading Buddhist sutras and other related material in English. During the particular semester I visited in 2013, the first-year students were reading Red Pine's translations of the essays attributed to Bodhidharma, but as it was a little difficult, they switched to an easier book by Thich Nhat Hanh.[30] Indeed, over twenty of Thich Nhat Hanh's books have been translated into Korean. Some have sold over a million copies and have perhaps inspired more Koreans to take an interest in Buddhism than any local teacher has.[31] At the time of my visit, the second-year students at Hwaunsa were reading *Women of the Way,* Jane Blanchard's personal account of her Christian spiritual pilgrimage to Spain.[32]

Student attitudes at this school certainly seemed to conform to the more liberal values found in these English books—a far cry from the formality and hierarchies that inevitably accompany the Korean language. When I was invited to join one afternoon session at the institution, I was surprised to discover students engaging in open classroom debates, which are often shunned in Korean monasteries. On that particular winter day, they were questioning, in English, some of the most basic Korean monastic behavioral norms, at the end of which it was decided—by popular vote—that it was unnecessary to wake up at 4 a.m. for the morning ceremonies, and from now on waking at 5 would be sufficient at this school. During the summer breaks the institution arranges communal trips to American and European Buddhist centers, where students get to meet prominent Western Buddhist leaders, and gain experience in Western-style Buddhist practice.

In 2015, in an additional effort to promote English study among the sangha, the Education Department of the Chogye Order initiated the first seminary foreign language speech contest. This fascinating competition took place in October at the headquarters in Seoul. Seminary students from all over the peninsula arrived on buses for an afternoon show of twenty-one creative Buddhist propagational speeches, original songs, dances, magic tricks, and skits, all performed by their peers. Sixteen of the twenty-one performances were done in English, two in Chinese, two in Japanese, and one in Korean—performed by a Russian monastic student from the seminary of Sudŏksa. Female novices were far more active in the performances than their male counterparts, and it was the large group of female monastic students from Unmunsa that ended up winning the first prize of a million wŏn for their remarkable postmodernist dance performance. It involved breaking mirrors symbolizing the collapse of the distinction between "self" and "other," all the while singing "I am everything" in several different languages. Male novices from Dongguk University composed a Buddhist English rap song with the rather catchy *huatou*-style chorus that repeatedly asked "Do you know what it means?" (fig. 5). My favorite group performance, however, was Pongnyŏngsa's English cup-dance song, "Live Like the Buddha" (fig. 6), which included an interesting choreographed basic English Dharma talk on stage.

The first prize in the individuals' category was given to a female monastic student from Tonghaksa by the name of Chinhŭng. Her English speech was titled "The Importance of the Modernization of the Sangha's Education," and its contents may well summarize our discussion of the relevance of

FIG. 5. Dongguk University novices' English rap performance.

FIG. 6. Pongnyŏngsa's seminary students' English cup-dance performance.

the English language to Korean monasticism today. Chinhŭng began her talk by recounting a time she overheard a certain mother, who was visiting the monastery, warning her daughter that if she did not keep her grades up she might end up becoming a nun. This shocked and saddened Chinhŭng immensely, and, upon reflection, she came to the realization that the best way to improve the reputation of the sangha may be the regeneration of the temple education system, placing particular emphasis on global contents and on English. She ended her speech exclaiming that she had resolved to become fluent in English so that parents who see her in the future would tell their children they hoped that they could grow up and be as great as this English-speaking Buddhist nun!

The Elementary Chan Hall (Kich'o Sŏnwŏn 基礎禪院)

The number of Chan Halls used for monastic meditation retreats in Korea more than doubled in the final years of the twentieth century—from thirty-five in the 1980s to seventy-seven by the turn of the century. The number of monastics sitting in Chan Halls has also steadily grown, and nowadays over two thousand—close to a fifth of the sangha—sit in each of the three-month retreat seasons. This demonstrates the increased interest in meditation by Korean monks in recent years. Still, as we have seen in the previous chapter, since the mid-1990s, seminary education has become a mandatory precondition for joining these Chan Halls. This has been a revolutionary change—rather different from the traditional system in which novices could choose either to study in a seminary, take a temple managerial position, or enter a Chan Hall, and it has been strongly opposed by those who were mainly interested in contemplative practice. Therefore, the Education Department agreed to a compromised vision and approved the establishment of the Elementary Chan Hall in Tonghwasa in 1997. It offers an alternative to the regular seminaries, fusing meditation—which is rarely practiced in the basic education system—along with textual study, both under the same roof. Like a seminary, it offers a four-year textual course required for full ordination, yet it also allows its novice students to sit in with fully ordained monastics at the seasonal Chan retreats (*kyŏlche* 結制) twice a year. It is during the retreat off-seasons (*haeje* 解制) that novices at this institution attend classes and study texts.

This school was very popular at first, with approximately three hundred novices enrolled in the early 2000s. Yet, due to the rather plausible perception that classroom education at this institution was relatively lax and insufficient, the Chogye Education Department has pressured monastic leaders to limit the number of novices they sent there, and its student body has consequently dropped to sixty students per year.[33] The Department also persuaded the school to extend its classroom sessions from thirty to fifty days during the retreat off-seasons, and add introductory textbook courses to traditional readings of Chan-related essays during these study periods.

Still, unlike in the regular seminaries of the Chogye Order, study sessions at the Elementary Chan Hall tend to pay particular attention to Chan-related treatises. The current official schedule of the institution[34] begins with an introductory class on early Buddhism and Chan, the study of a seventeenth-century admonitions text by Chan master Boshan (1575–1630),[35] and the reading of three additional Chan treatises by Xiyun (d. 850), Chinul, and Zhuhong (1535–1615)[36] for students of the first year. It continues with learning the *Platform Sutra,* Gaofeng's *Chan Essentials,* and three additional Chan treatises by Sengcan (d. 606), Huihai (eighth century), and Hyujŏng (1520–1604)[37] for students of the second year. And it culminates with the study of the history of Chogye (Caoxi) Chan, the collected sayings of Mengshan (夢山, see chapter one), and the records of fourteenth-century Korean Master, T'aego Pou (1301–1382), for students of the third year. Only in the fourth and final year does this curricular program step away from Chan and provide broader introductory classes on the Vinaya and on the history of Buddhism in India and in Korea.

Although this may indeed be the most localized Chan-focused program in existence on the peninsula today, the actual course schedules at the school have been constantly fluctuating, and it has been quite difficult to keep up. When I visited in February 2014, for example, the third- and fourth-year novices of the institution sat in joint classes on the *Awakening of Faith,* an introduction to Yogācāra and Tathāgatagarbha thought, and a ritual chanting practice seminar. They only studied one Chan treatise—Huihai's eighth-century *Treatise on the Essential Gate of Entering the Way through Sudden Awakening* (*Dunwu rudao yaomenlun* 頓悟入道要門論). The Education Department is making an effort to bring the curriculum of the Elementary Chan Hall as close as possible to the official seminary program, if only for the sake of administering unitary exams to all novices prior to their ordination.

Several years ago, the male novices of the Elementary Chan Hall relocated north, where they now attend retreats in the company of fully ordained monastics at Paektamsa or the nearby Yonghwasa Chan Halls. During the off-seasons they head down to Tonghwasa and attend classes with the female novices there. Some of the students explained that the male novices sit at the front of the class in order not to be able to see the nuns sitting in the back. The nuns in turn are forbidden to talk to or even look the male novices in the eyes. They sit through two hours of classes in the mornings and two in the afternoons. After spending a little time with these novices, my impression was that they evinced a freer and more outgoing demeanor than the students I usually encountered at seminaries. The strict hierarchies and working chain of command that stamp life in most seminaries seem to be looser in the Elementary Chan Hall—where novices of different grades sit alongside fully ordained monks in the meditation halls—and their self-confidence is unmistakably higher. When I asked two friendly novices at Tonghwasa whether they thought the short study sessions they held were sufficient, they laughed saying that "meditation raised their IQs," and that they were able, in these short sessions, to quickly comprehend the same amount of material that others study in the seminaries all year long.

The female novices of the Elementary Chan Hall reside in a large hermitage called Yangjin-am, located approximately a twenty-minute walk uphill from the main temple of Tonghwasa. Leading the female novices—yet still subordinate to the male head of the entire Elementary Chan Hall—is an impressive, charismatic nun by the name of Wŏnjŏng. When I visited, there were only twelve female students in the institution, and Wŏnjŏng explained that many of the elder nuns in Korea strongly believed that novices should begin with a seminary education before attempting to sit Chan; they therefore forbade their disciples to come. Some of her students, she laughed, ran away to join this center without permission. When I asked her what methods did she use to train novices in the Chan Hall, she modestly said that she did not actually do much, explaining that she was not allowed to give *huatou* to her disciples as she was not a "Great Monastic" (*k'ŭnsŭnim*).[38] She revealed that many of her students complained about the uselessness of the study sessions, and she simply told them that if they were bored in class, they could just sit there and meditate. The contemporary Korean word used for study—*kongbu* (工夫)—was in fact the term used by Song Chan masters, such as Dahui, to refer to *huatou* training, and for most of those involved with the Elementary Chan Hall today, *real* study (*kongbu*) still pertains to meditation practice rather than to textual learning. It is thus evidently not taken too seriously.

Foreign Students

As we have seen, the Chogye Order has been determined to educate its monastic community in the English language, whether for the sake of guiding foreigners at Temple Stays, for elevating their reputation and social status as global citizens, or for conducting other international Buddhist missionary activities. Resources have been allocated, for instance, for a campaign in support of spreading the Korean Kanhua Chan praxis throughout the world.[39] The Chogye Order also annually invites leading foreign Buddhist Studies scholars to come to Korea for propagational conferences and retreats. In recent years, the Order has moved forward with its globalization endeavors, establishing no fewer than sixteen temples in the United States and six in Canada, though at least some of these centers cater mainly to overseas Koreans.[40] Gi-wook Shin observed that, ironically, globalization was often promoted in Korea with patriotic motivations, and the attempts to spread Korean Buddhism throughout the world certainly convey similar nationalistic objectives.[41]

Korea may not have had a D. T. Suzuki, a Chögyam Trungpa, or an S. N. Goenka, but it did have one particularly successful missionary to the West, and most of the current foreign members of the Chogye Order have found their way into Korean Buddhism either due to an encounter with him directly or with one of his students. His name was Sungsan (commonly known as Seung Sahn, 1927–2004). He was a former Western philosophy student at Dongguk University who was ordained with the Chogye Order before moving to the United States in the early 1970s and opening small Buddhist centers in New York and Los Angeles. By the early 2000s, as many as 120 Buddhist groups were assembled under Sungsan's supervision in 30 countries—mainly in Europe and the

United States—all following his teachings, which blended traditional Korean practices of bowing and chanting with the global folk Buddhist emphasis on sitting meditation and kōan-encounter dialogues. Eventually, some of his students were ordained and moved to Korea, and it is his "grand-students" today who make up the majority of the foreign novices who internationalize Korean monastic seminaries.

To be sure, foreigners arrived on Korean shores wishing to study and practice Buddhism at least as early as the 1970s. Robert Buswell reports that fifty foreigners reached Songgwangsa at the time to practice Chan under the guidance of Master Kusan (1909–1983), who established the first international Buddhist facility on the peninsula, the Puril meditation center.[42] Other monasteries were quite reluctant to accept foreigners, and the international center at Songgwangsa was dispersed following the passing of Kusan. It was only years later, in 1991, that Sungsan established a new international meditation center in Korea, located at his home temple of Hwagyesa on the outskirts of Seoul, essentially initiating the pluralization of the Chogye Order's monastic community. In 1997, another international meditation center, the Lotus Lantern, was established on Kanghwa Island near Incheon by another Korean missionary monk named Wŏnmyŏng (1950–2003), who was especially active in Russia and Eastern Europe. Then, in 2000, Sungsan founded a mountain monastery called Musangsa exclusively for the use of foreigners, and it has been inhabited and managed by overseas monastics ever since. Musangsa is a rather unique institution in the global Buddhist scene: it looks and generally functions just like any other traditional monastery on the peninsula, yet its abbot and most of its monastic community is Western in origin and varied in gender, its chanting is done partially in English, its kitchen is equipped with salads and other Western-style vegetarian cuisine, and it is probably the monastery with the longest hours of daily communal meditation in Korea today.[43]

The new millennium has seen a steady increase in the numbers of Western Buddhist monastics all over East Asia. In Korea, in 2013, there were as many as 102 foreign monastics, all ordained with the Chogye Order and residing in its affiliated temples. Approximately half of these foreign monks were European or North American, the rest coming from traditionally Buddhist Asian cultures (table 10). Forty-five of these foreigners were in fact monastic students, enrolled in Dongguk University or in one of the monastic seminaries. Considering that up until the early 2000s overseas sangha members did not enroll in seminaries and simply studied on their own or with their individual teachers, this is obviously a rather new experiment. The first foreigner known to have graduated from a Korean monastic school is a monk from Kirgizstan who attended Songgwangsa's seminary in the early 2000s.[44] Since basic education in a seminary has recently become a required criterion for receiving the full precepts in the Chogye Order, international monastics are now obligated

Table 10 Chogye Order–Affiliated Foreign Monastics in Korea (2013)

Country	Novice Male Students	Novice Female Students	Fully Ordained Monks	Fully Ordained Nuns	Total
USA	6	2	11	5	24
Sri Lanka	9		1		10
Poland	2	1	3	2	8
Nepal	5		1		6
Russia	3		3		6
Czech Rep.	1	1	3		5
Taiwan		1		3	4
Bangladesh	2		2		4
India	2		2		4
China	2			2	4
Canada	1			3	4
Australia			1	2	3
Italy			2	1	3
Hungary	1		1	1	3
Lithuania			1	1	2
Malaysia	1			1	2
Argentina	1		1		2
Laos	1				1
Myanmar	1				1
Serbia			1		1
Estonia	1				1
England	1				1
Uzbekistan			1		1
Japan			1		1
France				1	1
Total	**40**	**5**	**35**	**22**	**102**

Source: Statistics received from the Chogye administration.

to enroll, and it is within these seminaries that foreigners are truly immersed in the realities of Korean Buddhist monasticism.

Acculturation has not been easy for these religious immigrants. Most overseas monks in Korea live and practice separately in one of the three foreign monastic centers of Musangsa, Hwagyesa's International Chan Center, or the Lotus Lantern temple at Kanghwa Island. As can be expected, decorum at these places is very different from that of traditional Korean monasteries, and I have heard of cases in which Korean monks visited, saw monks sitting down to eat together with female and male laypeople, and were so shocked they simply ran away. Entering a seminary involves not only adjusting to the rigid hierarchies of the early stages of the Korean monastic career, but also necessitates a good command of Korean and Chinese characters, which at least some of the foreign monks do not possess. On more than one occasion, seminary teachers complained to me that their foreign students do not understand anything in class, contending that they should have studied Korean before coming. Some do actually speak fluent Korean, but other foreign monastic students admit that all they do in class is sit quietly and meditate. To solve this problem, the Chogye Order is currently contemplating the establishment of a separate seminary for foreign novices in which communication will be in English. Its goal will be to foster monastics who will be able to propagate Korean Buddhism in their home countries.[45]

One particular seminary teacher also told me rather indignantly that all his foreign students want to do is meditate, and that they are not at all interested in studying texts. Meditation seems to be the Buddhist activity that attracts Westerners to the tradition most of all, and many are disappointed to discover that it is not going to be a major part of their lives as novices in Korea. Stuart Chandler has reported similar disillusions experienced by Westerners who were ordained in the Taiwanese Foguangshan, where only two out of every dozen foreigners ended up staying in the organization. Brooke Schedneck has likewise described the disenchantment of Western monks in Thailand, who often come to realize that the Buddhist culture they have joined is not very different from the Christian one they so eagerly left behind.[46] Not very many foreign monastics to date have actually remained ordained in the Korean tradition. A number of foreign students I encountered in monastic seminaries between 2012 and 2016 were unable to endure it and returned to their own countries without graduating. Probably the most famous foreign monastic in Korea—an American-born monk by the name of Hyŏn'gak, who became famous after publishing a bestseller in 1999 titled *Manhaeng: Habŏdŭ esŏ Hwagyesa kkaji* (Eternal travels: From Harvard to Hwagyesa)—made national news and instigated a minor scandal in 2016 when he opined that foreign monks were viewed as mere poster boys or "decoration" by the Chogye Order.

It is indeed quite challenging for a foreign monastic to enter a Chan Hall in Korea after graduating from a seminary, as these places are often dominated by cliques and are unwilling to allow unknown monastics to join. The international students thus return almost exclusively to Musangsa or Hwagyesa when finishing their classes. A Chan Hall monk from Haeinsa told me on a recent visit that monks there have never allowed a foreigner to join a retreat simply because foreigners "smelled different," which obstructs practice. I was rather startled by this at first, and asked him whether the fact that they were eating the same food did not have an effect on their body odors. He insisted that since the senses become exceptionally acute during retreats, even the slightest aroma lingering from a long time before would still be prohibitive to the common endeavor. Additionally, foreigners were not allowed to join the Elementary Chan Hall during its first several years of operation, but, in 2012, the first three foreign novices were finally granted entrance. They proved to be quite diligent and it has been decided that others will be permitted to join in the future. This could be viewed as a first sign of a greater integration between the local and international sangha in Korea, the basic educational facilities serving as crossroads of encounter, assimilation, and regeneration of a diversity of Buddhist cultural practices.

5

Monastic Examinations and Bureaucratic Ranks

> Although it seems that a secular system of exams is unfit for the life of those who left home, in actuality the four seasons continue to operate deep in the mountains, and in order to farm and eat there is a need for an ordered system and regulations, even among home-leavers.
>
> *Pŏpsan, a monk-professor at Dongguk University, 2002*[1]

> Examining the sangha on Buddhism is like testing a horse how it walks!
>
> *Koryŏ Dynasty monks criticizing the sangha exam system*[2]

CAN EXAMS EVALUATE BUDDHIST PRACTICE? ARE THEY the appropriate (and skillful) means for assessing the members of the sangha? Many would probably disagree with the notion that unified, objective examinations are able to determine individual Buddhist spiritual development. Yet, throughout history, Buddhist monastics in East and Southeast Asia have been repeatedly tested in various ways on their Buddhist learning and practice. At times, their own status as members of the sangha depended on passing such exams, and at other times, ranks and positions both inside and outside the sangha—as well as material rewards—were bestowed on those who managed to pass. Ironically, then, monastics who have left the secular structures of society often found that they have simply migrated into another society not very differently structured from the one they have left behind. As elucidated by Pŏpsan in the quote above, the four seasons continue to operate deep in the mountains and a hierarchic division of labor is still generally accepted there, too.

But are exams the best way to generate a bureaucratic administration for Buddhist monks? For the past several centuries, monastic hierarchies in Korea were based mostly on seniority in the sangha, on the number of Chan retreats one has taken, and probably on personal connections, rather than on exams. Nevertheless, as I hope this chapter will make clear, the criteria for promotion in Korean monasticism today is undergoing a great shift. Educational achievements have become paramount, and a modern, universal, objective examination system has been set as the main standard for both joining the Chogye Order and for advancing in rank and holding higher positions within its administration.

Historically, Buddhist monastic examinations in East Asia were operated and overseen by governments. In China, rulers often used qualifying exams in order to limit the number of monks, who were exempt from military service, from corvée labor in state projects, and from paying taxes. In Korea, the monastic exams were initiated and developed in parallel with the Civil Service exams, and as such, they served primarily for the selection of a few governmentally recognized position-holders.[3] The Chosŏn government discontinued the exam system permanently in the mid-sixteenth century, and it is only now, half a millennium later, that a monastic rank-examination system has been recreated on a large scale on the peninsula.

The new arrangement involves eight ecclesiastic ranks obtained through five successive exams. The first two operate as qualifying exams for taking the novice and full precepts and formally entering the sangha, and the following three serve as selection exams for obtaining higher ranks and positions. Specialized programs and institutions were recently developed to prepare monastics for these exams, and for the first time in Korean history, the system is now open to female monastics. As the examinations are neither managed nor overseen by the secular government, but are autonomously operated by the Chogye Order, they are not employed to control the sangha from the outside as they were in medieval times, but utilized for the internal structuring of the Order's bureaucracy. Their primary goal is not to limit the size of the sangha but to avoid cronyism and encourage overall monastic unity, objective impartiality, and continuous learning and development.

This chapter sets off by contextualizing the new system within the history of Buddhist monastic examinations in Korea and in broader East Asia, and later proceeds to provide a closer analysis of the new structure and of the contents of the various exams. As in the curricula discussed in previous chapters, the particular questions chosen to appear on these tests demonstrate what the current Chogye Order believes monastics should know about Buddhism, revealing the construction of a modern Korean Buddhist orthodoxy. I first explore the fifth-level assessments, which are based on a new postulant education program. Next, I analyze the fourth-level exams—required for taking the full precepts—exploring them in relation to the changing seminary curricula. Finally, I take a closer look at the contents of the three higher-level examinations and the new continuing education programs set up in order to prepare more senior monastics for these assessments. In addition to introducing this new intriguing Buddhist valuation system, my hope is that the chapter will provide the reader with a broader picture of the bureaucratic hierarchies and legalized procedures involved with the operation of a large Asian Buddhist monastic organization.

A Brief History of Sangha Examinations

The famous Chinese traveler, Xuanzang, who visited India in the seventh century, reported that monastic hierarchies in the motherland of Buddhism at the time were based on oral examinations rather than on seniority. He added that servants and elephants were awarded to those who were able to expound upon several texts and thus did exceptionally well in the exams.[4] In China, examinations of monastics on the sutras—imposed in order to purify the sangha from those who simply joined in order to avoid taxation and labor—were sporadically conducted in various localities beginning in the fourth century.[5] It is interesting to note that it was Emperor Zhongzong (656–710) of the Tang Dynasty, raised under the tutelage of Xuanzang, who was the first Chinese ruler to implement an examination system for all monastic aspirants on a national scale in 705.[6] Later, in the year 747, a system of monk certificates was inaugurated, and only those who passed a recitation exam, had connections to the royal family, or were wealthy enough to purchase a certificate, were allowed to ordain.[7] Various eighth-century royal regulations stipulated the number of pages to be recited for these exams (usually between five hundred and a thousand pages from the *Lotus, Vimalakīrti,* or *Mahāparinirvāṇa* sutras), and, in 773, the composition of short essays was added to the format.[8]

Research regarding Buddhist-related policies in later Chinese dynasties is relatively scarce, but in general it seems that monastic exams continued to take place, though mostly on the local administrative levels. In eleventh-century Song, for example, the Chief Rectifier of the sangha of Hangzhou, Hui Bian (慧辯, 1014–1073), created an exegetical examination system for those who wished to compete for vacant abbacy positions in small temples in the area, whereas abbots of larger public monasteries were typically appointed by recommendation.[9] Later, a Pure Rules text written in fourteenth-century Yuan (the *Jiaoyuan qinggui* 教苑清規) stipulated both oral and written exams for the Tiantai sangha.[10] The first Ming emperor is reported to have purged the sangha in the fourteenth century by imposing exams and laicizing any monastics whose knowledge of Buddhist texts was deemed insufficient.[11]

In Korea, there is some evidence that exams and ranks were issued at least locally in the late Silla era. Chajang (慈藏, 590–658) is said to have established a twice-yearly monastic examination system that sought to determine who kept the Vinaya rules. Epitaphs from late Silla reveal that the monastic ranks of *Taedŏk, Taesa,* and *Sŏnsa* (大德, 大師, 禪師) were already in use.[12] Nevertheless, it was Koryŏ king Kwangjong who nationally formalized the sangha examination procedures in 954, four years before the first Civil Service examinations were organized in Korea.[13] In normal circumstances both the Civil Service and the monastic examinations were administered once every three years during the dynasty, and we now have records of thirty-seven particular occasions of monastic exams, most of which took place in the twelfth and thirteenth centuries.

These records demonstrate that the assessment of the sangha was conducted in two or three consecutive stages. Only those who passed the first level of preliminary examinations were authorized to sit for the main exams, usually called the "Great Selection" (*Taesŏn* 大選).[14] Those who passed this "Great Selection" received the rank of "Great Virtue" (*Taedŏk* 大德), and were thus eligible for abbot positions.[15] Some records show that exam passers were also granted plots of land.[16] They could then continue to the third step, climbing the monastic hierarchies and attaining higher titles. The five additional ranks were: "Great Teacher" (*Taesa* 大師), "Notable Teacher" (*Chungdaesa* 重大師), "Eminent Teacher" (*Samjungdaesa* 三重大師), followed by either "Chan Master" (*Sŏnsa* 禪師) and "Great Chan Master" (*Taesŏnsa* 大禪師) in the Chan tradition, or "Head Priest" (*Sujwa* 首座) and "Monastic Minister" (*Sŭngt'ong* 僧統) in the "Learning" tradition.[17] There is evidence of at least two cases in which higher exams were held for the purpose of acquiring these higher titles, but it seems that personal recommendation remained the main channel through which monastics could climb further in the bureaucracy.[18]

More interesting, perhaps, are the actual proceedings and contents of the exams. Separate procedures were administered for the Chan and "Learning" traditions, and, in the late Koryŏ, a Tiantai exam was also set up for a certain time. Analysis of the tests has demonstrated that, until the mid-thirteenth century, the Chan exams focused on the explanation of key terms, while the "Learning" exams focused on Yogācāra. Yet, later, the *Huayan Sutra* became the center of the "Learning" exams, and short poems were written for its Chan counterpart.[19] Historians describe a special attempt to create a pan-sectarian exam in 1370 that involved testing all monks on various *huatou,* though the practice did not seem to catch on.[20] Nuns were excluded both from the exams and from holding official titles.[21] Examinations were generally oral, and often involved public debates. In fact, proposals for written exams both for the monastics as well as for the Civil Service were rejected by the Censorate in the eleventh century, based on the reasoning that this would simply enhance writing skills rather than the ability to discuss ideas. Nevertheless, there is evidence that soon afterward written components were, in fact, added to the format.[22]

It is important to note that these historical monastic examinations were conducted under the management and supervision of the central government. At least since the late Koryŏ, they all had to be presided over by a secular official who had passed the (Confucian) Civil Service exams. Monks seem to have spent a considerable amount of time preparing for them, and soon, criticism of the system began to be heard. The prominent monk Chinul, for instance, despite passing the sangha examinations himself, later voiced his disgust at the worldly atmosphere surrounding them, and attempted to create an alternative structure outside the royally sponsored hierarchies, deep in the Chogye Mountains.[23] In fact, both Confucian scholars and Buddhist monastics in the late Koryŏ expressed a degree of distrust toward the examination system, occasionally arguing that erudition ensured neither high moral standards nor spiritual attainments.[24]

Nevertheless, the exam system remained intact and continued to operate through the turmoil of the dynastic change of the fourteenth century. As pointed out in chapter one, the new Chosŏn government codified the monastic exam curriculum into a law stipulating that the Chan exams should involve the *Transmission of the Lamp* and Hyesim's *Enlightened Verses,* and the "Learning" exam should be on the *Huayan Sutra* and the *Ten Stages of the Bodhisattva.* Only roughly 30 percent of exam takers at the time were able to pass the tests, which were evaluated by ten distinguished monastics. Even those who passed still needed further recommendations and the sanction of the king in order to receive appointments as abbots.[25] Less than a century into the new dynasty, however, King Sŏngjong (1457–1494) abolished the monastic examinations altogether as part of the broader dynastic policy of marginalizing Buddhism from the central administration. The system was revived for about a decade in the mid-sixteenth century by Queen Munjong (1501–1565), a Buddhist sympathizer, and several hundred monastics sat for the examinations. However, this was probably the last time large-scale monastic exams took place on the peninsula prior to the current twenty-first-century reforms.

Monks in other East Asian localities likewise sat for Buddhist ecclesiastic exams. In Japan, monastic oral assessments had taken place in Kōfukuji since the eighth century, and were regulated by the governmental Office of Monastic Affairs.[26] These exams were first focused solely on recitation, but doctrinal mastery was gradually added to the syllabus.[27] In the ninth century, Saichō established an alternative examination system for Tendai on Mt. Hiei, and test passers in this tradition gradually came to occupy major positions in the government.[28] Tendai examinations continue to this day in Japan, and contemporary clerics climb through the eleven-rank system of the sect mainly through modern academic degrees and exams.[29] In contemporary Japanese Pure Land denominations, too, Jessica Starling reports, clerics must pass a qualifying exam at the headquarters before taking charge of a temple.[30]

In Tibet, a system of *Geshe* examinations that focuses on doctrinal debates was established in the seventeenth century. It was historically overseen by the government, and it is operated independently by several Tibetan schools to this day.[31] Nithiyanandam recalls how in his own *Geshe* exam in the twentieth century he was expected to memorize 1,500 pages of text, and prizes (hats, robes, scarfs, coins) as well as punishments (cleaning, whipping) were meted out according to the number of folios remembered.[32] Government-sponsored monastic exams were also established in seventeenth-century Thailand and Burma.[33] These exams focused on simple translations from Pāli to the local vernaculars, and were mainly used by the government to select a few elite ecclesiastic administrators who received royal stipends.[34] The system was reformed in nineteenth-century Thailand, and to this day involves a nine-level structure of increasingly more difficult translations from Pāli texts.[35] Secular British colonial rule in Burma put an end to the national sangha exams in the 1880s, and private monastic associations have assumed the role of administrating two levels of tests to those wishing to take leading positions in major temples throughout the country in the modern period.[36]

The Modern Revival of Monastic Examinations

A number of attempts to reorganize the monastic bureaucracy in Korea according to a formal rank system were made since the beginning of the twentieth century. The 1902 Detailed Rules for Operating Temples in the Country (*Kungnae sach'al hyŏnhaeng sech'ik* 國內寺刹現行細則) stipulated three sangha ranks—called *Sŏkp'um* (釋品)—based on seniority in the sangha.[37] Red patterned robes were to be worn by those of the highest rank; red non-patterned robes by those of the second; and violet robes by monks of the third level. Later, in 1912, the committee of abbots of the thirty main temples, which had just been organized by the Japanese colonialists, formulated a six-rank system with corresponding robe colors and headwear, and titles resembling the ones used during the Chosŏn Dynasty. It was still based primarily on seniority, yet, an additional educational stipulation—that is, graduating from the *Taegyo* course at a seminary—was added for those wishing to attain higher ranks.[38] The committee of abbots stipulated yet another five-rank system in 1941, in which sitting in a fixed number of Chan retreats—and not just seniority—had become essential in order to advance in the hierarchy.[39] The rank titles found in the regulatory documents of the 1940s are still in use by the Chogye Order today, but it seems that no actual exam system was operating at the time.

The current Chogye Order's Constitution, written in 1962, signaled the coming of change. This document generally maintained the same rank-system that had been promulgated in the 1940s—based on seniority and on the number of retreats a monastic had sat through—yet, it stipulated, in addition, the development of monastic exams. An Examination Committee was to be formed and take charge of both sangha and lay propagator exams.[40] Still, despite the occasional conferring of higher monastic titles on a number of individual monks in the late 1960s, no general examinations were actually administered.[41] Based on the constitution, the first Chogye Order Sangha Rank Law (Pŏpkye pŏp) was enacted in 1976, correlating monastic titles with specific qualifying exams, and more notably, adding for the first time a separate set of rank-titles for female monastics.[42]

It was a decade later, in 1985, that the Sangha Exam Law (Sŭngga kosi pŏp) finally fashioned the basic system we know today. It stipulated seniority, retreats, and specific exams as qualifications for climbing the bureaucratic ladder of Korean monasticism. The fifth-level exam would signal the end of the postulancy period, in which monastics would be tested on ritual texts, the *Ch'obalsim,* and the *Novice Precepts and Decorum* (*Shami luyi* 沙彌律儀; see chapter two). The fourth-level exam would qualify novices to take the full precepts and become full members of the sangha, and its contents would be the *Ch'imun, Sajip,* and *Sagyo* texts of the traditional seminary curriculum. The third-level exam would essentially be a qualification exam for abbacy, and would include questions on the *Transmission of the Lamp,* the *Enlightened Verses,* propagation methods, and comparative religion. The contents of the two higher exams were not yet specified.[43]

Although all of this was legally stipulated in the 1980s, examinations were still not held. One reason for this was the absence of a registration system able to keep track of the resumes of monastics, that is, their educational records, the number of retreats they have participated in, and so forth. Following the computation of the Chogye administration in the 1990s, this problem has been gradually eliminated. Another reason for the delay has probably been the need to convince skeptical sangha leaders of the necessity of such exams in the first place. Some monastics certainly put up a persistent opposition to an exam system, often echoing the appeals of Koryŏ Dynasty monks regarding the inadequacy of unified exams for the evaluation of Buddhist monastic practice. In a Chogye Order seminar in the year 2000, for instance, the head of the Elementary Chan Hall, Yŏngjin, contended that although exams may be appropriate for the seminary graduates, they were surely unsuitable for evaluating the practice of the graduates of the Elementary Chan Hall. Still, he did agree that there was a need for consistent assessment in the contemporary world, and suggested that the graduates of his institution would be graded based on their attitudes during Chan retreats.[44] One may well wonder if anyone sitting through a rigorous three-month retreat would ever deserve a B– for a lack of sincere attitude.

In order to solicit ideas and accommodate the wishes of its members, the Chogye administration distributed several opinion surveys among the sangha regarding the possible creation of an exam system between the years 1999 and 2001. The results of a 1999 survey among several hundred abbots, for example, illustrated that as many as 84 percent supported the implementation of the rank-examination system.[45] Other surveys, however, demonstrated less positive opinions. Perhaps unsurprisingly, a survey among seminary students in 2000 found that the majority was strictly opposed to any exam system.[46] Their rejection could be at least partly explained by the fact that, like most students, they simply dreaded having to cram for exams. The largest survey was conducted among seven thousand monastics and lay Buddhist academics in the same year. Sixty percent were found to support the plans for the new system. The remaining 40 percent objected to the whole idea of having ranks in the sangha, which they thought should be based on communality and equality.[47] The Korean sangha was evidently split in opinion regarding the need for a rank-exam system, though attitudes seem to have been somewhat more favorable toward such procedures among the more senior monastics of the Order.

Finally, in 2001, a decision was made. The head of the Chogye Order's Education Department, Mubi, announced:

> At first it was said that evaluating character through a test does not tally with Buddhism, but I think it is the best method [for making sure all monks have the proper attitudes]. Therefore, it is obvious that at least those who wish to be abbots or leaders in the Chogye administration should have the basic qualification of passing the third-level exam.[48]

The first fifth- and fourth-level monastic exams in modern Korea took place in 2000; the yearly third-level examination system began in 2001; the first second-level tests took place only in 2010; and the highest first-level assessments were first administered in 2016. Several changes and amendments were made in the early twenty-first century to the Sangha Examinations Law. A summary of the entire system as of 2016 is presented in table 11.

As may be easily gleaned from table 11, passing the fifth-level exams is currently the required condition for becoming a novice, and taking the fourth-level tests is a prerequisite for becoming a full member of the sangha. Afterward, monastics are generally not obligated to take the higher exams, and only those with political motivations who wish to become abbots and/or hold higher positions in the Chogye headquarters must first pass these tests. Still, when I asked a number of monastics who were about to sit for the higher exams their reasons for doing so, a common explanation has been that although they did not plan on actually holding a position, they felt pressure to advance in the hierarchy in order not to fall behind and stay in line with their peers. The Chogye is currently planning to make all those who pass the third-level examinations eligible to vote in the elections for the Order's leadership, a move that will surely encourage a growing number of monastics to study for and take the exams.[49]

Table 11 The Chogye Order's Rank-Examination System

Rank Title	Seniority	Education and Exams	Eligibility for Positions
Postulant (*Haengja* 行者)[a]	At least six months in a monastery	Postulant education program	
Novice (*Sami* 沙彌, m/ *Samini* 沙彌尼, f)	At least four years since ordination	After passing the fifth-level sangha exams and receiving the ten precepts for novices, monastics go through the basic education system[b]	
"Seeing Virtue" (m), "Virtuous Conduct" (f) (*Kyŏndŏk* 見德/ *Kyedŏk* 戒德)		After graduating from one of the basic education institutions, passing the fourth-level sangha exams, and receiving the full precepts	Formally recognized as a full member of the sangha
"Middle Virtue" (m), "Virtuous Concentration" (f) (*Chungdŏk* 中德/*Chŏngdŏk* 定德)	At least ten years since ordination	After completing at least four Chan retreats or receiving a PhD, and either passing the third-level sangha exams or graduating from a Monastic Graduate School	Eligible for abbacy or office director in branch monasteries
"Great Virtue" (m), "Virtuous Wisdom" (f) (*Taedŏk* 大德/ *Hyedŏk* 慧德)	At least twenty years since ordination	After passing the second-level sangha exams	Eligible for various posts in the Chogye Order's administration
"Religious Virtue" (m), "Sagacious Virtue" (f) (*Chongdŏk* 宗德/ *Hyŏndŏk* 賢德)	At least twenty-five years since ordination	After passing the first-level sangha exams	Eligible for abbacy in major monasteries and for central posts in the Chogye Order's administration
"Religious Teacher" (m), "Bright Virtue" (f) (*Chongsa* 宗師/ *Myŏngdŏk* 明德)	At least thirty years since ordination	Individual practice	Eligible to be head of the Chogye Order's General Assembly, Education Department, Propagation Department, etc.
"Great Religious Teacher" (m), "Bright Teacher" (f) (*Taejongsa* 大宗師/ *Myŏngsa* 明師)	At least forty years since ordination	Individual practice	Eligible to be Head of the Chogye Order and to serve in the Committee of Elders

Source: Adapted from: Taehan Pulgyo Chogyejong Kyoyugwŏn, "Sŭngga kyoyuk kwajong mit kyoyuk kigwan annae."

a It seems that the distinction between a monastic postulant (*haengja* 行者) and a novice (*sami* 沙彌, śrāmaṇera) did not exist in India, and Zurcher traces it to seventh-century China. See: Eric Zurcher, "Buddhism and Education in T'ang Times," 30–31.

b The basic education system consists of the mountain monastic seminaries, the Central Sangha College, Dongguk University's Buddhist Studies program, or the Elementary Chan Hall.

Monastic ranks have recently been more strictly differentiated by exterior attire. Postulants must wear brownish-colored (male) or orange (female) robes, and novices wear the Korean gray robes with a brown stripe in the collar. After passing the fourth-level exams and receiving the full precepts, monastics can remove the brown stripe and wear fully gray robes. Observing ancient Vinaya instructions, Korean monks are also expected to wear outer garments made of several scraps of cloth weaved together. In regulating these outer robes by rank, the idea of the Order seems to be that the more rags used for a robe, the closer affinity one will have with the Buddha. Novices' outer robes can thus only be made of a maximum of nine scraps of cloth, while passing the third-level exams entitles monastics to wearing outer garments made out of as many as fifteen patches. Finally, after passing the first-level exams, sangha members are allowed to wear robes made of twenty-five rags.[50] Since 2002, monastics also receive badges in different colors according to their ranks, though I have never encountered a monk or a nun actually wearing them.

A Postulant Canon for the Fifth-Level Exams

The modern rationalization of Buddhist monastic postulancy in Korea began with the establishment of a unified Chogye Order ordination system in the early 1980s, continued with the creation of national postulant-education programs in the 1990s, and culminated in the twenty-first century with the fifth-level exams required of all monastic postulants before taking the novice precepts. Until the 1980s, aspiring monastics would simply receive the novice precepts from their own guiding teacher at their home monastery—if at all—and perhaps travel to the provincial head monastery to receive the full precepts. Due primarily to the efforts of monastic reformer Ilt'a (1929–1999), the first unified Chogye ordination-system was inaugurated in T'ongdosa in 1981, and both novice and full-precept ceremonies have been conducted nationally ever since.[51] Soon, the sporadic and subjective manner of educating postulants came under attack, and calls for substantial systematized programs began to be heard. Essentially, these calls represent an attempt to make the individual-teacher-based apprenticeship-style postulancy period more equitable, and to eliminate regional differences.

Monastic critics in the late twentieth century frequently lamented the fact that many monasteries simply treated postulants as unpaid laborers and servants, and spent very little time actually educating them in the Buddhist teachings. Pŏpchang, a prominent monk who eventually served as head of the main assembly of the Chogye Order, reminded us in an article written in the early 1990s that, according to the *Platform Sutra,* the Sixth Patriarch Huineng himself began his monastic career doing manual work, and that, through labor, postulants can learn order, respect, frugality, simplicity, altruism, humility, and patience, as well as rid themselves of secular habits.[52] Nevertheless, Pŏpchang believed that overstressing labor creates excessively formalistic hierarchies and problematic relationships among the sangha. Too much labor may thus pose an obstacle to a smooth communal life, initiative spirit, and Buddhist contemplation. He argued for the need to create a unified postulant program, which balances labor with classes on Buddhist doctrines and rituals, and is supplemented by an hour of sitting meditation every evening.[53]

Pŏpchŏng (1932–2010), a well-known monk in Korea who has written several best-selling books on Buddhism, seems to have had similar ideas. He wrote in 1992 that postulants were typically found in an unstable and sensitive state of mind that could be easily influenced, and so their postulancy period should not be wasted on labor alone, and must be supplemented by a curriculum of Vinaya-related texts, basic Buddhist doctrine, ritual practice, confessionals, and sitting meditation.[54] An additional monk by the name of Chihwan further expounded on these notions. He suggested that the Korean sangha must rethink the traditional harsh postulant system, which he thought was more like a test, similar to the habit of lions known for throwing their young off a cliff, and raising only those who manage to crawl back up.[55] He deplored the fact that very large percentages of the postulants in Korea drop out disappointed before receiving the precepts (it is estimated that over half change their minds and return home in the first six months), and argued that the main reasons for this were the lack of affectionate role models, reliance on strict authoritarian structures, the scarcity of practice and study of Buddhism, the focus on work alone, and the absence of a systematized, unified program. As a solution, he offered a detailed plan for a postulant curriculum, which included teachings on (1) Buddha's life with the aid of *Jātakas* to emphasize altruism; (2) the *Heart Sutra* as a basis for the doctrine of emptiness; (3) several chapters of the *Huayan Sutra* to emphasize the importance of making vows (to save all beings) at the beginning of one's monastic career; (4) *Āgamas* and *Ch'imun* for learning about the early sangha in India and China respectively; (5) several Chan treatises; (6) admonitions literature and the *Novice Precepts and Decorum;* (7) daily chanting and confessionals; (8) Buddhist history; and also (9) learning respect for one's elders and devotion through labor and servitude.[56]

This particular proposal has not been implemented, but looking at the postulant curricula of today, it is possible to detect much continuity. To be sure, when the Chogye Order began organizing twenty-three-day unified education programs for postulants nationally in 1991, a more modest curriculum was utilized at first. It was comprised of the Buddha's biography—newly written by the Order—along with two Vinaya texts: the *Ch'obalsim* (examined in chapter one), and the *Bequeathed Teachings Sutra,* a Chinese apocryphal text that recounts the Buddha's final admonitions and encouragements before his passing (see chapter two). Later, with the creation of the Chogye Order's Education Department in early 1995, these three texts were codified into the

Postulant Textbook (*Haengja kyobon*), becoming the first official postulant canon of modern Korean Buddhism.[57]

Since then, this syllabus has been greatly broadened and diversified. The novice exam-preparation booklet published in 2006, for example, shows that basic Buddhist doctrine, Buddhist history, ritual procedures, and two additional disciplinary texts were added to the original three-text program.[58] The added Vinaya-related essays were the *Novice Precepts and Decorum* (which was composed in sixteenth-century China and details the ten novice precepts along with a lengthy list of requisite monastic decorum rules) and the *42-Section Sutra,* which focuses on ethical admonitions to the sangha (see chapter two). Postulants have had to study this curriculum mainly by themselves in their spare time or with the help of their tonsure teachers at first, but gradually, mandatory condensed weekend classes have been organized in head parish temples once every month or two to facilitate study. By the second decade of the twenty-first century, the new postulant system seems to have been normalized. Every monastic aspirant today needs to spend a period of at least six months as a postulant in his or her home temple, visit their local head temple for further training every couple of months, and join a several-week nationally unified course in preparation for the fifth-level sangha exams, which ends with precept ceremonies.[59]

Let us briefly review the procedures of becoming a monk in contemporary Korea. The process of joining the Chogye Order and becoming a postulant begins with an interview with the abbot of one's chosen monastery. Candidates submit documents ensuring they are of the right age (13–50), have graduated from high school, have neither a criminal record nor are wanted by the police, are not bankrupt, are unmarried or have been divorced for at least six months, and do not have underage dependents, mental illnesses, incurable diseases, remarkable disability, or visible scars and tattoos. Their role as spiritual cultivators and teachers is at least as important as their role as delegates of the Buddha and representatives of Buddhism in the world and, as such, Chogye Order monastics believe they must embody certain levels of physical and moral rectitude. If the physical exam and all documents are in order, new aspirants can officially take refuge in the Buddha, Dharma, and sangha before their chosen tonsure teachers, have their heads shaved, make official prostrations in front of their senior monks and their parents (if present), and chant the Four Great Vows to save all beings, end all afflictions, study all the dharmas, and complete the Buddha's path. They then receive a postulant package from the Chogye administration, which includes their monastic ID, a prayer-bead bracelet, a notebook and practice diary, and sixteen official postulant textbooks with which to study for their fifth-level examinations. Up until not very long ago, all postulants had to know was how to humbly sweep the grounds, diligently wash the dishes, dutifully tend to their seniors' wishes, and correctly chant during rituals. Now, they all must be aware of basic Buddhist doctrines, the history of the Chogye Order, the contents of select Pāli sutras, and the disciplinary admonitions found in historical Chinese texts.

In 2010, the *Brahma Net Sutra* was added to the postulant canon, and a bodhisattva precepts ceremony began supplementing the novice precept ritual at the end of the program. Up to this point, although bodhisattva precept ceremonies based on the *Brahma Net Sutra* were conducted sporadically on the peninsula for both monastics and laypeople, these rituals have not been a formal part of the monastic ordination process. In fact, as Lori Meeks has recently shown, in premodern China and Japan, the *Brahma Net Sutra* was more often used by Buddhists for conferring the precepts on lay, rather than upon monastic, audiences.[60] The fact that the bodhisattva precepts of the *Brahma Net Sutra* are often mentioned in contemporary Buddhist Studies materials as the Mahāyāna substitution for the Theravāda Vinaya surely must have inspired modern Korean Buddhist reformers to add this ritual to the Chogye Order's ordination process. Since 2010, all postulants are required to participate in separate novice- and bodhisattva-precepts rituals in order to officially become Chogye Order novices.

In the past decade or so, national postulant education programs have been taking place in the beautiful monastery of Chikchisa.[61] Twice a year, all postulants who have been living in temples throughout the country for at least five months assemble in Chikchisa along with roughly two dozen practice-guides (*sŭpŭija*) from several major Korean monasteries. Female and male postulants inhabit two separate huge halls for the program. The schedules are tight and full, involving classes, special lectures, ritual practices, robe-dressing guidance, and numerous confessional prostration sessions. Postulants do not eat after lunch during the two weeks; they participate in six hours of classes a day, perform 108-bow confessionals every morning and every evening, and take three-steps-one-bow and one-step-one-bow trips up the hill and toward the main Dharma Hall of Chikchisa once a week (fig. 7). Schedules for the program from 2014 show that the fifth-level examinations took place on the fifteenth day, followed by a bodhisattva precept ceremony. Participants told me that only the ten major precepts of the *Brahma Net Sutra* were taken during the ritual; the forty-eight minor rules were ignored. After the ceremony, the postulants gathered for an all-night three-thousand-bows vigil followed by the morning novice-precepts ritual that ended the program. The exhausted new novices were then allowed to return to their home monasteries.

Aside from sitting in lectures on the texts of the new postulant-curriculum discussed above, participants in the 2014 program were given several writing assignments, encouraging them to deliberate upon their own goals and aspirations in the form of letters to their parents and/or tonsure teachers. I was told that these letters were not really sent out, but served as exercises for the

FIG. 7. The one-step-one-bow procession of postulants in Chikchisa, 2014.

new monastics, meant to clarify their intentions to themselves, raise vows, and be retained as sort of time capsules useful for reconsidering their practice and measuring their progress in the future. The exact schedule for the postulant education program of 2014 is presented in Appendix B.

The unification of the monastic postulancy system has not always been smooth. Particular lineages have sometimes found it difficult to forgo their distinct identities, pride, and authority, and have resisted complete dissolution under the umbrella of the Chogye Order. One example of such a community is the Sŏn-hagwŏn, a monastic fraternity assembled in the early twentieth century by monks known for their opposition to the so-called secularization of Buddhism under Japanese influence. Its approximately one thousand currently affiliated monastics have been operating to a large extent under the auspices of the Chogye Order. In 2015, however, when they refused to surrender their exceptional privileges and control over several temples, Sŏn-hagwŏn novices were kicked out of Chogye seminaries and were forced to organize their own education programs and ordinations for new monks in the tiny temple of Kŭmjŏngsa in Pusan. As of 2017, it is still unclear whether this fraternity will end up realigning with the Chogye Order or splitting from it completely and administering its own autonomous education system.

Before concluding this section, let us take a closer look at the exams taken at the end of the postulant education programs. First, it is interesting to find that—at least in the last decade or so—very few postulants have actually failed these exams. An average of almost 99 percent of test-takers have passed. One foreign monk in Korea told me that his Korean language skills were so basic when he took the exam that he simply did not understand the questions and had to guess the answers throughout—yet he still passed. The only case I have encountered of someone failing the exam was when the postulant did not attempt to answer any questions at all and simply left the paper blank. This proves that unlike in certain historical circumstances, the main goal of the tests today is not to limit the number of new monastics, but to encourage learning from the very beginning of one's monastic career.

The exams incorporate both written and oral components. The written part involves short multiple-choice questions, which deal specifically with the contents of the texts of the postulant canon, as well as essay writing. The 2013 fifth-level exam essays, for example, included such prompts as: (1) Describe the person you respect the most and how do you intend to use your future practice to resemble him or her. (2) Describe the five precepts and your practice of them. (3) Use the Four Great Vows to describe the reasons you left home. (4) Describe the first and last teachings of the Buddha. (5) Describe the connection between your intentions in leaving home and *Śākyamuni*'s intention in leaving home. (6) Based on your own experience with the variety of desires and lifestyles people have, how would you put into practice the Four Great Vows of the bodhisattva path?[62]

These may certainly be great questions and *huatou* for new monastics. Rather than simply testing their knowledge and understanding of basic Buddhism, these questions force Korean postulants to contemplate their own motivations and goals in relation to the Buddhist teachings, and make vows for future practice. They are personal questions aimed to teach rather than to merely test. They demonstrate that what is understood as the most important thing new monastic postulants should know and understand about Buddhism is not intricate doctrine, but the right attitudes, objectives, and intentions appropriate for a future member of the Buddhist sangha.

The oral part of the fifth-level examinations is usually very short. Each postulant in turn moves forward to sit in front of two testers, who first ask a few questions regarding his or her personal motivation to become ordained. They may then ask the postulant to perform a short ritual chant using the traditional wooden-fish instrument. This is to be done from memory. The *Heart Sutra,* the morning and evening taking-refuge texts, or the first part of the *Thousand Hands Sutra* (used for the midday offering ceremonies) are commonly performed on this occasion. These three chants make for the basic ritual canon of the Chogye Order and are performed daily in all monasteries, and thus surely must be memorized prior to ordination. They are short enough, and many dedicated lay Buddhists in contemporary Korea and abroad memorize them as well.

The Seminary Curricula and the Fourth-Level Exams

The fourth-level sangha exams serve as qualification tests for novices before receiving the *bhikṣu/bhikkhuni* precepts and becoming full members of the Chogye Order. When novices from monasteries all over the peninsula gathered in Songgwangsa for the first of such exams in 2000, the curriculum reflected the traditional seminary programs. Ten questions were dedicated to the *Novice Precepts and Decorum* and to the *Huayan Sutra*, and five additional questions dealt with the *Ch'imun, Sajip, Sagyo,* and *Ch'obalsim* texts.[63] In subsequent years, the exam questions were altered according to the changing seminary curricula, reflecting the official Chogye understanding of the basic material every monastic was expected to be familiar with. In 2002, questions on Buddhist history and basic Vinaya were added to the exams. Test preparation booklets published by the Order in 2003 and 2006 show that exam questions on popular academic Buddhist topics—such as Mādhyamika, Yogācāra, the *Platform Sutra,* and the *Brahma Net Sutra*—were added to the program.

As Kanhua Chan gradually came to be regarded and promoted as the central hallmark of Korean Buddhism by the Chogye Order, two relevant Ming Dynasty Kanhua Chan treatises were appended to the fourth-level exam curriculum.[64] The first was *Admonitions to Practice Chan* (*Canchan jingyu* 參禪警語) written by Wuyi Yuanlai (無異元來, 1575–1630), and the second was *Changuan cejin* (禪關策進) written by Yunqi Zhuhong (雲棲袾宏, 1535–1615).[65] It has been argued that since exams have been constructed according to the seminary programs, they were unsuitable for the novice graduates of Dongguk University and the Central Sangha College, who studied a different, modern, curriculum.[66] While it is true that graduates of the Buddhist universities and the Elementary Chan Hall often must prepare individually for the exams using study notes and Chogye textbooks, this does not seem to pose a real problem. Approximately 95 percent of all fourth-level test-takers, including those preparing on their own, are regularly able to pass the exams.[67]

Following curricular reforms in 2010, the test has undergone considerable modifications. Only 50 percent of the exam questions now deal with the traditional curricular texts. The other half of the questions deal with early Buddhism, various Mahāyāna doctrines and texts, Vinaya and Buddhist ethics, temple management, and contemporary Buddhist issues.[68] Exams now take place once a year in the Central Sangha College and contain three parts: open essay questions, multiple-choice questions on specific doctrines, and short translations of key phrases from the texts. They also involve a ten- to twenty-minute interview with two testers. Like the interview of the fifth-level exams, the oral assessments here are centered on the evaluation of the novices' attitudes and motivation, and on short performances of the daily liturgy.

By 2014, the *Ch'imun* and *Sajip* Chan treatises had been completely dropped from these exams. Instead, Chan-related questions dealt mainly with the *Platform Sutra* and the abovementioned Kanhua Chan texts, conforming to the current Buddhist Studies' understanding of what the focal texts of Chan really are. Questions related to the four *Sagyo* sutras were limited to short phrase translations, while the only questions about the *Huayan Sutra* dealt with the ten bodhisattva stages. Instead, several questions on the historical Buddha were added, as well as inquiries on the four noble truths, the eightfold path, no-self and emptiness, and the eight consciousnesses. Accordingly, these exams have become increasingly comparable to the tests given at the end of "Introduction to Buddhism" courses in European or American universities, aligning Asian monastic knowledge of Buddhism with that of college students taking Buddhist Studies courses.

Still, the essay questions of the fourth-level examinations do show some interesting divergence from standard Buddhist Studies agendas. To be sure, some of the possible prompts involve typical Buddhist doctrinal history. A few instances are: "Compare and contrast the eightfold path and the six perfections." "Why do you think the Buddha allowed meat eating in three circumstances but the Mahāyāna forbids it altogether?" And: "How did the teaching of emptiness of the *Prajñā-paramitas* influence Chinese Buddhism?" Yet, other questions clearly attempt to encourage novices to contemplate Buddhist doctrines in light of their particular circumstances as Korean monastics. Examples include: "What is your opinion of the recent critique of 'praying for fortune Buddhism' (*kibok Pulgyo*)?" "How does faith in Buddhism differ from faith in other religions?" Or: "Compare the new *uposatha* system of the Chogye Order with the one described in the Vinaya."[69]

Most remarkable are the essay questions designed to force soon-to-be fully recognized Chogye monastics to consider how Buddhism could be propagated and skillfully used in order to benefit modern society. Some examples are: "Why do conflicts appear between religions and how could the Buddhist worldview help to solve them?" "Explain the best way for contemporary laypeople to practice Kanhua Chan in order to deal with social anxiety and disorganized values." "What would be the best method of propagation for the Korean urban population today?" And: "Discuss how chanting the names of Buddhas and bodhisattvas could be useful as a healing practice for dealing with the stress of modern society." Here, again, the point seems to be not simply to evaluate familiarity with Buddhist doctrines, but to encourage active contemplation of the ways one could put them into practice by teaching and propagating Buddhism. In other words, these questions propel new monastics to comply with the bodhisattva ideal and consider how they could utilize the Buddhist teachings to benefit society at large, rather than concentrate on their own individual path of salvation.

The Higher Rank Examinations

As pointed out earlier, the first third-level sangha exams took place in 2001. They serve as qualifying tests for those interested in abbacy in local branch monasteries, in directing offices in the major monasteries, and in climbing the ecclesiastical hierarchy of the Chogye Order. Unlike the fourth- and fifth-level exams, this test is not a mandatory part of the ordination process, and it is thus perhaps unsurprising that many Korean monastics choose to simply ignore it. Although anyone who has been a member of the sangha for at least ten years and who has participated in at least four retreats is eligible to sit for these exams, early statistics show that only about half of the qualified monastics have actually taken the test.[70] Yet, with the Order's encouragement and growing peer pressure, higher percentages of eligible monastics are gradually signing up for these exams.

Since it is a higher assessment for the selection of leaders, grading criteria have been stricter, and significant numbers of monastics have actually failed to pass. Between 11 and 13 percent of test-takers failed to pass in the early 2000s.[71] More recently, however, grading has become more lenient, and only 3 percent of the over four hundred home-leavers who took the 2013 third-level test failed to pass. In 2010, the Education Department announced that graduating from one of the various new sangha graduate schools discussed in the previous chapter would be considered equal to passing the third-level exams.[72]

The contents of these tests are not very different from those of the fourth-level exams, blending doctrinal and historical knowledge of Buddhism with personal essays on the way these doctrines could be put into practice. The 2003 third-level examination, for example, consisted of two parts. The first focused solely on the *Diamond Sutra,* while the second posed more general questions on Buddhist culture, propagation methods, and temple management.[73] More recently, the exam has been divided into three parts: fifty short questions on basic doctrines, one or two essay questions, and an oral interview evaluating the candidate's past activities and future plans as a leading member of the sangha.[74]

Examples of essay questions from recent exams include: "How would Buddhist values best be actualized in contemporary society?" "How does Buddhist compassion tally with the reluctance of many contemporary sangha members to participate in society?" "How could Buddhism today increase its competitiveness using its 'harmonizing controversies' (*hwajaeng sasang*) and bodhisattva ideals?" "How should the Chogye Order reform itself to be more transparent and pure?" "How can the Mahāyāna precepts be put into practice in modern society?" "Provide plans for financial expansion and fair management of temples." "What are the roles of abbots in their regional societies?" "Provide adequate propagation plans for the modern five-day work week and city life."[75] As these samples suggest, exam questions aim to encourage prospective monastic leaders to be involved in secular society and to ponder new, up-to-date propagation strategies for Buddhism to remain competitive in the religious marketplace of contemporary Korea.

The second-level exams, which qualify sangha members to hold higher executive positions in the central Chogye bureaucracy, have been held annually since 2010. Evaluating Buddhist doctrinal and textual familiarity has been almost completely relegated to the third- and fourth-level tests. The second-level assessments focus predominantly on the prior experiences and undertakings of the candidates, while evaluating their thoughts and plans regarding the development of the Order and its outreach in the future.

The interview portion of the exam, regarding past activities in the sangha, counts for more than the written section—two-thirds of the final grade. Essay topics include: the difference between the Buddhist belief in the Pure Land and the Christian belief in redemption; social activism in the spirit of Chan; possible modern applications of "no killing" and vegetarianism; Buddhist perspectives on social justice and human rights; problems with sticking excessively to traditional Korean Chan in trying to propagate in other cultures; propagation plans for males in order to correct the lay Buddhist gender imbalance toward females; modernizing and popularizing Buddhist rituals; propagation using smartphones and social networks, such as Twitter and Facebook; dealing with state laws that cause difficulties for the Order or for particular temples; the rights and duties of public temples and private hermitages; a welfare system for elderly monks and nuns; and so forth. These themes demonstrate that this exam is not intended to appraise monastics' fluency in Buddhist doctrines—nor to encourage individual cultivation—but rather to assess their ability to find creative solutions for the practical bureaucratic problems and propagational needs of the modern Korean sangha.

Twenty-six monks and twenty-five nuns registered for the first first-level examination, held in April 2016. The Order had hoped to administer it much earlier, but had to postpone it due to long discussions regarding the kind of assessment adequate for the respected elders of the community.[76] At first, the plan was for the exam to be based on preaching skills, but it was later decided that proposals for future activities would stand at the center of the evaluation process. To be exact, gauging one's monastic resume counted for a third of the score, and appraising written proposals for the Order's development along with specific plans for personal projects—for the remaining two-thirds.[77] All fifty-one test-takers passed the first-level exams that year, thus becoming eligible for abbacy positions in the twenty-five head district temples. Two won special monetary prizes for excellence in the exams, both of which were awarded for distinction in the creative management of propagation centers.

Continuing Education

In order to prepare monastics for the higher-level exams—as well as to provide them with an opportunity to keep up with the changing times and fortify their understanding of Buddhism—the Chogye Order established a system of short "continuing education" (*yŏnsu kyoyuk*) seminars. The first inchoate programs began in 1995 (right after the creation of the Education Department), and mainly targeted the needs of abbots and other bureaucrats. That year, 1,854 sangha members, comprising 58 percent of the invited monastics, participated in seminars dealing with temple management and accounting, Vinaya regulations, organizing the laity, and Buddhist environmentalism.[78] Since 1997, similar annual continuing education programs were separately created for foreign monastics in Korea, as well as for various temple position-holders.[79]

The programs gradually expanded, participant numbers grew, and today roughly four thousand monastics—a third of the entire sangha—take part in these educational programs each year. New seminars were soon added to the continuing education curricula on topics such as Buddhist education for children, the IMF and Buddhism, the modern roles of abbots, preaching methods, temple construction, and computers.[80] In 2001, taking part in continuing education programs became a requirement for all candidates of the higher-rank exams.[81]

In other words, these seminars have become firmly incorporated into the rank-exam system. All who wish to sit for the higher exams—as well as all abbots—must participate in at least one continuing education seminar per year, and at least three overall, before sitting for the third-level exams. In addition, beginning in 2014, continuing education seminars were divided according to sangha ranks: all monastics ranked "Seeing Virtue"/"Virtuous Conduct" are gathered once a year for seminars dealing with practice in modern society, propagation strategies, and the parish system. All monastics ranked "Middle Virtue"/"Virtuous Concentration" must participate in sessions about the future vision of the Chogye Order, counseling the laity, and strategies for regional propagation; while all "Great Virtue"/"Virtuous Wisdom"–ranked members of the sangha must take classes on world politics and economy, the role of the Chogye Order in the Korean national sphere, and the functions of head district/parish temples. Finally, highest-ranking, "Religious Teacher"/"Bright Virtue" monastics should participate in special lectures on the rather abstract topic of the "flow in human civilization," as well as in social leadership seminars.[82]

In recent years, most of these continuing education courses—as well as the higher exams themselves—take place in the newly built Traditional Buddhist Cultural Center (T'aehwasan Chŏnt'ong Pulgyo Munhwawŏn), located next to Magoksa. While this institution belongs to the Chogye Order, it looks more like a resort than a monastery, and often houses company membership training sessions for new employees (usually called MTs in Korea), given with a Buddhist flavor. Continuing education seminars usually last three to five days and cost between fifty and two hundred dollars. Apart from the obvious courses on Buddhist texts, temple management, and propagation, various fascinating new courses on Western philosophy, science, Korean history, the tea ceremony, Buddhist psychology, yoga, feminism, Christianity, Daoism, cinema, Darwinism, and so forth, have been arranged in recent years to broaden the horizons of the Chogye Order's monastic leaders.

In 2013, pilgrimage voyages were added to the system and, these days, four- to ten-day trips to famous Buddhist sites in India, China, Myanmar, Japan, Tibet, and the Silk Road are organized as continuing education for the Chogye sangha. The 2014 schedules also included some original courses in oratory skills and on using the internet and smartphone technologies for outreach.[83] I had a chance to participate in one interesting three-day seminar called "Practice and Coffee," in which monastics were taught to prepare tasty drip-coffee, mainly in order to enhance the hospitality of temples and better appeal to the public.[84] The 2016 schedules included seminars on temple cooking, propagation of Korean Buddhism abroad (including a course conducted completely in English), as well as a special trip to Dharamsala for a public talk by the Dalai Lama. These seminars further illustrate the changing fashions and trends of the Chogye Order that have been discussed throughout this book. They reconfirm the broader shift of Korean Buddhism from a particular kind of Chan toward a broader, more global, pluralistic, and inclusive style of Buddhism.

The Rank-Exam System of the T'aego Order

The second largest Buddhist organization in Korea, the T'aego Order, also operates a similar rank-exam system for its sangha. Its rank titles, in fact, almost fully match their Chogye counterparts, the only differences being that the T'aego does not issue distinct titles for females, and that the lowest rank of the fully ordained is called "Good Virtue" (*Sŏndŏk* 善德) rather than "Seeing Virtue," as it is in the Chogye. Ranks are based on seniority and on examinations, which have been administered once every two to three years since the early 1980s. Unlike the Chogye, there are no qualifying exams (and no mandatory qualifying education) for ordinations, and tests are strictly conducted for obtaining higher ranks. The contents of these exams, however, are very similar to the Chogye assessments, typically involving interviews on prior activities and future plans, as well as essays on devising new propagation methods and offering ways for sangha participation in modern society.[85]

The T'aego Order also runs yearly, intensive, one-day continuing education seminars according to rank. They are mandatory for all who wish to continue their climb up the monastic hierarchies of the organization. I participated in the 2013 program, which took place in the T'aego headquarters at Seoul's Pŏmnyunsa. In the first day, approximately three hundred clerics ranked "Good Virtue" huddled together in the lecture hall in order to listen to a law professor explain the intricacies of religious taxation laws in Korea (fig. 8). This was an important topic for many of the participants, who struggle to make a living in their small urban temples. The next day, roughly two hundred "Great Virtue"–ranked monastics gathered to listen to lectures regarding the T'aego's administration plans and policies for the following year. Original Buddhist welfare programs developed by individual temples were presented as examples to encourage creative propagation and economic activities.

To summarize briefly, in recent years, the Korean Chogye and T'aego Orders have endeavored to give structure to their monastic bureaucracies by creating fixed, unified rank-exam systems. Unlike their historical precedents, these new sangha exams are autonomously operated by the Buddhist institutions, and, rather than aiming to limit and control the sangha, they encourage learning and promote modern, curriculum-based scholarship. The fifth- and fourth-level exams of the Chogye Order serve as qualifying exams for taking the novice and full precepts, respectively, and are based on the new postulant and

FIG. 8. Continuing education day for T'aego monastics at Pŏmnyunsa.

seminary curricular canons. Passing the higher-level exams qualifies candidates for abbacies and other bureaucratic positions, though all eligible monastics are encouraged to sit for them regardless of their professional aspirations. Rather than testing fluency in texts and doctrines, these higher exams evaluate prior practice and management experience, and appraise the ability of candidates to serve as leaders and devise new skillful propagation methods in order to increase the Chogye Order's competitiveness in contemporary Korea's multi-religious society.

Evidently, contemporary Buddhist monastic bureaucratic hierarchies in Korea are based primarily on textual education and exams, rather than on meditation practice. Some sangha members criticize this system, believing that exam preparation could actually become an obstacle to genuine spiritual practice. Yet, as we have seen, the actual questions on the monastic exams often serve to encourage active contemplation about the way Buddhism should be practiced and propagated in the world today, rather than to confirm doctrinal fluency. The four seasons do continue to operate deep in the mountain monasteries, and the debates surrounding the exams essentially focus not on the existence of the hierarchies themselves, but on the conditions most appropriate for determining them.

Conclusions

IT IS SAID THAT DURING THE ANNUAL Korean university entrance examinations all construction work is halted, the police are busy driving tardy students, and even flights are restricted in order to avoid noise that may interrupt the examinees.[1] As in neighboring countries, Korean students tend to spend long hours in after-school academies (*hagwŏn*), and success in examinations generally ensures high social prestige.[2] The Chogye Order, too, seems to have been infected with this "education fever" (*kyoyugyŏl*). Buddhist monastic life in Korea today involves more hours of classroom education than ever before—beginning with a new three-week postulant program, continuing with four years of mandatory seminary study, gradually offering more opportunities for monastic graduate work, and lasting for the rest of one's monastic career in the form of continuing education seminars and rank-exam preparation courses. This certainly makes textual education quite central to the dominant Korean Buddhist monastic institution, fostering monks who do not focus on Chan meditation alone, but are knowledgeable in the histories, foundational texts, languages, and cultures of multiple Buddhisms. They are thus able to see beyond their local lineages and grasp themselves as part of a broader, pluralistic form of Buddhism.

As we have seen, what came to be known as the "traditional" Korean Buddhist monastic seminary curriculum may be traced back to the seventeenth century. The ten core texts that comprise this curricular canon have been the most commonly printed and studied Buddhist works in Korea for several centuries, and as such, exerted much influence on the way Buddhism has been understood and practiced on the peninsula. Yet, contrary to common opinion, this was only one among several pedagogical programs that existed side by side prior to the twentieth century. Only during the last hundred years or so was this particular syllabus systematized, unified, legitimized in history writing, propagated nationally, and finally institutionalized in Chogye law as the mandatory course for all monastic novices.

At the same time, this traditional program has also endured continual pressure to reform and restructure according to regional and global developments in Buddhist learning. In the early twentieth century, attempts were made to rearrange the curriculum by adding science classes, languages, and courses on Indian Buddhism according to the modern programs of the new Japanese sectarian universities. These efforts materialized in the establishment of pioneering Buddhist institutions of higher education in Korea. More severe attacks were sustained at the dawn of the twenty-first century, when the traditional curriculum was criticized for being outdated, skewed, incomprehensible, and intolerably lacking, and the entire system was pressured to conform to the hegemonic pedagogical dispositions of contemporary, Western-university-led, Buddhist Studies.

In 2010, a new mandatory national curriculum was introduced into Chogye monastic seminaries. Unlike the particular scholastic Huayan-Chan that characterized the traditional syllabus—and, with it, Korean Buddhist orthodoxy as a whole—the new program consists of broader introductory courses dealing with multiple Mahāyāna traditions, Pāli sutras, Indian Vinaya, English language study, propagation methods, history, and cultural courses. Simple recitation and memorization of Classical Chinese texts that once prevailed in the seminaries was replaced by textbook-based general introductions in the vernacular, and the program currently often involves exams and writing assignments. Interestingly, some of the historically more popular Chan texts of Korean Buddhism (such as the *Sutra of Perfect Enlightenment,* the *Śūraṃgama Sutra,* Zongmi's *Preface,* Chinul's *Excerpts,* etc.) have been mostly removed from today's curricula, and exchanged for the works that hold more weight in the canon of contemporary Chan studies (such as the *Platform* and *Vimalakīrti* sutras). This compulsory monastic program is increasingly supplemented with diverse options for graduate study, fostering Chogye Order specialists in multiple forms of Buddhism. Overall, these new educational agendas transform the identity of the Korean tradition from a specific kind of Chan to a more general, inclusive, and pluralistic Buddhism, similar to the one found in our English language textbooks.

In addition, a new system of rank-examinations ensures that monastic hierarchies in Korea are determined according to objective standards. While seniority and meditational experience remain important criteria for holding higher positions in the Order, pedagogical attainments now assume a more determinative role. The contents of the new monastic bureaucratic examinations bring to light what the Chogye Order considers to be its two main objectives today. The first is reinterpreting and updating Buddhist doctrines, practices, and disciplinary rules, making them more suitable for contemporary life. Exam questions, thus, often force monastics to contemplate possible ways to develop new modern organizational structures, rituals, cultivation practices, and monastery regulations, all the while retaining the spirit of the ancient sutras and Vinaya. The second major objective mirrored in the examinations is the development of new propagation methods for increasing the Order's competitiveness in the contemporary Korean religious marketplace. Hence, while preparing for the exams' essay questions, monastics are encouraged to ponder how new technologies, cultural agendas, and doctrinal flexibility may be used to attract more people to (Korean) Buddhism in the contemporary world.

The curricular shifts discussed in this volume certainly did not appear spontaneously out of thin air, nor did they result only from inner developments within the Korean Buddhist community. Rather, they were essentially mimetic responses to the values of significant others in the non-Buddhist outside world, be it Confucianism in premodern times, or modern Buddhist Studies, globalization, and cultural diversity today. The traditional Buddhist program, in which elementary instructions and admonitions (*Ch'imun*) are followed by four books (*Sajip*) and five sutras (*Sagyo* and *Huayan*), seems to mirror Zhu Xi's Confucian curriculum (where *Elementary Learning* is followed by the Four Books and the Five Classics), which was the dominant school syllabus in Chosŏn Korea. As a modern, rationalized, universal education system gradually replaced the elitist Confucian curriculum during the twentieth century, the Buddhist sangha followed suit, establishing its own parallel national seminary network with unified curricula for all monastics, both male and female, as well as its very own higher learning facilities. Finally, with accelerating globalization, the twenty-first century exposed the Korean sangha to the hegemonic canons of Buddhist Studies, which seem to endorse a differently centered, more pluralized version of Buddhism. In response, the Chogye Order has diversified its curricula, educational institutions, and personnel, encouraging more comprehensive study of Buddhism and an increasingly internationalized sangha.

Buddhist monastics are seldom completely detached from the outside world. Most have grown up in secular society and carry its values into the monasteries upon leaving home. In earlier times, East Asian monastics who have been educated within the Confucian tradition Confucianized Buddhist learning in the monasteries, and similarly today, young monastic matriculants carry with them democratic and globally oriented values when leaving to the mountains. The worldly values of the times, it seems, tend to infiltrate the religious sphere and transform spiritual beliefs and practices.

The Korean sangha continues to be as vibrant as ever, with new reforms constantly under way. At the time this book was going to print, the Education Department legislated several additional ordinances in an effort to further systematize seminary teacher qualifications, and new plans to squeeze the entire curriculum into three years of schooling in order to improve seminary financials have been proposed. In the summer of 2018 several leading monastic teachers were invited yet again to the Chogye Order offices to discuss educational reforms. Ilchin, a respected female monastic teacher from Unmunsa—the largest seminary in the country—reminded the participants that rationalization and legislation were not the ultimate objectives of monastic education. Perhaps it is appropriate to end this book with the sober words of this elderly nun:

> [Buddhist] practice is ultimately the mutual deployment of tension and relaxation. Making the most out of time and space is very important. Thus, perfect administration of monastic education is not dependent upon a [rational] system. The *system* is not the primary issue; what is at stake is [rather] how monastic students would be able to transform via the words of the Buddha through this education.[3]

Appendix A
Chogye Order Official Curricula for Monastic Graduate Schools

Below are the recommended schedules for the various new monastic graduate schools affiliated with the Chogye Order. These schedules appear on the Order's website. Schedules for the Pure Land and Yogācāra Graduate Schools, which have not yet been established, are also included as recommendations for the future. These schools are expected to house a minimum of twenty students, and accommodate both female and male monastics, as well as laypeople. Communal living in these schools is not mandatory, and students could simply commute to the monastery for classes.

A. Standard Curriculum for Vinaya Sangha Graduate Schools (ten currently exist)

Course	First Semester	Second Semester
Graduate first year	• *Dharmaguptaka Vinaya* in comparative perspective • General ethics * Designing novice-precept ceremonies	• *Dharmaguptaka Vinaya* in comparative perspective • Mahāyāna precepts * Designing full-precept ceremonies and meal regulations
Graduate second year	• *Brahma Net Sutra* • Buddhist ethics * Designing bodhisattva-precept ceremonies and confession rituals	• Baizhang's Pure Rules and the new Chogye Order Pure Rules • The Chogye Order Constitution and laws • Thesis writing
Research first year	• Indian Vinaya research	• Indian Vinaya research
Research second year	• Chinese Vinaya research	• Korean Vinaya research and modern ethics
Research third year	• Specialized research	• Thesis writing

B. Standard Curriculum for Chan Studies Sangha Graduate Schools (one currently exists in Yumasa)

Course	First Semester	Second Semester
Graduate first year	• Early Buddhism and Chan • Mahāyāna texts and Chan	• Laṅkāvatāra Chan • Patriarch Chan
Graduate second year	• Kanhua Chan • Korean Chan	• Methods of guiding Chan practice • Special lectures on Chan Lamp Anthologies • Thesis writing
Research first year	• Tathāgatagarbha thought • Chan Pure Rules	• Chan anthologies of the Five Houses • Chan chanting research
Research second year	• Dahui research • Huayan-Chan research	• Korean Chan textual research • Tiantai-Chan research
Research third year	• Chan culture research • Specialized research	• Thesis writing

C. Standard Curriculum for Chinese Buddhist Texts Sangha Graduate Schools (four currently exist)

Course	First Semester	Second Semester
Graduate first year	• Readings from the *Āgamas* • *Ch'imun* • Chinese characters 1	• Dahui's *Letters* • Chinul's *Excerpts* • Chinese characters 2
Graduate second year	• *Śūraṅgama Sutra* • *Diamond Sutra* • *Awakening of Faith*	• *Lotus Sutra* • *Nirvana Sutra* • *Vimalakīrti Sutra*
Research first year	• *Huayan Sutra* 1 • Sungchao's *Starting Treatises* (*Zhaolun* 肇論)	• *Huayan Sutra* 2 • Zhiyi's *Great Calming and Contemplation*
Research second year	• *Memorabilia of the Three Kingdoms* (*Samguk yusa* 三國遺事) • *Sutra of Infinite Life*	• Inscriptions of great monks • Wŏnhyo's *Treatise on the Diamond Samadhi Sutra*
Research third year	• Readings from the *Collected Works of Korean Buddhism* • Specialized research	• Thesis writing

D. Standard Curriculum for Early Buddhist Texts Sangha Graduate Schools (one currently exists in Sŏnunsa)

Course	First Semester	Second Semester
Graduate first year	• Pāli language 1 • History of Theravāda • *Sutta Nipata*	• Pāli language 2 • *Āgamas* and *Nikāyas* • *Mahasatipatthana Sutta*
Graduate second year	• Pāli language 3 • Readings from the *Samyutta Nikāya* • Readings from the *Mahavagga*	• Readings from the *Anguttara Nikāya* • Readings from the *Jātakas* • Readings from the *Dhammapada*
Research first year	• Readings from the *Digha Nikāya* • Buddhagosa's *Visuddhimagga* 1	• Readings from the *Majjhima Nikāya* • Buddhagosa's *Visuddhimagga* 2
Research second year	• Readings from the *Milindapanha* • Buddhagosa's *Samanthapasadika*	• Readings from the *Theragatha* • Readings from the *Abhidhamma* 1
Research third year	• Readings from the *Abhidhamma* 2 • Specialized research	• Thesis writing

E. Standard Curriculum for Huayan Sangha Graduate Schools (two currently exist)

Course	First Semester	Second Semester
Graduate first year	• Introduction to Huayan • The ten stages of the bodhisattva • Tathāgatagarbha thought	• *Awakening of Faith* • Chengguan's *Pure Conversations of Huayan* (*Hwaŏm hyŏndam* 華嚴玄談) • History of Huayan in China
Graduate second year	• Readings from Śikṣānanda's 80-scroll *Huayan Sutra* 1 • Huayan and Tiantai • History of Korean Huayan	• Readings from Śikṣānanda's 80-scroll *Huayan Sutra* 2 • Ŭisang's *Huayan Dharmadhatu Diagram* (*Pŏpkyedo* 法界圖) • Huayan and Chan
Research first year	• Early Huayan research • Wŏnhyo's Huayan research	• Fazang's Huayan research • Ŭisang's Huayan research
Research second year	• Chengguan's Huanyan research • Kyunyŏ's (均如) Huayan research	• Late Huayan research • Bodhisattva stages research
Research third year	• Vasubandhu's *Treatise on the Ten-Stages Sutra* • Specialized research	• Thesis writing

F. Standard Curriculum for Prajñā/Mādhyamika Sangha Graduate Schools (one currently exists in Paegyangsa)

Course	First Semester	Second Semester
Graduate first year	• Indian Buddhist thought • Prajñā/Mādhyamika thought 1 • Sanskrit 1	• Prajñā/Mādhyamika thought 2 • Sanskrit reading of the *Diamond Sutra* • Sanskrit 2
Graduate second year	• Chinese Prajñā/Mādhyamika thought • Nāgārjuna's *Mūlamadhyamaka-kārikā* • Candrakīrti's *Prasannapadā* 1	• Readings from the *8000-verses Prajñā-Paramitra Sutra* • Tibetan literature research • Candrakīrti's *Prasannapadā* 2
Research first year	• Readings from the *25,000-verses Prajñā-Paramita Sutra* 1 • Aryadeva's *Satasastra* 1	• Readings from the *25,000-verses Prajñā-Paramita Sutra* 2 • Aryadeva's *Satasastra* 2
Research second year	• Nāgārjuna's *Vigrahavyāvartanī* 1 • Śāntideva's *Bodhicaryavatara* 1	• Nāgārjuna's *Vigrahavyāvartanī* 2 • Śāntideva's *Bodhicaryavatara* 2
Research third year	• Yijing's Nāgārjuna translations • Specialized research	• Thesis writing

G. Standard Curriculum for Yogācāra/Tathāgatagarbha Sangha Graduate Schools (none exist to date)

Course	First Semester	Second Semester
Graduate first year	• History of Indian Buddhism • Yogācāra and Tathāgatagarbha thought 1 • Sanskrit 1	• *Abhidharmakośa* research • Yogācāra and Tathāgatagarbha thought 2 • Sanskrit 2
Graduate second year	• *Awakening of Faith* • Vasubandhu's *Thirty Verses of Consciousness-Only* • *Saṃdhinirmocana Sūtra*	• *Nirvana Sutra* • Maitreya's *Mahāyāna-Sutra-Alamkara-karika* • Tibetan literature research
Research first year	• *Yogācāra-bhumi-sastra* 1 • Sanskrit readings from Maitreya's *Mahāyāna-sutra-alamkara-karika*	• *Yogācāra-bhumi-sastra* 2 • The three Tathāgatagarbha sutras
Research second year	• Xuanzang's *Cheng weishi lun* (成唯識論) 1 • Sanskrit readings from Asanga	• Xuanzang's *Cheng weishi lun* 2 • *Treasure-Nature Treatise* (*Baoxing lun* 寶性論)
Research third year	• Asanga's *Mahāyāna-saṃgraha* • Specialized research	• Thesis writing

H. Standard Curriculum for Pure Land Sangha Graduate Schools (none exist to date)

Course	First Semester	Second Semester
Graduate first year	• Introduction to Pure Land • The three Pure Land sutras • Japanese 1	• *Pratyutpanna Sutra* • Indian Pure Land thought • Japanese 2
Graduate second year	• The Pure Land faith • Chinese Pure Land thought • Korean Pure Land thought	• Vasubandhu's *Sukhavati-vyuhopadesa* • Wŏnhyo's *The Path Where the Mind Plays in Bliss* (*Yusim-allakdo* 遊心安樂道) • Japanese Pure Land thought
Research first year	• Tan Luan's (曇鸞) Pure Land thought • Chanting Chan research	• Wŏnhyo's Pure Land thought • Maitreya's Pure Land thought
Research second year	• Pure Land during the Tang • Kyŏnghŭng's (憬興) Pure Land thought	• Fayan's (法演) Pure Land thought • Shinran's Pure Land thought
Research third year	• Chanting and death anticipation rituals • Specialized research	• Thesis writing

Appendix B
Schedule of the 2014 Chogye Order Postulant Education Program

Schedule of the 2014 Chogye Order Postulant Education Program
Day 1–Day 8

<table>
<tr><th>Time</th><th>Day 1</th><th>Day 2</th><th>Day 3</th><th>Day 4</th><th>Day 5</th><th>Day 6</th><th>Day 7</th><th>Day 8</th></tr>
<tr><td>3:00</td><td rowspan="14">Arrival</td><td colspan="7">Waking up</td></tr>
<tr><td>3:00–3:40</td><td colspan="7">Washing up and gathering in the Dharma Hall</td></tr>
<tr><td>3:40–4:00</td><td colspan="7">Morning chanting ritual</td></tr>
<tr><td>4:00–5:40</td><td colspan="7">108 bows and chanting practice</td></tr>
<tr><td>5:40–6:00</td><td colspan="7">Rest</td></tr>
<tr><td>6:00–7:00</td><td colspan="7">Formal four-bowl monastic meal</td></tr>
<tr><td>7:00–7:25</td><td colspan="7">Work/Rest</td></tr>
<tr><td>7:25–7:30</td><td colspan="7">Class beginning ritual</td></tr>
<tr><td>7:30–8:30</td><td>Monastic dress and posture practice</td><td colspan="3">Novice Precepts and Decorum</td><td colspan="2" rowspan="5">One step one bow</td><td>Novice Precepts and Decorum</td></tr>
<tr><td>8:30–8:50</td><td colspan="4">Rest</td><td></td></tr>
<tr><td>8:50–9:50</td><td>Monastic dress and posture practice</td><td colspan="3">Chanting rituals</td><td rowspan="3">Chanting rituals</td></tr>
<tr><td>9:50–10:50</td><td>Opening ceremony</td><td colspan="3">Thousand Hands Sutra chanting</td></tr>
<tr><td>10:50–11:00</td><td colspan="4">Rest</td></tr>
<tr><td>11:00–12:00</td><td colspan="7">Formal four-bowl monastic meal</td></tr>
</table>

12:00–12:30	Physical inspection	Free practice (reviewing studied material)						
12:30–13:40		Special lecture	Monastic dress and posture practice	*Novice Precepts and Decorum*		Monastic dress and posture practice		
13:40–14:00		Rest						
14:00–15:20		Life of the Buddha	*Admonitions to Beginners* (*Ch'obalsim*)	*42-Sections Sutra*	Basic doctrine	Life of compassion	The meaning of bowing	Work and developing faith
15:20–15:40	Rest							
15:40–17:00	Monastic dress and posture practice	Life of the Buddha	*Admonitions to Beginners* (*Ch'obalsim*)	History of the Chogye Order	Basic doctrine	Practicing Chan	The Vinaya of home-leavers	Social leadership
17:00–17:50	Cleaning/Work/Showers					Shaving heads	About Chikchisa Temple	Cleaning/ Work/ Showers
17:50–18:20	Monastic dress and posture practice	Religious practice (reviewing learned material)						
18:20–18:40		Practicing the use of the *mokt'ak* instrument						

(*continued*)

Schedule of the 2014 Chogye Order Postulant Education Program (*continued*)

Day 1–Day 8 (*continued*)

Time	Day 1	Day 2	Day 3	Day 4	Day 5	Day 6	Day 7	Day 8
18:40–18:50	Rest							
18:50–19:20	Evening chanting ritual							
19:20–20:10	Monastic dress and posture practice	108 bows confessional				Writing a letter to teachers or parents		108 bows confessional
20:10–20:30		Rest						
20:30–21:00	Writing a diary, bedtime							

Day 9–Day 16

Time	Day 9	Day 10	Day 11	Day 12	Day 13	Day 14	Day 15	Day 16
3:00	Waking up							All night 3000 bows
3:00–3:40	Washing up and gathering in the Dharma Hall							
3:40–4:00	Morning chanting ritual							
4:00–5:40	108 bows and chanting practice							
5:40–6:00	Rest							
6:00–7:00	Formal four-bowl monastic meal							
7:00–7:25	Work/Rest							
7:25–7:30	Class beginning ritual							

<table>
<tr><td>7:30–8:30</td><td colspan="2">Novice Precepts and Decorum</td><td colspan="2">Monastic dress and posture practice</td><td rowspan="5">3-steps-one-bow and head shaving</td><td>Chanting rituals</td><td>Free practice</td><td>Closing ceremony</td></tr>
<tr><td>8:30–8:50</td><td colspan="4">Rest</td><td rowspan="3">Receiving the robes ceremony</td><td rowspan="4">Fifth-level sangha exam (written part)</td><td>Rest</td></tr>
<tr><td>8:50–9:50</td><td colspan="4">Chanting rituals</td><td rowspan="3">Novice Precept ceremony</td></tr>
<tr><td>9:50–10:50</td><td colspan="4">Thousand Hands Sutra chanting</td></tr>
<tr><td>10:50–11:00</td><td colspan="4">Rest</td><td>Rest</td></tr>
<tr><td>11:00–12:00</td><td colspan="8">Formal four-bowl monastic meal</td></tr>
<tr><td>12:00–12:30</td><td colspan="6">Free practice (reviewing learned material)</td><td rowspan="4">Fifth-level sangha exam (oral part)</td><td rowspan="4">Ending</td></tr>
<tr><td>12:30–13:40</td><td>Novice Precepts and Decorum</td><td colspan="3">Monastic dress and posture practice</td><td>Brahma Net Sutra</td><td>Practice</td></tr>
<tr><td>13:40–14:00</td><td colspan="6">Rest</td></tr>
<tr><td>14:00–15:20</td><td>Q&A with an Elder</td><td>Various Buddhist practice methods</td><td>Admonitions to Beginners (Ch’obalsim)</td><td>Raising vows</td><td>Brahma Net Sutra</td><td>Video documentary on Indian Buddhist pilgrimages</td></tr>
</table>

(continued)

Schedule of the 2014 Chogye Order Postulant Education Program (*continued*)
Day 9–Day 16 (*continued*)

Time	Day 9	Day 10	Day 11	Day 12	Day 13	Day 14	Day 15	Day 16
15:20–15:40	Rest						Bodhisattva Precept ceremony	
15:40–17:00	The Huayan story of a novice (善財) in search of the Dharma	Buddhist practice methods	*Admonitions to Beginners (Ch'obalsim)*	Buddhism and mod-ern society	Monastic dress and posture practice	Video docu-mentary on prominent Korean monks		
17:00–17:50	Cleaning/Work/Showers					Cleaning	Commem-orative pictures	
17:50–18:20	Religious practice (reviewing material)					Free practice	Lecture on the monastic education system	
18:20–18:40	Practicing the use of the *mokt'ak* instrument							
18:40–18:50	Rest							
18:50–19:20	Evening chanting ritual							

19:20–20:10	108 bows confessional	Writing one's practice goals	Free practice	A talk by an Education Department officer	
20:10–20:30	Rest			All night 3,000 bows	
20:30–21:00	Writing a diary, bedtime				

Appendix C
Glossary of Principal Curricular Titles and Terms

Glossary of Principal Curricular Titles and Terms

Title Used in this Book	Full English Title	Chinese Characters	Pinyin	McCune-Reischauer	Notes
Awakening of Faith	*The Treatise on the Awakening of Faith in Mahāyāna Buddhism*	大乘起信論	*Dasheng qixin lun*	*Taesŭng kisin ron*	Part of the *Sagyo*
Bequeathed Teachings Sutra		遺敎經	*Yijiao jing*	*Yugyo kyŏng*	Vinaya-related
Chan Essentials		禪要	*Chanyao*	*Sŏnyo*	Part of the *Sajip*, written by Gaofeng
Chan Preface		禪源諸銓集都序	*Chanyuan zhuqhuanji douxu*	*Sŏnwŏn chejŏnjip tosŏ*	Part of the *Sajip*, written by Zongmi
Ch'imun	*Admonitions to the Gray-Robed Monks*	緇門警訓	*Zimen jingxun*	*Ch'imun kyŏnghun*	Song Dynasty compilation of admonitions and other essays
Ch'obalsim	*Admonitions to Beginners*	初發心自警文	*Chufaxin zijingwen*	*Ch'obalsim chagyŏngmun*	Collection of three Korean-written admonition essays
Diamond Sutra		金剛經	*Jingang jing*	*Kŭmgang kyŏng*	Part of the *Sagyo*
Enlightened Verses	*The Sŏn School's Enlightened Verses*	禪門拈頌	*Chanmen niansong*	*Sŏnmun yŏmsong*	Korean *gongan* collection

Excerpts	*Excerpts from the Dharma Collection and Special Practice Record with Personal Notes*	法集別行錄節要幷入私記	*Fajibiexinglu jieyao bingru Siji*	*Pŏpchippyŏrhaengnok chŏryo Pyŏngip sagi*	Part of the *Sajip*, written by Chinul
Huayan Sutra		華嚴經	*Huayan jing*	*Hwaŏm kyŏng*	Part of the *Taegyo*
Letters	*Dahui's Letters*	大慧書狀 (found in *Dahui's Recorded Sayings* 大慧普覺禪師語錄)	*Dahui shuzhuang*	*Taehye sŏjang*	Part of the *Sajip*, written by Dahui
Mirror of Sŏn		禪家龜鑑	*Chanjia guijian*	*Sŏn'ga kwigam*	Written by Hyujŏng
Novice Precepts and Decorum		沙彌律儀	*Shami luyi*	*Sami yurŭi*	Vinaya-related
Sagyo	The Fourfold Sutra Collection	四敎		*Sagyo*	*Diamond Sutra*, *Śūraṃgama Sutra*, *Sutra of Perfect Enlightenment*, and the *Awakening of Faith*
Sajip	The Fourfold Treatise Collection	四集		*Sajip*	*Chan Preface*, *Excerpts*, *Letters*, and *Chan Essentials*
Śūraṃgama Sutra		楞嚴經	*Lengyan jing*	*Nŭngŏm kyŏng*	Part of the *Sagyo*

(continued)

Glossary of Principal Curricular Titles and Terms (*continued*)

Title Used in this Book	Full English Title	Chinese Characters	Pinyin	McCune-Reischauer	Notes
Sutra of Perfect Enlightenment		圓覺經	*Yuanjue jing*	*Wŏn'gak kyŏng*	Part of the *Sagyo*
Taegyo	Higher Learning (Course)	大敎		*Taegyo*	Usually involving the *Huayan Sutra*
Transmission of the Lamp	*The Record of the Transmission of the Lamp of the Jingde Era*	景德傳燈錄	*Jingde chuandenglu*	*Kyŏngdŏk chŏndŭngnok*	Biographies of Chan patriarchs
42-Section Sutra		四十二章經	*Sishierzhang jing*	*Sasibijang kyŏng*	Vinaya-related

Notes

ACKNOWLEDGMENTS

1 Samuel Hawley, *Inside the Hermit Kingdom*, 98.

INTRODUCTION

1 Steven Collins, "On the Very Idea of the Pali Canon."

2 Anne M. Blackburn, "Looking for the Vinaya: Monastic Discipline in the Practical Canons of the Theravāda."

3 Justin Thomas McDaniel, *Gathering Leaves and Lifting Words: Histories of Buddhist Monastic Education in Laos and Thailand.*

4 The *Koryŏ Canon,* often mistranslated in English as the *Tripitaka Koreana* (the Korean title reads "Great Storehouse of 80,000 Buddhist Texts," *P'alman taejang-gyŏng* 八萬大藏經) was printed for the most part in the twelfth century, although some texts were added later on. For an analysis of its contents see: Lewis Lancaster and Sung-bae Park, *The Korean Buddhist Canon: A Descriptive Catalogue.* See also the entry for *Dazangjing* in: Robert Buswell and Donald Lopez, *The Princeton Dictionary of Buddhism,* 225–226. A more explicit discussion of the Korean canon as a talisman has been recently offered in: Jiang Wu and Ron Dziwenka, "Better Than the Original: The Creation of Goryeo Canon and the Formation of Giyang Bulgyo 祈禳佛敎." On the modern valorization of this canon see: Hwansoo Ilmee Kim, *The Korean Buddhism Empire: A Transnational History (1910–1945),* chapter one.

5 Cited in: Jiang Wu, "Knowledge for What? The Buddhist Concept of Learning in the Śūramgama Sūtra."

6 It is often lamented that Buddhist Studies lacks sufficient ethnographic work and mainly concentrates on textual analysis. See, for example: Gareth Fisher, "Fieldwork on East Asian Buddhism: Toward a Person-Centered Approach." I believe that this is gradually changing. In fact, the twentieth century has seen several ethnographic publications on Buddhism in Southeast Asia, and in the new millennium some anthropological studies of East Asian Buddhism have been conducted as well. See also: David Gellner, "Introduction: What Is the Anthropology of Buddhism About?"

7 George Marcus, *Ethnography through Thick and Thin,* 91. The idea of a "multi-locale" ethnography first came up in: George Marcus and Michael Fischer, *Anthropology as Cultural Critique: An Experimental Moment.*

8 I made initial visits to some of the seminaries in the summer of 2012, but did most of the fieldwork between August 2013 and December of 2014. I returned to Korea in July of 2015 and made additional visits to seminaries and other educational events described in this manuscript throughout 2016.

9 Helen Hardacre, "Fieldwork with Japanese Religious Groups," 71–88.

10 Richard Irvine, "The Experience of Ethnographic Fieldwork in an English Benedictine Monastery: Or, Not Playing at Being a Monk."

11 It is estimated that about half of the Korean postulants and novices return to the laity before receiving the full precepts, and much smaller numbers leave later in their monastic careers. Still, I believe the situation is different for the foreign sangha, many of whom seem to have been disrobing even after years of monastic life.

12 See: B. J. Terwiel, "A Model for the Study of Thai Buddhism."

13 Gary Fine, "Ten Lies of Ethnography: Moral Dilemmas in Field Research."

14 The "practical Vinayas" of Korean Buddhism often condemn frivolous speech. For more details see chapter one.

15 Anne M. Blackburn, *Buddhist Learning and Textual Practice in Eighteenth-Century Lankan Monastic Culture;* McDaniel, *Gathering Leaves and Lifting Words.*

16 Georges Dreyfus, *The Sound of Two Hands Clapping: The Education of a Tibetan Buddhist Monk.*

17 Hayashi Makoto, "Religious Studies and Religiously Affiliated Universities."

18 Mark Rowe and Hiroki Kikuchi, "Round-Table Discussion: The Current State of Sectarian Universities."

19 For the case of Sōtō see: Griffith Foulk, "The Zen Institution in Modern Japan." In addition, Kaoru Nonomura recalls a summer lecture series on Dōgen's *Treasury of the True Dharma Eye* when he attended Eiheiji in the 1990s: Nonomura, *Eat Sleep Sit.* In regard to Rinzai, Victor Sogen Hori discussed the practice of choosing "capping phrases" for various kōans, as well as the writing of explanations and poetic verse as part of the kōan curriculum. Nevertheless, Hori admitted that such practices vary in different monasteries and sometimes no writing exercises are involved in the training at all. In any case, very few of the Rinzai priests stay in training monasteries long enough to go through such advanced scholarly practices, and most simply select the appropriate "capping phrases" out of a phrase-book. See: Hori, "Zen Koan Capping Phrase Books: Literary Study and the Insight 'Not Founded on Words or Letters.'"

20 Jørn Borup, "Contemporary Buddhist Priests and Clergy," 114–115.

21 Philip Nicoloff, *Sacred Kōyasan: A Pilgrimage to the Mountain Temple of Saint Kobo Daishi and the Great Sun Buddha,* 191–195. See also: John Nelson, *Experimental Buddhism: Innovation and Activism in Contemporary Japan,* 131.

22 Jessica Starling, "Family Temples and Religious Learning in Contemporary Japanese Buddhism."

23 Holmes Welch, *The Buddhist Revival in China.*

24 Don Alvin Pittman, *Toward a Modern Chinese Buddhism: Taixu's Reforms.*

25 Raoul Birnbaum, "Buddhist China at the Century's Turn."

26 Lei Kuan Rongdao Lai, "Praying for the Republic: Buddhist Education, Student-Monks, and Citizenship in Modern China (1911–1949)."

27 Onoda Shunzō, for instance, argued that upon visiting the newly established Buddhist Ōtani University in Japan, Taixu was inspired to model his seminaries on the Chinese mainland according to this pioneering modern Buddhist institution. See: Onoda, "Meiji jidai no Bukkyō sō ga suishin shita Bukkyō kyōiku seido no kaikaku."

28 Holmes Welch shortly discusses the demise of these seminaries under Mao and the creation of a new official Buddhist school in Beijing in the 1950s. See: Welch, *Buddhism Under Mao,* 156–159.

29 Darui Long examined the establishment of various seminaries in Sichuan in the 1980s and 1990s, including the first female seminary in China and a governmentally funded Tibetan Buddhist seminary. See: Long, "Buddhist Education in Sichuan." Borchert has recently written a detailed ethnography of a Buddhist school established by the Dai-lue minority in Yunnan: Thomas Adams Borchert, "Educating Monks: Buddhism, Politics and Freedom of Religion on China's Southwest Border."

30 Ji Zhe, "Buddhist Institutional Innovations," 741.
31 Sueki Fumihiko, "Gendai Chūgoku Bukkyō no kenkyū," 317–318.
32 Mochizuki Kaie, "Gendai Chūgoku niokeru Bukkyō kyōiku kikan no chōsa hōkoku."
33 On my visit in summer 2014 I learned that although approximately half of the program consisted of traditional Tiantai texts, the other half included courses on Indian Buddhism, Pāli sutras, and other Mahāyāna doctrines such as Mādhyamika, Buddhist histories, calligraphy, and contemporary politics. See also: Wanniansi, *Zhejiang Fuxueyuan Tiantaizong Fuxueyuan*.
34 Chun-fang Yu, *Passing the Light: The Incense Light Community and Buddhist Nuns in Contemporary Taiwan,* 115–116.
35 A thorough analysis of the Tzu Chi movement is available in: Richard Madsen, *Democracy's Dharma: Religious Renaissance and Political Development in Taiwan.*
36 Stuart Chandler, *Establishing a Pure Land on Earth: The Foguang Buddhist Perspective on Modernization and Globalization,* 119, 156.
37 Daniel Ryan Tuzzeo, "Education, Invention of Orthodoxy, and the Construction of Modern Buddhism on Dharma Drum Mountain," 122–123.

CHAPTER ONE: THE TRADITIONAL CURRICULUM

1 Chongbŏm, "Kangwŏn ŭi kyoyuk ch'egye wa kaesŏn panghyang," 61.
2 This stage is often called the *Śrāmaṇera* (Novice) Stage (K. *Sami kwa* 沙彌科) in the literature, but among Korean monastics it is most often referred to simply as the *Ch'imun* class.
3 Blackburn, "Looking for the Vinaya: Monastic Discipline in the Practical Canons of the Theravāda."
4 See, for example: Yifa, *The Origins of Buddhist Monastic Codes in China,* chapter two.
5 *Zimen jingxun,* T. 2023.48. I follow the English translation of the traditional curricular titles found in Robert Buswell, *The Zen Monastic Experience,* 96–97.
6 Wŏnil, for example, demonstrated that the first three chapters of the *Ch'imun* were written by a Mazu-line Chan teacher (Guishan 潙山), a Yunmen-line Chan master (Cijue 慈覺), and the Sixth Patriarch of Pure Land, Zhijue (智覺), respectively. See: Wŏnil, "Ch'imun kyŏnghun e taehan sogo," 127–129.
7 Shiina Kōyū, "Shimon keikun no bunken shi teki kōsatsu." Shiina adds that it was the earlier text, the *Zilin baoxun,* that made it to Japan in the Kamakura and Muromachi periods, and attempts to link the text to a particular Rinzai lineage, that of Xueyan Zuqin (雪巖祖欽, 1215–1287).
8 Sin Hoe-jŏng, "Ch'imun kyŏnghunju ŭi kyoyukchŏk kach'i e kwanhan yŏn'gu," 24–29. For an English biography of T'aego Pou see: J. C. Cleary, *Buddha from Korea: The Zen Teachings of T'aego,* 64–77.
9 Wang Sŏn-yŏp, "Yŏngnamdae tosŏgwan tongbin mun'go sojang p'yohun sap'an Ch'imun kyŏnghun ŭi Sŏji mit Kugyŏl," 148.
10 For more details see: ibid., 150–153. The *Ch'imun* was published six times in the sixteenth century (in 1524, 1532, 1537, 1539, 1549, and 1588) and five times in the seventeenth century (in 1614, 1638, 1664, 1682, and 1695).
11 Chun-fang Yu, "Ch'an Education in the Sung: Ideals and Procedures," 98. According to these particular Pure Rules, after learning the admonitions, new monks were to be instructed in the *Śūraṃgama, Diamond, Sutra of Perfect Enlightenment,* and other Buddhist texts, after which the monastic curriculum ended with the study of the Confucian Classics!
12 Lee Jong-su, "Chosŏn hugi Pulgyo illyŏk kwamok ŭi sŏnjŏng kwa kŭ ŭimi," 127.
13 Sin, "Ch'imun kyŏnghunju ŭi kyoyukchŏk kach'i e kwanhan yŏn'gu," 35–42.

14 Blackburn, *Buddhist Learning and Textual Practice in Eighteenth-Century Lankan Monastic Culture,* 12.
15 It includes an essay on Emperor Ming of Han, believed to be the first to have received Buddhism in China, along with a short royal message (*Chiwen* 勅文) on the virtues of Buddhism by Emperor Wen of Sui (541–604), a piece on a Jin Dynasty (third-century) king receiving the bodhisattva precepts, and a couple of other chapters written by Song Dynasty emperors in favor of Buddhism.
16 Sin, "Ch'imun kyŏnghunju ŭi kyoyukchŏk kach'i e kwanhan yŏn'gu," 67–72.
17 Myoŏm is the one quoted here. See: Yogyŏng, "Piguni kyoyuk toryang Pongnyŏngsa sŭngga taehak e taehan koch'al," 83–136.
18 Sin, "Ch'imun kyŏnghunju ŭi kyoyukchŏk kach'i e kwanhan yŏn'gu," 80–81.
19 A partial translation of *Guishan's Admonitions* is found in: Mario Poceski, "Guishan Jingce and the Ethical Foundations of Chan Practice," 15–41.
20 Minh Thi Nguyen, "Buddhist Monastic Education and Regional Revival Movements in Early Twentieth Century Vietnam," 73–74.
21 Hyewŏn, "Hyŏndae Han'guk sŏnwŏn Ch'ŏnggyu ŭi mosŭp kwa naagal pangyang," 265–267.
22 Kim Chi-hyŏn, "Chogyejong kibon kyoyuk kigwan p'yojun kyogwa kwajŏng e taehan yŏn'gu," 335.
23 I have read through some of the chapters using the following modern Korean translation to the text: An Chae-ch'ŏl, *Ch'imun kyŏnghun*. This particular quote is found in the fourth chapter of the compilation: Mingjue's (明覺, 988–1052) "The Remaining Writings on the Wall" (*Bijianyiwen* 壁間遺文), on page 106.
24 This is the first line of the chapter "Encouraging Study" (*Quanxuewen* 勸學文) found in: ibid., 191. It also appears in other essays in the *Ch'imun*. It reads: 玉不啄不成器 人不學不知道.
25 On the *Saja sohak* see: Uri Kaplan, "The Present-day Korean Confucian Primer: Annotated Translation of the Four-Character Elementary Learning (*Saja sohak,* 四字小學)."
26 See, for example: Kwangmyŏng, "Suhaengmyŏn esŏ pon kangwŏn kyoyuk," 96.
27 Taehan Pulgyo Chogyejong, *Sinp'yŏn Ch'imun*.
28 Yonghak, "Kangwŏn kyoyuk ŭi hyoyulchŏgin haksŭp ŭl wihan kangwŏn kyoje kaesŏnan."
29 Translated by Robert Buswell, "Arouse Your Mind and Practice!," 154–157. See also: Charles Muller, "Awaken Your Mind and Practice (Balsim suhaeng jang) 發心修行章," 261–269.
30 Translated by Robert Buswell, "Admonitions to Neophytes (Kye ch'osim hagin mun 誡初心學人文)."
31 Kim Pang-yong, "Kojungse Han'guk sŏnwŏn Ch'ŏnggyu ŭi t'ŭkching kwa ŭiŭi," 207–212. Kim argues that Chinul actually referred to the Pure Rules in his essay.
32 Ibid., 212. An English translation of the *Chagyŏngmun* is found in: Richard McBride, "Watch Yourself! (Jagyeongmun 自警文) By Yaun."
33 Ko Hŭi-suk, "Han'guk Pulgyo kangwŏn samigwa kyoje ŭi sŏjijŏk yŏn'gu," 913.
34 Note, however, that in Tibetan monastic schools the curriculum usually begins with logic and debate manuals, then turns to Mahāyāna treatises, and only ends after many years of study with Vinaya texts. See: V. Nithiyanandam, *Buddhist System of Education,* 75–91; Dreyfus, *The Sound of Two Hands Clapping,* 112–131.
35 Tibetan programs seem to spend more time on commentaries than on sutras. For details see: Dreyfus, *The Sound of Two Hands Clapping,* 112–133.
36 Zongmi's *Chan Preface* 禪源諸銓集都序, T. 2015.48. Full English translation is available in: Jeffrey Lyle Broughton, *Zongmi on Chan.*
37 Chinul's *Excerpts* 法集別行錄節要并入私記, is not found in the Taishō Canon. Full English translations are available in: Robert Buswell, *The Korean Approach to Zen: The Collected Works of Chinul,* 262–374; Robert Buswell, *Numinous*

Awareness Is Never Dark: The Korean Buddhist Master Chinul's Excerpts on Zen Practice.

38 Dahui's *Letters* 大慧書狀 is found within the larger *Dahui's Recorded Sayings* 大慧普覺禪師語錄, T. 47.1998. A full translation of its Japanese *Gozan* edition has recently appeared in: Jeffrey Lyle Broughton, *The Letters of Chan Master Dahui Pujue.*

39 The *Chan Essentials* 禪要 is not found in the Taishō Canon. We are still awaiting its first complete English translation.

40 On the division of the four *Sajip* treatises into "Chan" and "teaching" see, for example: Taehan Pulgyo Chogyejong Kyoyugwŏn, "Chigwan sŭnim int'ŏbyu," 384.

41 The entire quote is: 若導初學 則先以禪源集別行錄立如實知見次以禪要語錄掃除知解之病 而指示活路也. It is found in Hyujŏng's collection of Chiŏm's essays titled *Pyŏksongdang Yarohaengnok* (碧松堂野老行錄). Note that the expression "maladies of knowing and understanding" is found several times in essays by Chinul, usually referring to the "ten maladies of Chan practice" depicted by Dahui. Also note that although the passage refers to the *Recorded Sayings* rather than to Dahui's *Letters,* it is most likely that this is the text in question, as the *Letters* constitutes the last part of Dahui's *Recorded Sayings.*

42 Yong-tae Kim argued that in the sixteenth century Buddhists tended to form lineages mimicking Confucian practices and that Hyujŏng was considered to be a successor of a particular branch of Chiŏm's lineage. See: Yong-tae Kim, *Glocal History of Korean Buddhism,* 134–135. Still, evidence suggests that monks traveled and studied under several masters throughout their lives, and although certainly keeping allegiance to their tonsure teacher, their spiritual viewpoints may not have been confined to that of one particular lineage.

43 先以都序節要 決釋佛法之知見 以固其基本 次禪要書狀 擊碎佛法知解之病. This quote is extracted from a comprehensive collection of education-related references assembled in: Nam To-yŏng, "Han'guk Pulgyo chŏnsŏ rŭl chungsimŭro pon Chosŏn sidae sawŏn kyoyuk."

44 Son Sŏng-p'il, "16–17 segi Pulgyo chŏngch'aek kwa Pulgyogye ŭi tonghyang."

45 Note that the Dunhuang version of the *Preface* appears under a different title: 大乘禪門要錄 ("Important Records of the Mahāyāna Chan Gate"). See: Peter Gregory, *Tsung-mi and the Sinification of Buddhism,* 315–316. On the text's inclusion in the formal Ming Canon see: Broughton, *Zongmi on Chan,* 190.

46 For China and Japan see: Broughton, *Zongmi on Chan.* For Korea see: Yonghak, "Tosŏ ŭi ot'alcha chijŏk e taehan kyŏnhae."

47 For the fifteenth-century printings of the *Preface* see: Yonghak, "Tosŏ ŭi ot'alcha chijŏk e taehan kyŏnhae." For the sixteenth and seventeenth centuries see: Son Sŏng-p'il, "16 segi Chosŏn ŭi Pulsŏ kanhaeng."

48 This could very well be the first historical mention of this famous Chan slogan.

49 There are several generic terms used in East Asia to refer to the kind of sutra-based scholastic Chan in which sutra study and Chan practice complemented one another: *Chanjiao yizhi* (禪教一致) and *dinghui shuangxiu* (定慧雙修) seem especially common in references to the thought of Zongmi, Yongming Yanshou (永明延壽, 904–975), and Chinul, though I was unable to locate actual use of the term *Chanjiao yizhi* prior to the sixteenth century (it appears in Hanshan Deqing's *Hanshan laoren mengyouji* 憨山老人梦游集). The second term, *dinghui shuangxiu,* is more common, and it actually appears in Yanshou's well-known *Zongjing lu* (宗鏡錄). The complementary nature of wisdom and meditation has been repeatedly emphasized in the Chan tradition at least as early as the *Platform Sutra.* Another term that is often used in the scholarship to refer to the same kind of Chan (that *does* depend on words and letters) is *wenzi Chan* (文字禪), but as it turns out, this term was coined by Huihong (1071–1128) to connote the poetic, lettered Chan of later Song, rather than the notion of a sutra-based Chan practice.

See the entry for *wenzi Chan* in: Buswell and Lopez, *The Princeton Dictionary of Buddhism,* 995.

50 Zongmi says: "If one practices without yet being awakened, this is not real practice" (若未悟而修非真修也, T. 2015.48 0406a07). For a detailed discussion see: Peter Gregory, "Sudden Enlightenment Followed by Gradual Cultivation: Tsung-mi's Analysis of Mind," 279–320.

51 Robert Buswell, *Tracing Back the Radiance: Chinul's Korean Way of Zen,* 50.

52 Buswell, *The Korean Approach to Zen,* 262.

53 "Dharma Collection and Special Practice Record" 法集別行錄. This title does not appear in any Buddhist catalogue and Buswell contended that perhaps it connoted an earlier proto-version of Zongmi's "Chan Collection" (sometimes called "Chan Canon"). See his: "The Identity of the Pŏpchip pyŏrhaeng nok," 11.

54 Buswell, *Tracing Back the Radiance,* 156–164.

55 Ibid., 61–72.

56 Dahui did not actually use the terms Kanhua or *huatou* in his *Letters*—rather he commonly says he is doing *gongfu* 工夫, practice/work—and Morten Schlütter argued that these terms may have been first coined by modern Japanese researchers. See: Schlütter, *How Zen Became Zen: The Dispute over Enlightenment and the Formation of Chan Buddhism in Song-Dynasty China,* note 27 on page 215. Broughton argued that there is in fact some evidence in favor of the claim that Dahui inherited his *huatou* method from his teacher, Yuanwu Keqin, who seems to have used it when instructing a laywoman saying: "no mind, no Buddha, no sentient beings—what is it?" See his: *The Letters of Chan Master Dahui Pujue,* 21–22.

57 Hwang Kŭm-yŏn, "Taehye Chonggo sŏnsa ŭi Sŏjang yŏn'gu," 90–92.

58 The two Korean commentaries to the *Letters* are Hyesim's (1178–1234) *Notes on the Letters* (*Sŏjang ki* 書狀記) and the anonymous *Notes on Plucking Out Difficulties from the Letters* (*Sŏjang chŏngnan ki* 書狀摘難記).

59 Dahui presided over the monasteries of Ayuwangshan and Jingshan. For details see: Miriam Levering, "Dahui Zonggao (1089–1163): The Image Created by His Stories about Himself and by His Teaching Style," 91–116. For his students see her: "Ch'an Enlightenment for the Laymen: Ta-hui and the New Religious Culture of the Sung," 76–81. On his relationship with Zhang Shangying see her: "Dahui Zonggao and Zhang Shangying: The Importance of a Scholar on the Education of a Song Chan Master." Further discussions of Zhang Shangying's Buddhist agendas are found in Uri Kaplan, *Buddhist Apologetics in East Asia: Countering the Neo-Confucian Critiques in the* Hufa lun *and the* Yusŏk chirŭi non.

60 Further evidence for the intended lay audience of this text may be found in the fact that although the *Letters* was first compiled by one of Dahui's monastic disciples, Huiran, the final edition was made by a scholar-official by the name of Huang Wenchang (1128–1165). Broughton quotes the Japanese commentary to this text, the *Pearl in the Wicker Basket,* in which the author, Mujaku (1653–1744), argues that the letters in this compilation are mainly addressed to laypeople simply because monastics had the opportunity to receive face-to-face direct instruction from Dahui, whereas laymen did not. See: Broughton, *The Letters of Chan Master Dahui Pujue,* 51.

61 Quiet sitting was recommended by Luo Congyan (1072–1135) and other Confucian literati in the eleventh and twelfth centuries. For details see: Xinzhong Yao, *An Introduction to Confucianism.* On quiet sitting in Neo-Confucianism see also: Rodney Taylor, *The Religious Dimensions of Confucianism,* 77–114; *The Confucian Way of Contemplation: Okada Takehiko and the Tradition of Quiet-Sitting,* 35–41.

62 See: Schlütter, *How Zen Became Zen.* This is the main argument of the book, but see in particular pages 116–182.

63 The entire quote is 若學坐禪 禪非坐臥 若學坐佛 佛非定相 於無住法 不應取捨 汝

若坐佛 即是殺佛 若執坐相 非達其理. Cited in Hwang, "Taehye Chonggo sŏnsa ŭi Sŏjang yŏn'gu," 253–256.

64 Ibid., 106–108.

65 Robert Buswell, "The Transformation of Doubt (Ŭijŏng 疑情) in Kanhwa Sŏn 看話禪: The Testimony of Gaofeng Yuanmiao 高峰原妙 (1238–1295)."

66 Kim Suk-hyŏn, "Kobong hwasang Sŏnyo yŏn'gu," 1, 56–60, 77.

67 Ibid., 118–121. See also: Ha Chŏng-nyong, "Sinpyŏn Sajip ŭi ŭiŭi wa kwaje," 359–360.

68 Chŏn Chae-gang, "Sŏnyo haesŏk ŭi oryu wa parŭn haesŏk," 395–397.

69 My discussion of the three essentials relies mainly on: Kim, "Kobong hwasang Sŏnyo yŏn'gu"; Buswell, "The Transformation of Doubt (Ŭijŏng 疑情) in Kanhwa Sŏn 看話禪: The Testimony of Gaofeng Yuanmiao 高峰原妙 (1238–1295)." The following translation from the text given by Buswell summarizes the process succinctly: "If we are speaking about authentic Sŏn contemplation, there have to be three essentials. The first essential is to have the faculty of great faith: This matter should be so patently obvious that it is just as if you are leaning against Mt. Sumeru. The second essential is to have great fury, which is just as if you've come across the villain who murdered your father and right then and there you want to cut him in half with a single strike of your sword. The third essential is to have the sensation of great doubt, which is just as if you've done a heinous act in secret and are about to be exposed." 若謂着實叅禪.決須具足三要. 第一要有大信根 明知此事如靠一座須彌山. 第二要 有 大憤志 如遇殺父冤讎. 直欲便與一刀兩段. 第三要有大疑情 如暗地做了 一件極事 正在欲露未露之時.

70 On subitism in the *Platform Sutra* and its comparability to the *Vimalakīrti* and *Laṅkāvatāra* see: Peter Gregory, "The Platform Sutra as the Sudden Teaching," 77–108.

71 *Diamond Sutra* 金剛般若波羅蜜多經, T. 8.235. Various English translations are readily available.

72 The *Diamond Sutra* was published over thirty times in Korea during the sixteenth and seventeenth centuries alone. See: Son, "16–17 segi Pulgyo chŏngch'aek kwa Pulgyogye ŭi tonghyang."

73 Charles Muller, "A Korean Contribution to the Zen Canon: The Oga Hae Seorui (Commentaries of Five Masters on the Diamond Sutra)," 43–64.

74 *Sutra of Perfect Enlightenment* 大方廣圓覺修多羅了義經, T. 17.842. A complete English translation is available in: Charles Muller: *The Sutra of Perfect Enlightenment: Korean Buddhism's Guide to Meditation.*

75 Ibid., 3–60.

76 *Śūraṅgama Sutra* 大佛頂如來密因修證了義諸菩薩萬行首楞嚴經, T. 19.945. An English translation is now available by the Buddhist Texts Translation Society, *The Śūraṅgama Sūtra: With Excerpts from the Commentary by the Venerable Master Hsüan Hua.* On the sutra's association with the *Sutra of Perfect Enlightenment* see: James Benn, "Another Look at the Pseudo-Śūraṃgama Sūtra," 63–64.

77 Ibid. Note, however, that some of these metaphors appear in other texts, too. The *Laṅkāvatāra Sutra,* for example, uses both the fingers pointing at the moon and the sky flowers metaphors.

78 Ronald Epstein, "The Shurangama Sutra (T. 945): A Reappraisal of its Authenticity."

79 Kim Chin-yŏl, *Nŭngŏm kyŏng yŏn'gu immun,* 381–388.

80 Jiang Wu, *Enlightenment in Dispute: The Reinvention of Chan Buddhism in Seventeenth-Century China,* 59–60. Wu suggests that perhaps the *Śūraṅgama Sutra* was so popular because the literati could easily identify themselves with its progenitor, Ānanda, who just like them was very knowledgeable in the Buddha's words, but was lacking in spiritual cultivation.

81 The curriculum of Wenhui's Jetavana Hermitage can be found in: Lai, "Praying for the Republic: Buddhist Education, Student-Monks, and Citizenship in Modern China (1911–1949)," 113–114.

82 Yonghak, "Kangwŏn kyoyuk ŭi hyoyulchŏgin haksŭp ŭl wihan kangwŏn kyoje kaesŏnan," 41.

83 John Jorgensen reported that the *Śūraṃgama* was translated into the vernacular in 1461, only fifteen years after the new script was officially introduced in the peninsula and a few years before the *Lotus, Diamond,* and *Amida* sutras were translated. See: John Jorgensen, *A Handbook of Korean Zen Practice: A Mirror on the Sŏn School of Buddhism (Sŏn'ga kwigam),* 60. In December 2015, the Korean media announced the discovery of an additional *Śūraṃgama* vernacular translation dated to 1462.

84 Kim, *Nŭngŏm kyŏng yŏn'gu immun,* 114.

85 *Treatise on the Awakening of Faith in Mahāyāna* 大乘起信論, T. 32.1666. D. T. Suzuki translated this treatise in the early twentieth century, but what has now become the standard is: Yoshito S. Hakeda, *Awakening of Faith—Attributed to Aśvaghoṣa, with commentary by Yoshito S. Hakeda.* Note that Hakeda and Suzuki translated different versions of this essay.

86 Yonghak, "Kangwŏn kyoyuk ŭi hyoyulchŏgin haksŭp ŭl wihan kangwŏn kyoje kaesŏnan," 42.

87 Son, "16–17 segi Pulgyo chŏngch'aek kwa Pulgyogye ŭi tonghyang."

88 *Huayan Sutra* 大方廣佛華嚴經, T. 9. 278, 279. English translation available in: Thomas Cleary, *The Flower Ornament Scripture: A Translation of the Avatamsaka Sutra.*

89 *Jingde Transmission of the Lamp,* T. 51.2076. This influential compilation of biographies, sermons, dialogues, and poems of Dharma teachers was the first work of the "Transmission of the Lamp" genre (*Chuandeng lu*), which is believed to be inspired by official Chinese dynastic histories. It was compiled by Daoyuan (道源) in 1004, and Albert Welter argued that it generally presented a Wuyue-region Chan, dominated by the non-radical, scholastic, sutra-based approach of Yongming Yanshou (and Zongmi), which certainly fits the general attitudes of the Korean curriculum. For a detailed analysis see: Albert Welter, *Monks, Rulers, and Literati: The Political Ascendancy of Chan Buddhism,* chapter five.

90 This Korean *gongan* collection is not included in the Taishō Canon. One hundred out of its 1,463 cases were translated into English by Juhn Ahn, "Gongan Collections."

91 In the early Chosŏn, the Korean sangha was generally divided into doctrinal and Chan monks, yet, it is believed that by the sixteenth century these two were merged into one unified school. On the texts cited by the Great Code of Administration see, for example: Sem Vermeersch, *The Power of the Buddhas: The Politics of Buddhism during the Koryo Dynasty (918–1392),* 199.

92 Dahui explained that practice must begin with awakening (*wu* 悟). See: Levering, "Ch'an Enlightenment for the Laymen," 6.

93 Guishan claimed that even if one suddenly gained wisdom, he or she would still need to practice in order to rid themselves of habitual karmic tendencies. See: Poceski, "Guishan Jingce and the Ethical Foundations of Chan Practice," 32.

94 T. 19.945 0155a08–9: 理則頓悟乘悟「銷 事非頓除因次第盡. For additional discussions of the sudden-awakening-followed-by-gradual-cultivation approach as it is found in the *Śūraṃgama Sutra* see: Kim, *Nŭngŏm kyŏng yŏn'gu immun,* 141–146, 426–427.

95 English translations of the *Mirror of Sŏn* are available: Mark Mueller, Won-yoong Sunim, and Mujin Sunim, *Mirror of Zen: A Korean Buddhist Classic by Sŏsan;* Jorgensen, *A Handbook of Korean Zen Practice.* Jorgensen noted that the *Chan Essentials* is also cited in this text several times.

96 Chinul's commentary of the *Huayan Sutra* has been particularly influenced by Li Tongxuan's (李通玄, 635–730) *Exposition of the Huayan*. See: Buswell, *Tracing Back the Radiance,* 47–54.

97 For Dahui's biography see: Levering, "Dahui Zonggao."

98 Muller, *The Sutra of Perfect Enlightenment,* 16.

99 Levering, "Ch'an Enlightenment for the Laymen," 207.

100 Hwang, "Taehye Chonggo sŏnsa ŭi Sŏjang yŏn'gu," 97–105. Hwang found twenty-one references to the *Huayan Sutra* in the *Letters,* fifteen to the *Śūraṃgama,* fourteen to the *Transmission of the Lamp,* eight to the *Diamond Sutra,* and five to the *Sutra of Perfect Enlightenment,* the most oft-quoted other text being the *Vimalakīrti Sutra*—five times. Note, however, that another Korean scholar found a different number of references in the *Letters:* thirty from the *Huayan Sutra,* sixteen from the *Śūraṃgama*, eight from the *Nirvana* and *Vimalakīrti* each, seven from the *Diamond* and *Lotus* each, six from the *Sutra of Perfect Enlightenment,* and at least eight more from other Mahāyāna texts. The dominance of the *Huayan* and *Śūraṃgama,* though, is consistent in both sources. See: Yi Tŏk-chin, "Taesŭng kyŏngjŏn i Sŏn Pulgyo e mich'in yŏnghyang."

101 The essay was translated in: Robert Buswell, "Preface and Conclusion from Condensation of the Exposition of the Avatamsakasūtra (Hwaŏm non chŏryo 華嚴論節要)," 355–367.

102 Kim Suk-hyŏn found five quotes from the *Huayan Sutra* in the *Chan Essentials,* three from the *Śūraṃgama, Lotus,* and *Nirvana* sutras each, four from the *Transmission of the Lamp,* two from Dahui, and five from the Confucian *Analects*. See: Kim, "Kobong hwasang Sŏnyo yŏn'gu," 87–92.

103 The title is: 四集四敎傳燈拈頌華嚴.

104 The poem is found in the *Yŏngwŏldang Taesa Munjip* (詠月堂大師文集), Tongguk Taehakkyo, *Han'guk Pulgyo chŏnsŏ*, vol. 8. I would like to thank Yi Sang-min for his useful comments on earlier drafts of this translation.

105 This is a reference to Dahui's discussion of the famous "Wu" 無 *huatou* ("does the dog have a Buddha nature? Wu") where he explains that one can err in ten different ways while keeping this *huatou*. Dahui actually seems to have had only eight errors listed, but Chinul systematized the eight into ten in his *Excerpts,* and he often refers to them as the "ten maladies of knowledge and understanding" (十種知解之病). The ten errors of thinking about the *huatou* are: (1) Understanding it to mean yes or no. (2) Considering it in relation to doctrinal theory. (3) Pondering over it logically at the consciousness base. (4) Considering the master's raising of his eyebrows or twinkling of his eyes as instructions. (5) Making stratagems for solving the *huatou* through the use of words. (6) Busying oneself inside a shell of unconcern (this refers to the defect of silent illumination). (7) Transforming the doubt toward the *huatou* to a doubt about the mind itself. (8) Looking for evidence in the wording itself. Chinul adds (9) Taking it as the "Wu" of true nonexistence. (10) Grasping at a deluded state and simply waiting for awakening (without positive practice). See also: Buswell, *The Korean Approach to Zen,* 338, 373–374.

106 The three teachings here refer to Yogācāric Dharma characteristics 法相, Mādhyamic refutation of characteristics 破相, and Dharma nature 法性.

107 This probably refers to the Five Chan Houses or lineages of the Tang: *Linji* 臨濟, *Guiyang* 潙仰, *Caodong* 曹洞, *Yunmen* 雲門, and *Fayan* 法眼.

108 The three kinds of emptiness (三空) are the emptiness of self (我空), emptiness of dharmas (法空), and emptiness of emptiness (空空).

109 The six perfections (六度) are generosity, discipline, tolerance, rigor, concentration, and wisdom.

110 The *Diamond Sutra* describes the three minds (三心) as the pure mind (清淨心), the material mind (色生心), and the mind of the five senses (聲香味觸法生心), T. 235 08.0749c21–23. It also depicts—or rather dismisses—the three minds of

past, present, and future (過去心 不可得 現在心 不可得 未來心 不可得), T. 235 08.0751b27–28.

111 Searching for the mind in seven places (七處窮心) is a reference to the Buddha's instructions to Ānanda in the first fascicle of the *Śūraṃgama Sutra*. Upon his return from his seduction by a prostitute, the Buddha asked Ānanda whether the mind was (1) Inside the body? (2) Outside the body? (3) Within the eyes (or other body-sense organs)? (4) Of the body? (5) In all of the above combined? (6) In between the senses and sense objects? (7) In none of those places? As can be expected, the mind was not found in any of these. Upon hearing this teaching Ānanda weeps and repents his mischief with the prostitute, deploring that his body left home but his mind was still entangled. He vows to not only learn the Way but also practice it, as one who only speaks of food will never get full.

112 The eight transformations (八還) are explained in the second fascicle of the *Śūraṃgama Sutra*. They are the various cases in which things "return to their sources," or in other words, the causes for conditions in the world: light returns to (or is caused by) the sun, dark returns to the black moon (!), circulation returns to an open window, blockage returns to fenced walls, conditions return to making distinctions, stubborn void returns to emptiness, stuffiness returns to dust, and freshness to clear air. The Buddha's point here seems to be that all things that are transforming and return to something else (i.e., are conditioned by something else) are not really themselves, but only that which does not return to anything is the real seeing nature, which is also the true nature. See: T. 16.945— 阿難此諸變化明還日輪. 何以故. 無日不明明因屬日. 是故還日. 暗還黑月. 通還戶牖. 擁還牆宇. 緣還分別. 頑虛還空. 鬱還塵. 清明還霽.

113 The five aggregates (五陰) out of which a "self" is made are form, sensation, perception, mental formations, and consciousness.

114 The *Śūraṃgama Sutra* lists the seven elements (七大) as water, fire, earth, wind, space/ether, sight (and other senses), and consciousness.

115 The ten directions (十方) are north, northeast, east, southeast, south, southwest, west, northwest, up, and down.

116 This refers to the second case of the *Enlightened Verses,* which tells the story of Śākyamuni taking seven steps immediately after his birth, pointing to all directions, and proclaiming himself to be the only honored one, and Chan master Yunmen (雲門, 862–949) commenting that if he had been there and seen that, he would have killed him with a single blow and given him to a dog to devour! Translation of this case is available in: Ahn, "Gongan Collections," 73–74.

117 This probably refers to Linji's (臨濟, ninth century) saying that some never leave home yet are always "on the way" (途中) and some leave home but are not "on the way." This case was not translated into English in the *Complete Works of Korean Buddhism,* but it is found in Ruth Fuller Sasaki's translation of Linji's Records: *The Record of Linji,* 143.

118 This probably refers to Linji's saying that the Bodhisattva Mañjuśrī was not found on Mt. Wutai as was commonly thought, but simply in the moment-to-moment activity. See: ibid., 202.

119 The green Paulownia trees and great phoenixes are mythological flora and fauna symbolizing rarity.

120 A short and rather abstract treatment of the four noble truths as they manifest in various realms is given in the *Huayan Sutra*. I was unable to track down any mention of the eightfold path or the twelve-linked chain of causation in these curricular texts.

121 J. Z. Smith, "Canons, Catalogues, and Classics," 307.

122 Hō Sōkoku, "Kankoku Bukkyō shosi kenkyū," 269–271. Details for all 908 extant woodblock editions of Buddhist texts made in Korea between the fourth and nineteenth centuries are found in: Pak Sang-guk, *Chŏn'guk sach'al sojang mokp'an chip.*

123 Both "Recorded Sayings" (*yulu*) and Chan genealogies (*denglu*) were published in an increased pace in sixteenth- and seventeenth-century China. Just as in Korea, the works of Dahui and Gaofeng were especially popular, though they gradually lost favor in Qing China. See: Wu, *Enlightenment in Dispute*, 3–6.

124 Recent scholarship sheds doubt on the traditional narrative of the suppression of Buddhism during the Chosŏn Dynasty, noting that in fact both kings and scholar-officials often continued to visit monasteries, donate money to Buddhism, and maintain personal contacts with monks, even in the later years of the dynasty. Although Buddhism was mainly pushed out of the capital and from official participation in the government, and the number of (registered) monks and monasteries were gradually limited, non-registered monks and monasteries continued to function in the mountains, Buddhist texts were continuously published, and legislation completely proscribing the religion was never passed. See, for example: Boudewijn Walraven, "A Re-Examination of the Social Basis of Buddhism in Late Chosŏn Korea"; Sangkil Han and Matty Wegehaupt, "The Activities and Significance of Temple Fraternities in Late Chosŏn Buddhism"; Hee-suk Nam and Inga Diederich, "Publications of Buddhist Literary Texts: The Publication and Popularization of Mantra Collections and Buddhist Ritual Texts in the Late Chosŏn Dynasty"; Sung-Eun Thomas Kim, "Buddho-Confucian Rituals, Filial Piety, and Ritual Monks: Sketching the Social-Cultural Dynamics of Later Joseon Buddhism"; Seong-uk Kim, "Korean Confucianization of Zen: Ch'oui Uisun's Affirmation of a Confucian Literati Approach to Buddhism in Late Chosŏn"; Don Baker, "Privatization of Buddhism in the Chosŏn Dynasty"; and Juhn Ahn, *Buddhas and Ancestors: Religion and Wealth in Fourteenth-Century Korea*. Still, Hwansoo Kim reminds us that although the suppression may not have been complete, the mainstream conception of Buddhist monastics as inferior resulted in a collective trauma that lasted for decades. See: Hwansoo Ilmee Kim, "Buddhism during the Chosŏn Dynasty (1392–1910): A Collective Trauma?"

125 Son Sŏng-p'il, "16 segi chŏnban Pulgyogye ŭi silt'ae: Chŏllado chiyŏk ŭl chungsim ŭro." The increase in printing could be partially related to a development in woodblock manufacturing technologies that may have made mass production easier.

126 *Mengshan's Sermon Summary* (蒙山和尚法語略錄)—also published in the Korean *Hangŭl* script—has been printed eight times in this period, and his *Sermon on the Six Destinies* (蒙山和尚六道普說) was published twelve times in the sixteenth century alone. See: Son, "16 segi Chosŏn ŭi Pulsŏ kanhaeng," 64–65. It seems that these two treatises have been preserved only in Korea. See also: Kang Ho-sŏn, "Chosŏn chŏn'gi Mongsan hwasang yukto posŏl kanhaeng ŭi paegyŏng kwa ŭimi." It is unclear whether this is the same Mengshan who wrote the *Mengshan Rite for Feeding the Hungry Ghosts* (*Mengshan shishi yi* 蒙山施食義), which has flourished since the Ming and is still popular in contemporary China. Although this text was published in tandem with the *Sermon on the Six Destinies* in Korea and both were probably written in the thirteenth century, the author of the *Shishi yi* is identified as Budong. Jiang Wu recently suggested that he was of Tangut origins and his ritual manual was involved in the "tantrification" of Chinese Buddhism. See: Wu, "The Rule of Marginality: Hypothesizing the Transmission of the Mengshan Rite for Feeding the Hungry Ghosts in Late Imperial China."

127 Kim, "Kobong hwasang Sŏnyo yŏn'gu," 108.

128 Son, "16 segi Chosŏn ŭi Pulsŏ kanhaeng," 64–65.

129 The 2001 "Sangha Examination Preparation Booklet" lists questions regarding Mengshan intended for the graduates of the Elementary Chan Hall program. See: Taehan Pulgyo Chogyejong Kyoyugwŏn, *4 kŭp sŭngga kosi yesang munjejip*. For additional information on the Elementary Chan Hall see chapter four.

130 Son, "16 segi Chosŏn ŭi Pulsŏ kanhaeng," 17.
131 Data was extracted from the list of educational references found in Nam, "Han'guk Pulgyo chŏnsŏ rŭl chungsimŭro pon Chosŏn sidae sawŏn kyoyuk."
132 O Yong-sŏp, "Hyesun i kanhaengan Yongboksa Pulsŏ."
133 The five are Ch'ŏnghak (淸學, 1570–1654), Ŏn'gi (彦機, 1581–1644), Hyŏnbyŏn (懸辯, 1616–1684), Ch'aekhŏn (策憲, b. 1623), and Toan (道安, 1638–1715). Data extracted from the biographical list in Nam, "Han'guk Pulgyo chŏnsŏ rŭl chungsimŭro pon Chosŏn sidae sawŏn kyoyuk."
134 This information is extracted from the list found in ibid.
135 It seems that the connection between the Confucian and the Buddhist curricula was first pointed out by Nam To-yŏng, "Han'guk sach'al kyoyuk chedo," 33–34. See also: Nam, "Ch'ŏnt'ong munhwa wa kyoyuk: Sach'al kyoyuk ŭl chungsimŭro"; and Jong-su Lee, "Monastic Education and Educational Ideology in Late Chosŏn Buddhism," 78–79.
136 Ibid.
137 Son, "16–17 segi Pulgyo chŏngch'aek kwa Pulgyogye ŭi tonghyang," 125.
138 I found the first reference to the *Awakening of Faith* instead of the *Lotus Sutra* in the record regarding the textual studies of Hyewŏn (海源, 1691–1770).
139 I utilized the reference list extracted from the *Han'guk Pulgyo chŏnsŏ* and found in: Nam, "Han'guk Pulgyo chŏnsŏ rŭl chungsimŭro pon Chosŏn sidae sawŏn kyoyuk." Nam's collection may be incomplete and there is certainly a possibility that other, unrecorded monastics, have gone through the same syllabus. Nevertheless, it does illustrate that according to what we do know, not very many premodern sangha members had studied the entire traditional curricular texts.
140 Ibid.
141 Ibid.

CHAPTER TWO: MONASTIC EDUCATION IN TWENTIETH-CENTURY KOREA

1 Eric Hobsbawm and Terence Ranger, *The Invention of Tradition*. Liu Zhiji's quotation is found in the opening pages of: Kiri Paramore, *Japanese Confucianism: A Cultural History*.
2 Chandler, *Establishing a Pure Land on Earth*, 1.
3 I borrow this revealing phrase about the way the colonized seem to fall in love if not with the colonizer itself then at least with the ideologies it carries with it from: Wendy Doniger, *On Hinduism*, 17.
4 Yi Nŭnghwa argued that the curriculum was completed by Sŏngch'ong (性聰, 1610–1666), Kim Yŏngsu pointed to Wŏldam (月潭, 1632–1704) as the figure who first put together the whole program, and Kwŏn Sangno thought it was Toan (道安, 1638–1715) who synthesized the curriculum. See, for example: Nam, "Han'guk sach'al kyoyuk chedo," 27–40.
5 Cho Sŏng-t'aek, *Pulgyo wa Pulgyohak: Pulgyo ŭi yŏksajŏk ihae*, 256–258.
6 Jongmyung Kim, "Yi Nŭnghwa, Buddhism, and the Modernization of Korea," 92, 99. Nam, "Han'guk sach'al kyoyuk chedo," 27–40.
7 The entire work has been translated in: Vladimir Tikhonov and Owen Miller, *Selected Writings of Han Yongun*. The section on education paraphrased above is found on pages 58–64.
8 Mark Andrew Nathan, "Buddhist Propagation and Modernization: The Significance of P'ogyo in Twentieth-Century Korean Buddhism," 44–51.
9 Tuzzeo, "Education, Invention of Orthodoxy, and the Construction of modern Buddhism on Dharma Drum Mountain," 55–56. See also: Pittman, *Toward a Modern Chinese Buddhism*, 234–236.
10 Chŏng Yŏng-hoe, *Kaehwagi chonggyogye ŭi kyoyuk undong yŏn'gu*, 131–133.
11 For Southeast Asian temples' historical role as primary schools see, for example:

Stanely Tambiah, *World Conqueror and World Renouncer: A Study of Buddhism and Polity in Thailand against a Historical Background,* 202.

12 Yi Ki-un, "Kŭndaegi Pulgyogye ŭi 30 ponsan kyoyuk ch'eje chŏngbi wa injae yangsŏng," 438–442; Pori Park, *Trial and Error in Modernist Reforms: Korean Buddhism under Colonial Rule;* "Korean Buddhist Reforms and Problems in the Adoption of Modernity during the Colonial Period."

13 Chŏng, *Kaehwagi chonggyogye ŭi kyoyuk undong yŏn'gu,* 132–133.

14 Hwarang, "Pŏmŏsa kangwŏn ŭi yŏksa wa munhwa."

15 Chŏng, *Kaehwagi chonggyogye ŭi kyoyuk undong yŏn'gu,* 132.

16 Anonymous, "Chosŏn Pulgyo ch'ongbo."

17 Taehan Pulgyo Chogyejong Kyoyugwŏn, *Chogyejongsa: kŭnhyŏndae p'yŏn,* 139–140.

18 Ibid.

19 Hwarang, "Pŏmŏsa kangwŏn ŭi yŏksa wa munhwa," 4.

20 Yanggwan, "T'ongdosa sŭngga taehak ŭi yŏksa wa chŏnt'ong," 5–6.

21 This interview is available in: Kyesŏng, "Chŏn'gyeda hwasang Pŏmnyong sŭnim."

22 The *42-Section Sutra* (T. 17.784) was traditionally believed to be the first Buddhist scripture brought to China from India, but is now widely thought to be apocryphal. An introduction and translation are found in: Robert Sharf, "The Scripture in Forty-two Sections," 360–371.

23 The *Yijiao jing* (full title 佛垂般涅槃略說教誡經, or 佛臨般涅槃略說教誡經, or 佛臨般涅槃經, T. 12.389) was supposedly translated by Kumārajīva but there is no extant Sanskrit version and it was probably another Chinese apocryphal work. It shares much of its contents with the Pāli *Nirvana Sutra* and with Aśvaghoṣa's *Buddhacarita*. The text has often been published as part of a three-text Vinaya collection called the *Fuzu san jing* (佛祖三經) alongside *Guishan's Admonitions* (see chapter one) and the *42-Section Sutra*. The precepts especially emphasized in this text are: do not buy and sell goods, do not manage houses and fields, do not raise animals, do not read stars or fortunes for people, do not take more food than is sufficient for you, and so on. It also discusses the importance of controlling hunger, laziness, anger, pride, and sycophancy, and ends by explaining the various merits for this. It is interesting to find that the *Bequeathed Teachings Sutra* and the *42-Section Sutra* seem to have also been the practical Vinayas in the first year of Yang Wenhui's early-twentieth-century school in China. For the curriculum of Yang's seminary see: Lai, "Praying for the Republic," 113–114.

24 Ch'ŏlun, "Kangwŏn kyoyuk kwa chedo kaesin."

25 This reform proposal is found in: Kim Kwang-sik, "1930 yŏndae Pulgyogye ŭi kangwŏn chedo kaesŏn munje."

26 Richard Jaffe demonstrated the growing interest in *Śākyamuni* and in Indian Buddhism in Japan in the late nineteenth and early twentieth centuries. See: Jaffe, "Seeking Sakyamuni: Travel and the Reconstruction of Japanese Buddhism"; *Seeking Sakyamuni: South Asia in the Formation of Modern Japanese Buddhism.* For a treatment of the growing orientalist interest in Sanskrit among early-modern Chinese Buddhists see: Francesca Tarocco, *The Cultural Practices of Modern Chinese Buddhism: Attuning the Dharma,* 66–71.

27 My discussion of the study abroad of Korean Buddhist monastics during the Japanese colonial era is based primarily on: Yi Kyŏng-su, "Ilche sidae Pulgyo yuhaksaeng ŭi tongyang."

28 Cho, *Pulgyo wa Pulgyohak,* 29.

29 Ibid., 7.

30 On the practice of clerical marriage in modern Japan, which has made an impact on the Korean sangha in colonial times, see: Richard Jaffe, *Neither Monk nor Layman: Clerical Marriage in Modern Japanese Buddhism.*

31 Scholars have noted that monks in Southeast Asia, Nepal, and South China often

use their ordination as an avenue for social mobility, joining the sangha for its free educational opportunities in order to enhance their secular status, and many disrobe right after graduation from universities. Stanley Tambiah noted that approximately half of the Thai monastic university graduates disrobed after graduation: Tambiah, *World Conqueror and World Renouncer,* 293, 358–359. For similar tendencies in Cambodia see: Bruce Mathews, "Buddhism in Extremis: The Case of Cambodia," 61–62. For minorities in South China see: Borchert, "Educating Monks," 189. For Laos see: McDaniel, *Gathering Leaves and Lifting Words,* 65. In Nepal, too, most monastics who pursued higher education abroad tended to disrobe after graduation. See: Sarah Levine and David N. Gellner, *Rebuilding Buddhism: The Theravada Movement in Twentieth Century Nepal,* 152–168.

32 Holmes Welch noted a similar focus on Japanese-influenced Abhidharma study in the new Chinese monastic seminaries of Taixu in the 1930s. See: Welch, *The Buddhist Revival in China,* 113.

33 It is estimated that there were forty to fifty Korean monastics who received PhD degrees abroad in the second half of the twentieth century, most from Japanese universities. See: T'aegyŏng, "Chongdan sŭngga chŏnmun illyŏk yuksŏng mit hwaryong pangan e taehayŏ," 308–309.

34 A detailed discussion of the modern Buddhist focus on propagation is found in: Nathan, "Buddhist Propagation and Modernization"; *From the Mountains to the Cities: A History of Buddhist Propagation in Modern Korea.*

35 Tongguk Taehakkyo, *Tongguk taehakkyo paengnyŏnsa,* 61–69. For the establishment of Japanese sectarian schools see: Makoto, "Religious Studies and Religiously Affiliated Universities," 167.

36 Tongguk Taehakkyo, *Tongguk taehakkyo paengnyŏnsa,* 71.

37 For a detailed discussion of the Jōdo's activities in late-nineteenth- and early-twentieth-century Korea see: Hwansoo Ilmee Kim, *Empire of the Dharma: Korean and Japanese Buddhism, 1877–1912,* chapter three.

38 Vladimir Tikhonov, "The Japanese Missionaries and Their Impact on Korean Buddhist Developments (1876–1910)," 265.

39 Tongguk Taehakkyo, *Tongguk taehakkyo paengnyŏnsa,* 74–80.

40 For an analysis of the infamous, planned Korean Sōtō-alliance see: Kim, *Empire of the Dharma,* chapter six.

41 Tongguk Taehakkyo, *Tongguk taehakkyo paengnyŏnsa,* 84–93.

42 The Jetavana Hermitage set a maximum quota of ten students a year. See: Lai, "Praying for the Republic," 97.

43 Ibid., 99–100.

44 In early-twentieth-century China the government confiscated temple lands to create schools and many of the new Buddhist seminaries were built in temples in order to avoid such governmental encroachment. The situation seems to have been similar in Korea, and thus the Myŏngjin School offered special courses in land measurement for protecting monastic landholding. Note that the most well-known students at the Jetavana Hermitage have been Taixu and Renshan, who were later involved in the establishment of numerous other Buddhist seminaries in China.

45 Tongguk Taehakkyo, *Tongguk taehakkyo paengnyŏnsa,* 94–97.

46 Ibid., 107–111.

47 Ibid., 128, 150.

48 For information on the Tongguk seminary see: Yi, "Kŭndaegi Pulgyogye ŭi 30 ponsan kyoyuk ch'eje chŏngbi wa injae yangsŏng," 445–452.

49 Tongguk Taehakkyo, *Tongguk taehakkyo paengnyŏnsa,* 138–158.

50 Hayashi Makoto demonstrated how Japanese sectarian schools also dropped the name of their sect from their titles in the early twentieth century. See: Makoto, "Religious Studies and Religiously Affiliated Universities," 169, 176.

51 Tongguk Taehakkyo, *Tongguk taehakkyo paengnyŏnsa,* 164–178.

52 Secularization may mean one of the following three modes of discourse and practice: a separation of the public sphere from religion (which becomes privatized), a decline in religion, and a new kind of belief—a secular one. See: Charles Taylor, "Modes of Secularism," and *A Secular Age*. All three modes are relevant to understanding the secularization of Dongguk and other religious universities. They were partially separated from religion (teaching non-religious courses), they host declining numbers of religious students, and they pose secularism as the general consensus for modern education and research.

53 In the mid-nineteenth century 80 percent of the students at British universities were pursuing a clerical career, and 60 percent of American college presidents were ministers. Demands for specialization and a more practical, scientific education, as well as increased participation of non-Christian intellectuals in higher education in the twentieth century have created a separation between private faith and public lectures at universities. See, for example: Christian Smith, "Secularising American Higher Education: The Case Study of Early American Sociology"; David Bebbington, "The Secularization of British Universities since the Mid-Nineteenth Century"; and George Marsden, "The Soul of the American University: A Historical Overview."

54 At Ryūkoku, Risshō, and Komazawa universities, only 2 percent of the students come from temple families; in Aichi Gakuin only 0.5 percent, in Jōdo's Bukkyo 3 percent, in Hanazono 5 percent, in Taishō 10 percent, and in Ōtani 16 percent. See: Rowe and Kikuchi, "Round-Table Discussion: The Current State of Sectarian Universities."

55 Ibid., 438–451. Jørn Borup noted that in reality very few students participated in morning rituals and Zen practice offered in the sectarian colleges, and that only the poorest of the soon-to-be priests lived in the special dormitory and obligingly took part in communal Buddhist practices at Hanazono University. See: Borup, *Japanese Rinzai Zen Buddhism: Myoshinji, a Living Religion,* 138–139.

56 Male monastics live in Paeksangwŏn dormitory near Hwagyesa, and female students in Hyegwangsa.

57 T'aegyŏng, "Chongdan sŭngga chŏnmun illyŏk yuksŏng mit hwaryong pangan e taehayŏ," 308.

58 Vladimir Tikhonov recently showed that young monastics studying in Dongguk often prefer doing their required military service as Buddhist chaplains helping to relieve the stress of other soldiers. There are currently 135 Buddhist chaplain positions in the Korean army. See: Tikhonov, "Militarized Masculinity with Buddhist Characteristics: Buddhist Chaplains and their Role in the South Korean Army."

59 Pak Il-sŭng elucidated that in the 1970s 25 percent of monastic Dongguk graduates became military chaplains, 25 percent returned to their monasteries, 23 percent took jobs at the main Chogye headquarters, and 20 percent continued to a graduate school abroad. See: Pak, "Sŭngga ŭi taehak kyoyungnon."

60 For the story of Masan College see: Ko Yŏng-sŏp, "Pulgyogye ŭi Haein-masan taehak (1946–1967) kyŏngyŏng."

61 Sŏran, "Han'guk Pulgyo sŭngga kyoyuk ŭi palchŏn panghyang e taehan yŏn'gu," 299.

62 Although the monastic seminaries are not officially recognized as universities in Korea, some have recently been able to create exchange programs with recognized universities abroad. Unmunsa, for example, established exchange programs with Qinghua University in China and Hanazono in Japan in 2007. See: Ko, "Pulgyogye ŭi Haein-masan taehak (1946–1967) kyŏngyŏng," 398, note 18.

63 Examples of Asian Buddhist schools that distribute secular degrees abound. The Sikkim Institute of Higher Nyingma Studies began granting secular degrees to the sangha in 1983: Chowang Achrya, "Aspects of Monastic Education in Sikkim," 4–5. Several Bhutanese monastic colleges began granting secular degrees in

the 1990s: Brian Denman and Sigye Namgyel, "Convergence of Monastic and Modern Education in Bhutan?" 482. A degree-granting monastic university was established in Singapore in 2006: Jack Meng Tat Chia, "Teaching Dharma, Grooming Sangha: The Buddhist College of Singapore." Laos also hosts one such degree-granting monastic university, and Thailand has two, both founded in the mid-1990s. For Thailand, see: David Gosling, "Visions of Salvation: A Thai Buddhist Experience of Ecumenism," 36–37; Tambiah, *World Conqueror and World Renouncer*. For Laos, see: Cho Pyŏng-wal, "Segye sŭngga kyoyuk ŭi ŏje wa onŭl," 269–270. In India, too, the Central University of Tibetan Studies near Benares recently received full university status: Michael Lampert, *Discipline and Debate: The Language of Violence in a Tibetan Buddhist Monastery,* 156.

64 John Jorgensen, "Minjung Buddhism: A Buddhist Critique of the Status Quo," 281.

65 Taehan Pulgyo Chogyejong Kyoyugwŏn, *Chogyejongsa: kŭnhyŏndae p'yŏn,* 211, 236–237.

66 Statistics provided in Chŏng Pyŏng-jo, "Han'guk Pulgyo ŭi hyŏnhwang kwa munjejŏm," 200–201.

67 For the history of Songgwangsa's seminary see: Yi Kye-p'yo, "Songgwangsa kangwŏn ŭi yŏksa."

68 For Pŏmŏsa see: Taehan Pulgyo Chogyejong, "Irhwan sŭnim int'ŏbyu"; Hwarang, "Pŏmŏsa kangwŏn ŭi yŏksa wa munhwa," 6–7. For T'ongdosa see: Yanggwan, "T'ongdosa sŭngga taehak ŭi yŏksa wa chŏnt'ong," 19–20.

69 Chongmuk, "Sŭngga taehak (kangwŏn) kyogwa kwajŏng unyŏng e kwanhan sogo."

70 Ibid.

71 Sugyŏng, "Samsŏn kangwŏn ŭi paltalsa," 216.

72 Taehan Pulgyo Chogyejong Kyoyugwŏn, "Irhwan sŭnim int'ŏbyu," 412–413.

73 "Chigwan sŭnim int'ŏbyu," 365–375.

74 Nŭnghŏ, "Sŏnjisik ŭl ch'ajasŏ ch'odae kyoyukwŏnjang Wŏnsan sŭnim," 399–400.

75 Buswell, *The Zen Monastic Experience,* 100.

76 For the detailed proposal see: Ko, "Haein kangwŏn: Haeinsa sŭngga taehak (1900–2009) ŭi yŏksa wa munhwa," 89–94.

77 Kim Kwang-sik, "Hwaŏmsa sŭngga taehak ŭi yŏksa."

78 Yi Ki-yŏng, "Sŭngga kyoyuk ŭi chemunje."

79 Wŏn Ŭi-bŏm, "Sŭngga kyoyuk ŭi yŏksajŏk chŏn'gae."

80 Chŏng, "Han'guk Pulgyo ŭi hyŏnhwang kwa munjejŏm," 205.

81 Chongmuk, "Sŭngga taehak (kangwŏn) kyogwa kwajŏng unyŏng e kwanhan sogo."

82 Kim, "Hwaŏmsa sŭngga taehak ŭi yŏksa," 5.

83 Kim Chŏng-ja, "Unmunsa haginsŭng ŭi suhaeng mit kyoyuk ch'egye yŏn'gu," 197.

84 Taehan Pulgyo Chogyejong Kyoyugwŏn, "(Untitled Report)," 1995, 57–61.

85 Woncheol Yun, "Zen Master T'oe'ong Sŏngch'ŏl's Doctrine of Zen Enlightenment and Practice," 199–222.

86 Gregory, "Sudden Enlightenment Followed by Gradual Cultivation," 283.

87 Pak Sŏng-bae, "Sŏngch'ŏl sŭnim ŭi tono chŏmsusŏl pip'an e taehayŏ," 238–241.

88 Yun, "Zen Master T'oe'ong Sŏngch'ŏl's Doctrine of Zen Enlightenment and Practice," 222.

89 Jae-ryong Shim, *Korean Buddhism: Tradition and Transformation,* 215.

90 Taehan Pulgyo Chogyejong Kyoyugwŏn, "(Untitled Report)," 1999.

91 Eun-su Cho, "Female Buddhist Practice in Korea: A Historical Account," 29–34. Interestingly, Sujŏng claims that while male students in the early twentieth century studied the *Sagyo* with the *Awakening of Faith,* female students focused on the *Lotus Sutra* instead! These gender curricular differences are hard to explain. Was the *Lotus* viewed as less philosophical and more feminine? Was this related to the famous nāga girl story of the *Lotus,* which points to the ability of females to attain enlightenment (though going through maleness first)? See: Sujŏng, "Tonghaksa sŭngga taehak ŭi yŏksa wa hyŏnhwang," 61.

92 Pomunsa distanced itself from the Chogye Order in 1972 and formed an independent female Buddhist school called the Pomun School. See: Pori Park, "The Establishment of Buddhist Nunneries in Contemporary Korea," 166–168.

93 Sugyŏng raises the rather scandalous idea that some of the female seminaries were closed down in the 1940s due to the concern that assembling too many virgins together at one spot would drive the Japanese military to collect "comfort women" from these monasteries! See: Sugyŏng, "Samsŏn kangwŏn ŭi paltalsa."

94 Regrettably, in contemporary Korea it is very often the case that monks occupy the main monastery and female monastics (sometimes in larger numbers than the male monks) are relegated to smaller surrounding hermitages.

95 Sujŏng, "Tonghaksa sŭngga taehak ŭi yŏksa wa hyŏnhwang," 65–66.

96 Unsan, "Unmun sŭngga taehak ŭi chŏnt'ong kwa hyŏnjaesŏng," 16.

97 Myŏngsŏng transmitted the teachings to two additional nuns. See: Kim Chŏng-ja, "Unmunsa haginsŭng ŭi suhaeng mit kyoyuk ch'egye yŏn'gu," 192.

98 For the most extensive discussion of the Purification Movement in English see: Chanju Mun, *Purification Buddhist Movement 1954–1970: The Struggle to Restore Celibacy in the Jogye Order of Korean Buddhism.*

99 Yogyŏng, "Piguni kyoyuk toryang Pongnyŏngsa sŭngga taehak e taehan koch'al," 93.

100 Sugyŏng, "Samsŏn kangwŏn ŭi paltalsa," 212.

101 Yogyŏng, "Piguni kyoyuk toryang Pongnyŏngsa sŭngga taehak e taehan koch'al," 103. On Myoŏm's life see also: Inyoung Chung, "Crossing Over the Gender Boundary in a Gray Robe: The Life of Myoŏm a Korean Buddhist Nun."

102 Interestingly, the Vinaya offers an almost identical story in which Sudinna is urged by his mother to sleep with his ex-wife just once in order to continue the family line, yet, after he does so, he is harshly rebuked by the Buddha. See: Achim Bayer, "A Case for Celibacy: The Sudinna Story in the in the Pāli Vinaya and Its Interpretation."

103 Yogyŏng, "Piguni kyoyuk toryang Pongnyŏngsa sŭngga taehak e taehan koch'al," 98–99.

104 Samsŏn has been the only monastic seminary in the country in which students did not actually live together as a community but commuted daily for morning classes, and left in the afternoon. It was also the only seminary located in Seoul, aside from the Central Sangha College. It was intended to serve as an alternative for older and ill nuns, for female students of Dongguk University who wished to go through the traditional curriculum alongside their modern program, and for nuns with temple obligations in Seoul who could not leave for the mountains. It has been continually criticized for not being a *true* seminary with communal life, and was finally closed down by the Chogye Order for this reason in 2014. For a general history of this institution see: Sugyŏng, "Samsŏn kangwŏn ŭi paltalsa."

105 On Ch'ŏngamsa's seminary see: Pullim, "Ch'ŏnamsa sŭngga taehak ŭi pyŏnch'ŏnsa mit apŭro ŭi palchŏn panghyang."

106 See, for example, an essay by a Ssangyesa seminary student: Chehaeng, "Taechung saenghwal kwa hagŏp sŏngch'wido."

107 Lampert, *Discipline and Debate,* 108–124. On the history of the Tibetan disciplinarian see also: Berthe Jansen, "The Disciplinarian (*dge skos/ dge bskos/ chos khrims pa/ zhal ngo*) in Tibetan Monasteries: His Role and his Rules."

108 Yogyŏng, "Piguni kyoyuk toryang Pongnyŏngsa sŭngga taehak e taehan koch'al," 126–127.

109 Jeffrey Samuels, "Toward an Action-Oriented Pedagogy: Buddhist Texts and Monastic Education in Contemporary Sri Lanka."

110 Songgwangsa's Study Supervisor stressed a very similar point in his essay: Wŏngyŏng, "Chŏnt'ong kangwŏn hagin ŭi kibon kyoyuk e taehan insik koch'al," 90.

111 The four-bowl meal rituals only take place in monastic seminaries, in some of the Chan Halls, and in some of the touristy Temple Stay programs. Other than

novices, tourists, and during retreats, monks simply eat in regular dining halls. There have been attempts to trace this dining ritual to an episode in which Buddha *Śākyamuni* received one bowl from each of the Four Heavenly Kings (*Sach'ŏnwang* 四天王) to use for his meals. *Paru* (鉢盂) means rice bowls, and *kongyang* (供養, literally offering) is the word used for eating in Korean Buddhist circles. The ritual involves various chants. Every monk in Korea possess a set of four bowls to use in these rituals: one is used only for rice, one for vegetables, one for soup, and one for water. Most crucially, the food itself is used to wash off and wipe clean the bowls at the end of the meal, and special attention is given to not leaving even tiny bits of food in the bowls. The leftover water is used to feed the hungry ghosts with their needle-thin throats, and so if even tiny bits of food are left in the water they might choke! In case there are too many chunky pieces of food left in the water, novices are sometimes made to drink the leftover watery food of the entire community themselves. A detailed description of the actual procedures of this ritual can be found in: Buswell, *The Zen Monastic Experience,* 123–125.

112 Chehaeng, "Taechung saenghwal kwa hagŏp sŏngch'wido," 146.

113 The *Thousand Hands Sutra* (*Ch'ŏnsu kyŏng* 千手經) is a modern Korean collection of numerous mantras/*dharani* in praise of Bodhisattva Avalokiteśvara. It was compiled in 1969 in the seminary of T'ongdosa and soon became the standard liturgy for the midday rituals in monasteries throughout the country. See: Chŏnggak, *Ch'ŏnsu kyŏng yŏn'gu,* 99–109.

114 Memorization has been the dominant premodern style of schooling in many if not most religious traditions. Scholars of Korean Buddhism sometimes cite the early-twentieth-century record of Hoemyŏng that depicts seventeenth-century teacher Chian (志安, 1664–1729) asking all his *Ch'imun* and *Sajip* students to chant these texts out loud and try to memorize them, while his *Sagyo* and *Huayan* students were expected to analyze the texts quietly. However, I have found no evidence for this in either of Chian's extant works that contain some biographic material, the *Hwansŏng sijip* (喚惺詩集) and the *Sŏnmun ojong kangyo* (禪門五宗綱要). Unlike in Korea, Dreyfus illustrated how even in the late twentieth century, memorization of the core curricular texts in order to be able to draw them out quickly in oral debates, was still the major pedagogical method in Tibetan monastic schools. See: Dreyfus, *The Sound of Two Hands Clapping,* 85–92.

115 For debates in ancient Indian monasteries see: Nisha Singh, *The Origin and Development of Buddhist Monastic Education in India.* Paul Groner discussed debates in the medieval Japanese Tendai tradition: Groner, "Training Through Debates in Medieval Tendai and Seizan-ha Temples."

116 A comprehensive description and analysis of the debate system in Tibetan monasteries is offered in Dreyfus, *The Sound of Two Hands Clapping.* See also: Lambert, *Discipline and Debate,* chapters two and three.

117 Ko Pyŏng-ch'ŏl, "Taehan Pulgyo Chogyejong kyoyuk ŭi t'ŭkching kwa chŏnmang," 205.

118 Ibid., 206.

119 My portrayal of the 1994–1995 reforms is based primarily on Kim Sun-sŏk, "1994 yŏn Taehan Pulgyo Chogyejong kaehyŏk chongdan ŭi sŏngnip kwa ŭiŭi"; Kim Pong-jun, "94 yŏn Pulgyo kaehyŏk undong ŭi pansŏngjŏk chŏmgŏm"; and Cho Ki-yong, "Taehan Pulgyo Chogyejong kaehyŏk chongdan ŭi inyŏm chŏngch'esŏng kwa sŭngga kyoyugŭi chŏngyang."

120 Demonstrations erupted a day before Ŭihyŏn was expected to win the elections and take office for a third straight term. Aside from the issue of reelection, the main charge against him was his suspected involvement with a huge money-laundering scheme, in which large sums of Korean tax money were supposedly misused for the construction of a large Buddhist statue in Tonghwasa in 1992.

121 Thirteen monks were suspended from the Order, and sixty others were demoted.

The Buddhist media announced in 2015 that the aging Ŭihyŏn was allowed to return to the Chogye Order after repenting for twenty-one years.

122 On the democratization of the Chogye Order see also: Uri Kaplan, "Updating the Vinaya: Writing Monastic Laws and Pure Rules in Contemporary Korea."

123 In Thailand, only 5 percent of the northern sangha, for example, was enrolled in the new Buddhist universities in the early twentieth century, and systematized doctrinal education still remains mostly restricted to the Bangkok elites. See: McDaniel, *Gathering Leaves and Lifting Words,* 107–113. In the Tibetan Gelukpa School only about 20 percent of the monastic community was involved in any kind of scholastic practices in the late 1950s. See: Dreyfus, *The Sound of Two Hands Clapping,* 48–49.

124 I found no clear data regarding the exact educational qualifications for the Japanese clergy, but perhaps some anecdotal information may be able to point us toward more general trends. A Japanese Rinzai monk I met on a recent visit to Kyoto's Kenninji explained that there is no mandatory Buddhist education for new monks in the Rinzai School, and although most do go to university, there are sometimes problems when those who did not receive formal doctrinal education have to speak to the public and propagate. A Japanese Tendai priest from Hiei's Enryakuji I met on the same visit explained that the only mandatory education for the Tendai clergy was a two-month-long training session in the basic ritual texts of the sect. Most Shingon priests at Kōya-san go through a yearlong program at a seminary (Senshu Gakuin for males or Niso Gakuin for females) on the mountain, but this is not mandatory and some may still choose to receive training in a university or in their own temple. See: Nicoloff, *Sacred Kōyasan,* 191–195.

125 Statistics show that in 1994 only 44 percent of new monastics received education either in a seminary, at Dongguk, or in the Central Sangha College. By 2002 the number jumped to over 80 percent. See: Taehan Pulgyo Chogyejong Kyoyugwŏn, "Sŭngga kyoyuk ŭi sŏnggwa wa chŏnmang," 261.

126 Hyŏnŭng, "Chonghŏn-chongbŏp kwa sŭngga kyoyuk," 111.

CHAPTER THREE: BUDDHISM SIMULATING BUDDHIST STUDIES

1 Myŏngbŏp, "Suhaengja paech'ul esŏ kangwŏn ŭi silsang kwa kaesŏnjŏm," 147.

2 Taehan Pulgyo Chogyejong Kyoyugwŏn, "Chongdan sat'ae ŭi kyohun kwa sŭngga ŭi kwaje," 30.

3 It is estimated that several hundred Chogye monastics fought in and around Chogyesa the day before the Order's planned elections in 1998, repeating similar incidents that occurred at the previous 1994 elections. The police had to put an end to the fighting, about forty were injured, and both the local and foreign media ridiculed Korean Buddhism for the event.

4 This discussion about postulant education is found in: Taehan Pulgyo Chogyejong Kyoyugwŏn, "Chongdan sat'ae ŭi kyohun kwa sŭngga ŭi kwaje," 17–54.

5 Sŏran, "Han'guk Pulgyo sŭngga kyoyuk ŭi palchŏn panghyang e taehan yŏn'gu," 316.

6 Kim Chi-hyŏn, "Chogyejong kibon kyoyuk kigwan p'yojun kyogwa kwajŏng e taehan yŏn'gu," 321.

7 See, for example: Yanggwan, "T'ongdosa sŭngga taehak ŭi yŏksa wa chŏnt'ong," 24.

8 Haewŏl, "Kangwŏn kyoyuk, Pulgyo rŭl al su innŭn'ga," 60.

9 In the early twentieth century, Taixu wrote that his main objective in establishing the Wuchang Buddhist Academy was "to produce talent that can propagate the Dharma in modern times." Quoted in: Rongdao Lai, "The Wuchang Ideal: Buddhist Education and Identity Production in Republican China," 57.

10 Pŏpsŏng, "Sŭngga kibon kyoyuk ŭi ch'egyehwa rŭl wihayŏ," 81–83.

11 See, for example, a paper by one of Haeinsa's teachers: Mugwan, "Chibang sŭngga taehak kyoyuk chedo palchŏn kwaje wa panghyang," 130.
12 Victor Sogen Hori uses this hot and cold metaphor (found in the *Platform Sutra*) to point out the difference between knowing for oneself and explaining to others. See: Hori, *Zen Sand: The Book of Capping Phrases for Koan Practice,* 11.
13 Pŏbin, "Sŭngga kyoyuk, sahoi wa sot'ong hago yŏksa e puhap haeya."
14 Ibid.
15 Pŏpchang, "Kangwŏn kyogwa kwajŏng chŏnban e taehan munjejŏm mit kaesŏnan."
16 These proceedings are found in: Taehan Pulgyo Chogyejong Kyoyugwŏn, "Ch'ogi Pulgyo kyosupŏp yŏnch'anhoe."
17 Taehan Pulgyo Chogyejong Kyoyugwŏn, *Sŭngga kibon kyoyuk kigwan kyogwa kwajŏng mit kyogwamok kaep'yŏnan maryŏn ŭl wihan kongch'ŏngoe,* 5–8.
18 Zongmi is known for his five-level classification of the teachings (*pan jiao* 判教), in which the Small Vehicle is classified as the second most shallow teaching after the Teaching of Men and Gods. On Zongmi's system see: Peter Gregory, *Inquiry Into the Origin of Humanity: An Annotated Translation of Tsung-Mi's Yuan Jen Lun with a Modern Commentary.*
19 Chimun, "Sŭngga kyoyuk ŭi hyŏndaehwa," 108.
20 Ryan Bongseok Joo, "Countercurrents from the West: 'Blue-Eyed' Zen Masters, Vipassana Meditation, and Buddhist Psychotherapy in Contemporary Korea," 627.
21 T'oehyu, "Taesŭng Pulgyo wa onŭl ŭi sŭngga kyoyuk."
22 Chongmuk, "Sŭngga taehak (kangwŏn) kyogwa kwajŏng unyŏng e kwanhan sogo."
23 Taehan Pulgyo Chogyejong Kyoyugwŏn, "Sŭngga kyoyuk chedo kaesŏn ch'ujin wiwŏnhoe hwaltong kyŏnggwa," 90–91.
24 See, for example: Pŏpchang, "Kangwŏn kyogwa kwajŏng chŏnban e taehan munjejŏm mit kaesŏnan," 21–26; Taehan Pulgyo Chogyejong Kyoyugwŏn, "2000, 2001 yŏndo Kyoyugwŏn saŏp hyŏnhwang mit kwaje," 24.
25 Taehan Pulgyo Chogyejong Kyoyugwŏn, "Sŭngga kyoyuk chedo kaesŏn ch'ujin wiwŏnhoe hwaltong kyŏnggwa," 92.
26 Sŏngbon, "Kibon kyoyuk kigwan kongt'ong kyogwamok sŏnjŏng kwa sŭngga kyoyuk ŭi munjejŏm," 316.
27 Kwŏn O-min, "Kyohak kwa chongak—hyŏnhaeng Pulgyo kangwŏn ŭi kyogwa kwajŏng e taehae tasi saenggak handa."
28 Myŏngbŏp, "Suhaengja paech'ul esŏ kangwŏn ŭi silsang kwa kaesŏnjŏm," 152–153.
29 Chongmuk, "Sŭngga taehak (kangwŏn) kyogwa kwajŏng unyŏng e kwanhan sogo."
30 Kwŏn, "Kyohak kwa chongak—hyŏnhaeng Pulgyo kangwŏn ŭi kyogwa kwajŏng e taehae tasi saenggak handa"; Chimun, "Sŭngga kyoyuk ŭi hyŏndaehwa," 112–113.
31 Taehan Pulgyo Chogyejong Kyoyugwŏn, "Sŭngga kyoyuk chedo kaesŏn ch'ujin wiwŏnhoe hwaltong kyŏnggwa."
32 Mugwan, "Chibang sŭngga taehak kyoyuk chedo palchŏn kwaje wa panghyang," 141.
33 See, for example: Sŏran, "Han'guk Pulgyo sŭngga kyoyuk ŭi palchŏn panghyang e taehan yŏn'gu," 316.
34 Sŏngbon, "Kibon kyoyuk kigwan kongt'ong kyogwamok sŏnjŏng kwa sŭngga kyoyuk ŭi munjejŏm," 302–303.
35 A 2012 teachers' seminar, for example, had one lecture on e-learning, one on making lesson plans, one on giving writing assignments, and one on using discussions and debates in class. See: Taehan Pulgyo Chogyejong Kyoyugwŏn, "Kyoyuk kyoyŏkcha kyosubŏp yŏnch'anhoe."
36 *Hangŭl* is the name of the vernacular Korean script invented in the fifteenth century, and so *Hangŭlization* means Koreanization in terms of the written language.
37 Taehan Pulgyo Chogyejong Kyoyugwŏn, *Sŭngga kibon kyoyuk kigwan kyogwa kwajŏng mit kyogwamok kaep'yŏnan maryŏn ŭl wihan kongch'ŏngoe.*
38 Yi Kye-p'yo, "Songgwangsa kangwŏn ŭi yŏksa."
39 To be sure, as the curriculum involves numerous new courses, not much time is

left for studying the *Ch'imun* and *Huayan Sutra,* and seminaries often end up going through only a chapter or two out of these texts. At Songgwangsa, for example, in 2014 the fourth-year class only read the last chapter of the *Huayan Sutra,* the *Lifajie pin* 立法界品.

40 In 2014, Songgwangsa seminary was teaching Dahui's *Letters* and the *Platform Sutra* instead of the full *Sajip,* but read through another shorter text by Chinul, *Secrets of Cultivating the Mind* (*Susim kyŏl* 修心訣).

41 The following are partial results of my fieldwork survey in 2014 regarding the actual study of the eight texts of the *Sajip* and *Sagyo* in seminaries: at Hwaŏmsa only Dahui's *Letters,* the *Awakening of Faith,* and the *Sutra of Perfect Enlightenment* were studied, and at Songgwangsa and Sudŏksa the same three were studied together with the *Platform Sutra.* At Tonghwasa, Dahui's *Letters,* Gaofeng's *Chan Essentials,* and the *Awakening of Faith* were studied; at Pŏpchusa, Dahui's *Letters,* Gaofeng's *Chan Essentials,* and the *Śūraṃgama*; at Haeinsa, Zongmi's *Preface,* Gaofeng's *Chan Essentials,* the *Awakening of Faith,* and the *Sutra of Perfect Enlightenment* were read*;* at Ssanggyesa, Dahui's *Letters* and Gaofeng's *Chan Essentials* were the only texts studied out of the *Sajip;* and at Pongnyŏngsa Dahui's *Letters,* Zongmi's *Preface,* the *Śūraṃgama Sutra,* and the *Awakening of Faith* were studied. The absence of Chinul's *Excerpts* from these programs is especially conspicuous.

42 Although Introduction to Buddhism may involve various contents beyond the Indian origins of the religion, the focus of this particular course, as can be deduced from the *Teacher Guides,* is clearly the teachings of the Pāli Canon.

43 Taehan Pulgyo Chogyejong Kyoyugwŏn, *Buddhist English* (vols. 1, 2). Note that in Taiwan, too, an English textbook for the sangha (titled *Sangha Talk*) was published in 1998, offering short reading comprehension excerpts from the sutras and *Jātakas,* and even from Dōgen. See: Corporate Body of the Buddha Educational Foundation, *Sangha Talk.*

44 The Temple Stay program is a new popular semi-governmental tourist-Buddhist project, in which many of the larger temples throughout the country now operate special overnight schedules for foreign and local visitors. For details on the history and contents of the program see: Uri Kaplan, "Images of Monasticism: The Temple Stay Program and The Re-branding of Korean Buddhist Temples."

45 Chang Yŏng-sŏp, *Ttŏnamyŏn kŭman inde,* 25.

46 Some examples are in order: in 2014 Songgwangsa employed a lay Buddhist professor to teach Early Buddhism and Mādhyamika Thought; Tonghaksa had a lay teacher coming in to teach Yogācāra Thought; and almost all schools had external lay English teachers coming in the mornings to teach. Some seminaries, T'ongdosa for example, remain strictly against this new practice, and refuse to invite lay teachers into their classrooms.

47 Chang, *Ttŏnamyŏn kŭman inde,* 118, 149.

48 At Pongnyŏngsa, for example, female novices study for two hours in the mornings and an additional two hours most afternoons. T'ongdosa and Haeinsa also added some class time in the afternoons. Many of the seminaries hold video lectures during the weekends.

49 Oliver Freiberger, "The Buddhist Canon and the Canon of Buddhist Studies," 262.

50 According to a recent survey, Gethin's *The Foundations of Buddhism* was still by far the most widely used textbook in academic Buddhist courses. Its focus is India, Pāli, and Sanskrit with very little discussion of the religion's development elsewhere. See: Stephen Berkwitz, "Textbook Buddhism: Introductory Books on the Buddhist Religion."

51 Jean Baudrillard, *The Gulf War Did Not Take Place,* 2.

52 My discussion of the powers gained through mimetic contagion is drawn from: Michael Taussig, *Mimesis and Alterity: A Particular History of the Senses.*

53 Lampert, *Discipline and Debate,* 154.

54 Seminary teachers often told me privately that these *Teacher Guides* offer syllabi that are simply too complicated for the simple study in the seminaries, and it would be very difficult to actually follow them in class. Some claimed they do consult them, though, in preparation for their lectures.

55 See: Taehan Pulgyo Chogyejong Kyoyugwŏn, *Ch'ogi Pulgyo: kangŭi kyehoegan 1; Taesŭng Pulgyo: kangŭi kyehoegan 2; Sŏn Pulgyo: kangŭi kyehoegan 3; Hanmun Pulchŏn: kangŭi kyehoegan 4; Ŭngyong Pulgyo: kangŭi kyehoegan 5; Pulgyosa: kangŭi kyehoegan 6;* and *Kyeyul kwa Pulgyo yulli: kangŭi kyehoegan 7.*

56 McMahan interestingly deconstructed *What the Buddha Taught* to argue that it is not that Rahula's Buddhism is not "real," but it is not simply what the Buddha taught. It selects from the canon those extracts that can be interpreted to resonate with modernity and obscures the parts that do not, and this idealized, textualized, orientalist Buddhism has little to do with the lives and rituals of living Buddhists. See: David McMahan, *The Making of Buddhist Modernism,* 50–51.

57 Paul Williams, *Unexpected Way: On Converting from Buddhism to Catholicism.*

58 Taehan Pulgyo Chogyejong Kyoyugwŏn, *Hanmun pulchŏn.*

59 For an overview of Buddhist reverse-orientalism see: Jørn Borup, "Zen and the Art of Inverting Orientalism: Religious Studies and Genealogical Networks."

60 For Ceylon see, for example: McMahan, *The Making of Buddhist Modernism,* 99–103. For Thailand see: Patrick Jory, "Thai and Western Buddhist Scholarship in the Age of Colonialism: King Chulalongkorn Redefines the Jatakas."

61 Joo, "Countercurrents from the West," 623.

62 Nelson, *Experimental Buddhism,* 198–200.

63 Donald Lopez, *Curators of the Buddha: The Study of Buddhism Under Colonialism,* 7.

64 John Makransky, "The Emergence of Buddhist Critical-Constructive Reflection in the Academy as a Resource for Buddhist Communities and for the Contemporary World." Note that some, however, reject such attempts to establish Buddhist theological schools arguing that they will harm the integrity of the discipline, which needs to at least aim for objectivity—see, for example: Ian Reader, "Buddhism and the Perils of Advocacy."

65 The shift of East Asian Buddhist hegemony toward Japan began in the early twentieth century, when Buddhist leaders from China and Korea flocked to Japanese universities, often retransmitting Japanese forms of Buddhism back into their homelands. For the Chinese case see: Eric Schickentanz, "Wang Hongyuan and the Import of Japanese Esoteric Buddhism to China during the Republican Period."

66 D. T. Suzuki has probably been one of the most influential architects of our received Zen Buddhist Studies canon.

67 See: Schlütter, *How Zen Became Zen,* 156–160; Jamie Hubbard, "Premodern, Modern, and Postmodern: Doctrine and the Study of Japanese Religion."

68 Taehan Pulgyo Chogyejong Kyoyugwŏn, "Kangwŏn kyogwa kwajŏng t'ongil mit kaesŏn ŭl wihan sŏlmun chosa punsŏk kyŏlgwa," 49–54; "Kangwŏn kyogwa kwajŏng t'ongil mit kaesŏn ŭl wihan sŏlmun chosa punsŏk pogosŏ," 33–55.

69 Ibid., 39–45.

70 Pŏbin, "Sŭngga kyoyuk, sahoi wa sot'ong hago yŏksa e puhap haeya," 281.

71 H. M. Vos, "The Canon as a Straitjacket."

72 All Chogye Order main directors to date have been Haeinsa-related monks, and many of the prominent monastics in the headquarters, including the contemporary head of the Education Department, have been students and teachers at the Haeinsa seminary.

73 Sŏran, "Han'guk Pulgyo sŭngga kyoyuk ŭi palchŏn panghyang e taehan yŏn'gu," 191–192.

74 Ibid.

75 Wŏlho, "Chŏnt'ong kangwŏn kyoyuk kwa hyŏndaesik taehak kyoyuk e taehan pigyo koch'al." 157–158.

76 Ibid.

77 Paul Griffiths, *Religious Reading: The Place of Reading in the Practice of Religion,* preface.

78 Ibid., 182.

79 Sangjŏng, "Kangwŏn, kwayŏn kibon kyoyuk in'ga," 153–154.

80 The Korean sangha is an aging community. In the late 1990s only 7 percent of novices were over forty years old, in the early 2000s 17 percent of new home-leavers were over forty, but since 2007 the numbers have risen to above 30 percent and in 2010 in particular over 40 percent of new novices were over forty years of age! This troubles the Chogye Order, which does not want its monasteries to turn into senior citizens' homes, and hopes for monastics who are still in their prime and are able to study, develop spiritually, lead, and propagate. Therefore, in 2002, the Order decided to lower the maximum age for new monastics to forty, explaining that older monks were having difficulties adapting to seminary study and communal life. Nevertheless, as new monastic numbers continued to drop in the 2000s this rule was reversed in 2005, and the maximum age for ordination was set again at fifty. See: Taehan Pulgyo Chogyejong Kyoyugwŏn, "Kyoyugwŏn 10 yŏn ŭi saŏp pogo mit ch'omgp'yŏng." For monastic age statistics in the late 1990s see: Taehan Pulgyo Chogyejong Kyoyugwŏn, "Chogyejong sŭngga kyoyuk hyŏnhwang," 59. For age statistics in the 2000s see: Pogwang, "Taehan Pulgyo Chogyejong ŭi ch'ulgaja hyŏnhwang kwa ch'ulga chedo ŭi kaesŏn pangan," 221.

81 Statistics show that over 60 percent of Koreans are now university graduates. Meanwhile, between 1995 and 1998 only 32 percent, and by 2012 only 28 percent of new Chogye novices graduated from a university. Almost all new novices leave home at an age in which they could have already graduated. These statistics illustrate that unfortunately it is often those who failed to succeed in education-based modern Korean society who find an alternative in the monasteries. For monastic educational statistics in the 1990s see: Taehan Pulgyo Chogyejong Kyoyugwŏn, "Chogyejong sŭngga kyoyuk hyŏnhwang," 59. For the 2000s see: Pogwang, "Taehan Pulgyo Chogyejong ŭi ch'ulgaja hyŏnhwang kwa ch'ulga chedo ŭi kaesŏn pangan," 223.

82 Chehaeng, "Taechung saenghwal kwa hagŏp sŏngch'wido," 148.

83 Cho Ŭn-su, "Han'guk Pulgyo chŏnsŏ ŭi p'yŏnch'an kwa kwaje."

84 Jun Jing, *The Temple of Memories: History, Power, and Morality in a Chinese Village,* 110.

85 Paul Griffiths similarly demonstrated that metaphors of tasting, digesting, sucking, chewing, and savoring the sweet words of the Bible were prevalent in medieval Christian discourse. See: Griffiths, *Religious Reading,* 43.

86 http://blog.daum.net/whoami555/13741990. Accessed October 2013.

87 Kim Chi-hyŏn, "Chogyejong kibon kyoyuk kigwan p'yojun kyogwa kwajŏng e taehan yŏn'gu."

88 Statistics received directly from the T'aego Order.

89 Mun, *Purification Buddhist Movement 1954–1970.*

90 When I visited Pŏpchusa in 2013, two T'aego monks were enrolled in the seminary. The Chogye Order generally allows up to two monastics from other institutions to be enrolled in each seminary, though apart from the two in Pŏpchusa I did not encounter other T'aego monks in Chogye institutions.

91 Sŏnamsa is located on Chogye Mountain not far from Songgwangsa, and its ownership is still disputed. The Chogye Order continues to claim it, though it is obviously operated by the T'aego.

92 Statistics found in: Munhwa Ch'eyuk Kwan'gwangbu, *Han'guk ŭi chonggyo*

hyŏnhwang. For general information on the Korean Ch'ŏnt'ae Order see: Taehan Pulgyo Ch'ŏnt'aejong, *Ch'ŏnt'ae sinhaeng ŭi ch'ŏkkŏrŭm*.

93 There is at least one major sutra that recommends avoiding sleep and cultivating mindfulness during all three watches of the night—the *Laṅkāvatāra*. See: Red Pine, *The Lankavatara Sutra: A Zen Text*, 79.

94 Kim Hun, "Taehan Pulgyo Ch'ŏnt'aejong ŭi chonggyo kyoyuk e taehan koch'al."

95 The Ch'ŏnt'ae Order skips the novice (*sami*) stage, and new home-leavers remain postulants (*haengja*) until they graduate from the seminary. They then take the ten bodhisattva precepts and become full Ch'ŏnt'ae monastic members.

CHAPTER FOUR: TOWARD BUDDHIST PLURALISM

1 Eun-su Cho, "The Uses and Abuses of Wŏnhyo and the 'T'ong Pulgyo' Narrative." See also: Robert Buswell, "Imagining 'Korean Buddhism': The Invention of a National Religious Tradition."

2 Tomoko Masuzawa, *The Invention of World Religions: Or, How European Universalism Was Preserved in the Language of Pluralism*, 122.

3 Urs App, *The Birth of Orientalism*, 124–125.

4 It is interesting to discover that some of the large mountain monastic seminaries in Taiwan today similarly offer ecumenical curricula that include Pāli, Chinese, and Tibetan material. See: Tuzzeo, "Education, Invention of Orthodoxy, and the Construction of Modern Buddhism on Dharma Drum Mountain," 21.

5 Jorge Ferrer and Jacob Sherman, *The Participatory Turn: Spirituality, Mysticism, Religious Studies*.

6 For a definition of pluralism see also: J. Milton Yinger, "Pluralism, Religion, and Secularism." For a taxonomy of religious pluralism see: Jorge Ferrer, "The Plurality of Religions and the Spirit of Pluralism: A Participatory Vision of the Future of Religion."

7 Pogwang, "Taehan Pulgyo Chogyejong ŭi ch'ulgaja hyŏnhwang kwa ch'ulga chedo ŭi kaesŏn pangan," 221.

8 For a detailed analysis of the current lay education system see: Uri Kaplan, "Assembling the Laity: Standardizing Lay Buddhist Affiliation via Education in Contemporary Korea." For an introductory essay on the history of the Temple Stay program see: Kaplan, "Images of Monasticism." Numbers of participants in the Temple Stay have grown steadily from approximately 50,000 in 2005 to close to 220,000 in 2015. One hundred and twenty major Korean monasteries now take part in this program.

9 These new 2014 regulations are found in: Taehan Pulgyo Chogyejong, *Ch'ulgaja, irŏk'e madihago indohamnida*.

10 See, for example: Hyŏnŭng, "Chogye chongdan sŭngga kyoyuk ŭi tangmyŏn kwaje e tehayŏ," 173–174.

11 This reform was offered in a Chogye Order seminar by a Ch'ŏngamsa teacher in 2002: Taehan Pulgyo Chogyejong Kyoyugwŏn, "Sŭngga kyoyuk ŭi sŏnggwa wa chŏnmang," 252–253.

12 Both the Hwaŏm Academy and Hwangak Buddhist Academy have been closed since the end of the century. See: Taehan Pulgyo Chogyejong Kyoyugwŏn, *Chogyejongsa: kŭnhyŏndae p'yŏn*, 281.

13 Chongmuk, "Ch'ongnim ŭi chindan, naagal panghyang: Haein ch'ongnim chungsim ŭro," 197–210.

14 Although Holmes Welch reported the existence of Vinaya institutions in early-twentieth-century China, he noted that these were mainly places of ritual study rather than textual research. See: Welch, *The Buddhist Revival in China*, 104–105. Likewise, Don Alvin Pittman demonstrated that the Chinese Vinaya schools of the time offered fifty-three-day preparatory courses for ordination, rather than

advanced study. See: Pittman, *Toward a Modern Chinese Buddhism*, 54–55. It was recently reported that there are currently two operating Vinaya Schools in China, though no details were given about their actual programs or locations. See Cho, "Segye sŭngga kyoyuk ŭi ŏje wa onŭl."

15 Note that Sudŏksa received the prestigious status of the fourth Korean "Comprehensive Chan Center" (Ch'ongnim 叢林) with plans to establish a Vinaya School as early as 1984, though no such institution has been erected to date.

16 See, for example: Chongmuk, "Ch'ongnim ŭi chindan, naagal panghyang: Haein ch'ongnim chungsim ŭro," 210–211.

17 For a comprehensive discussion of the contemporary Chogye Order Pure Rules and other regulatory codes see: Kaplan, "Updating the Vinaya."

18 Taehan Pulgyo Chogyejong Kyoyugwŏn, *Sŭngga kibon kyoyuk kigwan mit chŏnmun kyoyuk kigwan chojŏngan maryŏn ŭl wihan kongch'ŏngoe.*

19 On Samsŏn seminary see also chapter two, note 103.

20 Kim Kyu-bo, "Chŏngwŏn midal sŭngga taehak, taehagwŏn ŭro chŏnhwan hwallo mosaek."

21 *Pŏmp'ae* is mentioned in Chinese sources as early as the second century, and Ennin's diary of his travels to the Tang tells of three styles of *pŏmp'ae* performed at Korean temples in Shandong at the time: Silla style, Tang style, and a style similar to what was practiced in Japan. Notably, Ennin is said to have created the Tendai *pŏmp'ae* (called *Tendai shōmyō*) on his return to Japan. See: Byong Won Lee, "A Short History of Pomp'ae: Korean Buddhist Ritual Chant." According to the pamphlets given out in these ritual institutions, the Korean *pŏmp'ae* lineage began with a Ssangyesa monk by the name of Chingam who brought the right ways of chanting the rituals back from Tang China. The name of the school, Ŏsan (魚山), is another term used for *pŏmp'ae.*

22 See, for example: Pŏpsan, "T'ŭksu hakkyo kaesŏl kwa kwalli unyŏng e taehayŏ," 195–198.

23 Khammai Dhammasami, "Idealism and Pragmatism: A Dilemma in the Current Monastic Education Systems of Burma and Thailand."

24 Minae Mizumura, *The Fall of Language in the Age of English*, 62.

25 Jung Mi Nam, "The Changing Role of English in Korea: From English as a Tool for Advancement to English for Survival." An interesting treatment of the first public English school in Korea is found in: Leighanne Kimberly Yuh, "The Royal Academy: Korea's First Instance of American-Style Education and the Making of Modern Korean Officials, 1886–1994."

26 Dennis Letts, *In Pursuit of Status: The Making of South Korea's "New" Urban Middle Class*, 164–165.

27 Jin-kyu Park, "English Fever in South Korea: Its History and Symptoms."

28 Samuel Collins illustrated how English has been associated with conservative militarism in the Korea of the 1950s and 1960s, but by the turn of the millennium it has come to symbolize liberal values. See his: "Who's This Tong-il? English, Culture, and Ambivalence in South Korea."

29 McMahan, *The Making of Buddhist Modernism*, 262.

30 Red Pine, *The Zen Teaching of Bodhidharma*. I believe that the Thich Nhat Hahn book in question was *Peace in Every Step: The Path of Mindfulness in Everyday Life*.

31 Joo, "Countercurrents from the West."

32 Jane Blanchard, *Women of the Way: Embracing the Camino.*

33 The 2010 plan to lower the annual quotas of the Elementary Chan Hall to ten new matriculants has not yet been followed. See: Taehan Pulgyo Chogyejong Kyoyugwŏn, *Sŭngga kibon kyoyuk kigwan mit chŏnmun kyoyuk kigwan chojŏngan maryŏn ŭl wihan kongch'ŏngoe*, 20–22.

34 This schedule was received personally from the Tonghwasa office.

35 The *Canchan jing yu* (參禪警語, X63.1257), written by Boshan (博山) in the seventeenth century, repeats many of the Chan ideas about nourishing doubt found in the earlier works of Dahui and Gaofeng. It is not included in the Taishō Canon but it has recently appeared in English translation: Jeff Shore, *Great Doubt: Practicing Zen in the World.*

36 The three are: a collection of sayings by Huanbo Xiyun (黄檗希运) from the ninth century titled *Essentials of Mind Transmission* (*Chuanxin fayao* 傳心法要, T. 48.2012); Chinul's *Treatise on Resolving Doubts about Observing the Keyword* (*Kanhua kyŏlŭi ron* 看話決疑論, not in the Taishō); and a sixteenth-century treatise by Zhuhong (祩宏) titled *Progress through the Gate of Chan* (*Changuan cejin* 禪關策進, T. 48.2024).

37 The three are: Jianzhi Sengcan's (鑑智僧璨) *Xinxinming* (信心銘, T. 48.2010), which has been translated into English numerous times; the *Treatise on the Essential Gate of Entering the Way through Sudden Awakening* (*Dunwu rudao yaomenlu* 頓悟入道要門論, X63.1223) by Dazhu Huihai (大珠慧海); and a sixteenth-century work by Korean Chan master Hyujŏng, the *Sŏn kyo kyŏl* (禪敎訣, not in the Taishō Canon).

38 There are only two monks in Korea today who are regarded as "Great Monastics" and have received the official stamp (*inga* 印可) for their attainments. The first is Chinje, who spends most of his time at Tonghwasa, and the second is Songdam, who lives in a temple in Incheon.

39 Bernard Senécal, "A Critical Reflection on the Chogye Order's Campaign for the Worldwide Propagation of Kanhwa Sŏn 看話禪."

40 Aside from the Chogye Order, there are several Won Buddhist centers operating in North America. In addition, the T'aego Order operates the Institute of Buddhist Studies in California.

41 Gi-Wook Shin, *Ethnic Nationalism in Korea: Genealogy, Politics, and Legacy,* 184–205.

42 Buswell, *The Zen Monastic Experience,* 19–20.

43 Brooke Schedneck reports that ordained Buddhist foreigners have similarly established separate communities in Thailand. See her: "Religious Encounters in Thailand: The Integration of Foreign Monks into Thai Monastic Life."

44 Chang, *Ttŏnamyŏn kŭman inde,* 110.

45 Ŏ Hyŏn-gyŏng, "Sinnyŏn hoegyŏn ŭro pon 2014 sŭngga kyoyuk pangyang."

46 Chandler, *Establishing a Pure Land on Earth,* 293–294; Schedneck, "Religious Encounters in Thailand."

CHAPTER FIVE: MONASTIC EXAMINATIONS AND BUREAUCRATIC RANKS

1 Paraphrased from: Pŏpsan, "Han'guk Pulgyo sŭngga-pŏpkye chedo ŭi koch'al kwa chongdan sŭngga kosi chedo ŭi sihaeng," 205.

2 Paraphrased from: Sem Vermeersch, *The Power of the Buddhas: The Politics of Buddhism during the Koryo Dynasty (918–1392),* 203.

3 Ibid., 202.

4 Nisha Singh, *The Origin and Development of Buddhist Monastic Education in India,* 178–180.

5 Eric Zurcher, *The Buddhist Conquest of China: The Spread and Adaptation of Buddhism in Early Medieval China,* 259–260.

6 Stanely Weinstein, *Buddhism Under T'ang,* 49, 165–166.

7 Kenneth Ch'en, *Buddhism in China: A Historical Survey,* 243.

8 Eric Zurcher, "Buddhism and Education in T'ang Times," 31–33.

9 Chi-chiang Huang, "Elite and Clergy in Northern Sung Hang-chou: A Convergence of Interest," 311–313.

10 The *Jiaoyuan qinggui* is found in: X57n0968.

11 Ch'en, *Buddhism in China,* 434–435.
12 Pankaj Mohan, "The Roles of Monks Won'gwang and Chajang in the Formation of Early Silla Buddhism," 53–55, 63; Hŏ Hŭng-sik, "Koryŏ sidae ŭi sŭnggwa chedo wa kŭ kinŭng," 112–113.
13 Vermeersch, *The Power of the Buddhas,* 188. Note that although the Civil Service examination system was not formalized until 958, there is evidence for exams on the Chinese Classics taking place occasionally in Korea at least since 788. Dozens of Koreans also traveled to sit for the exams in Tang China. See: Yŏng-ho Ch'oe, *The Civil Examinations and the Social Structure in Early Yi Dynasty Korea: 1392–1600,* 1–2.
14 Other terms for these exams found in the sources are: *Sŏnsŏn* (禪選), *Sŏndo* (選度), *Sŏnbuljang* (選佛場), *Sŏngwa* (禪科), *Kuksi* (國試), *Sŭngsŏn* (僧選), and so on. See: Pŏpsan, "Han'guk Pulgyo sŭngga-pŏpkye chedo ŭi koch'al kwa chongdan sŭngga kosi chedo ŭi sihaeng," 208.
15 Hŏ Hŭng-sik, "Koryŏ ŭi sŭngjik kwa sŭngjŏng," 176–177.
16 Hŏ, "Koryŏ sidae ŭi sŭnggwa chedo wa kŭ kinŭng," 130.
17 For Koryŏ monastic ranks see, for example: Vermeersch, *The Power of the Buddhas,* 191.
18 Hŏ, "Koryŏ sidae ŭi sŭnggwa chedo wa kŭ kinŭng," 117.
19 Ibid., 124–131.
20 Ibid., 137.
21 Eun-su Cho, "Female Buddhist Practice in Korea: A Historical Account," 29.
22 Vermeersch, *The Power of the Buddhas,* 199.
23 Buswell, *Tracing Back the Radiance,* 19–21.
24 Ch'oe, *The Civil Examinations and the Social Structure in Early Yi Dynasty Korea,* 18–22.
25 Yi Pong-ch'un, "Chosŏn sidae ŭi sŭngjik chedo," 184.
26 Richard Bowring, *The Religious Traditions of Japan 500–1600,* 98.
27 Groner, "Training Through Debates in Medieval Tendai and Seizan-ha Temples," 234.
28 Paul Groner, *Ryogen and Mount Hiei: Japanese Tendai in the Tenth Century,* 128–143.
29 Ibid., 144. For the Tendai rank system see: Sŏran, "Han'guk Pulgyo sŭngga kyoyuk ŭi palchŏn panghyang e taehan yŏn'gu," 314.
30 Starling, "Family Temples and Religious Learning in Contemporary Japanese Buddhism."
31 Dreyfus, *The Sound of Two Hands Clapping,* 144–146, 317.
32 V. Nithiyanandam, *Buddhist System of Education,* 92–96.
33 Khammai Dhammasami explains that sangha examinations in Southeast Asia were first established in order to limit the numbers of the sangha at times of war in order to prohibit potential conscripts from joining the sangha. See: Dhammasami, "Growing But As A Sideline: An Overview of Modern Shan Monastic Education," 39; and "The Impact of Political Instability on the Education of the Saṅgha in the 17th Century Siam," 181–192.
34 Stephen J. Zack, "Buddhist Education Under Prince Wachirayan Warorot," 54–57.
35 Yoneo Ishii, *Sangha, State, and Society: Thai Buddhism in History,* 84–87.
36 Pyi Phyo Kyaw, "Foundations of Criticality: Applications of Traditional Monastic Pedagogy in Myanmar."
37 Pak Kyŏng-hun, "Kŭndae Pulgyo ŭi sŭngjik chedo," 208.
38 Ibid., 211.
39 This system is part of the Chosŏn Pulgyo Chogyejong ch'ongbonsa T'aegosa pŏp 朝鮮佛敎曹溪宗總本寺太古寺法. See: Pŏpsan, "Han'guk Pulgyo sŭngga-pŏpkye chedo ŭi koch'al kwa chongdan sŭngga kosi chedo ŭi sihaeng," 215.
40 Ibid., 217; Mubi, "4 kŭp sŭngga kosi ŭi hyŏnhwang kwa palchŏn panghyang." For

the lay propagation exams and the contemporary lay Buddhist education system in Korea see: Kaplan, "Assembling the Laity."

41 Mubi, "4 kŭp sŭngga kosi ŭi hyŏnhwang kwa palchŏn panghyang."

42 Taehan Pulgyo Chogyejong, "Pŏpkye pŏp."

43 Pon'gak, "4 kŭp sŭngga kosi chedo ŭi kaesŏn ŭl wihan chean."

44 Yŏngjin, "Sagŭp sŭngga kosi kaesŏn panghyang e taehan kich'o sŏnwŏn ŭi ipchang," 23–26.

45 Taehan Pulgyo Chogyejong Kyoyugwŏn, "Pon-malsa chuji yŏnsu sŏlmun chosa pogosŏ," 126.

46 Taehan Pulgyo Chogyejong Kyoyugwŏn, "Kangwŏn kyogwa kwajŏng t'ongil mit kaesŏn ŭl wihan sŏlmun chosa punsŏk pogosŏ," 36–37.

47 Han Myŏng-u, "Pŏpkye kubun hwijang naenyŏn put'ŏ ch'agyong."

48 Mubi made this announcement at a 2001 Chogye Order seminar. The proceedings of the seminar are found in: Taehan Pulgyo Chogyejong Kyoyugwŏn, "Sŭngga kyoyuk ŭi sŏnggwa wa chŏnmang," 257.

49 Currently only 320 members of the entire Chogye sangha are eligible to vote (the 81 assembly members along with 10 members out of each of the 24 parishes). Giving the right to vote to all *Taedŏk/Hyedŏk*-ranked passers of the third-level exam would raise the number of eligible voters to about 6,000, or approximately half of all affiliated monastics. On these recent plans see: Sin Sŏng-min, "Chogyejong ch'ongmuwŏnjang sŏngŏ indan hwaktae toena."

50 Taehan Pulgyo Chogyejong Kyoyugwŏn, "Sŭngga poksik yut'ong hyŏnhwang kwa kaesŏn pangan sŏlmun chosa punsŏ pogosŏ," 89.

51 Chanju Mun, "Kim Ilta's (1929–99) Systemization of the Current Jogye Order's Orthopraxy," 376–377.

52 Pŏpchang, "T'ongil toen haengja kyoyugŭi chedo hwangnip pangyang."

53 Ibid., 330–331.

54 Pŏpchŏng specified the Vinaya-related texts to be studied as the *Ch'obalsim,* the *42-Section Sutra,* the *Novice Precepts and Decorum,* and the *Bequeathed Teachings Sutra.* See: Pŏpchŏng, "Haengja kyoyuk ŏttŏk'e hal kŏdin'ga."

55 Chihwan, "Paramjikhan suhaengjasang hwangnip ŭl wihan haengja kyoyuk naeyong," 283.

56 Ibid.

57 Taehan Pulgyo Chogyejong Kyoyugwŏn, *Haengja kyobon.*

58 Taehan Pulgyo Chogyejong Kyoyugwŏn, *5 kŭp sŭngga kosi yesijip.*

59 For the schedules of these preparatory courses in the early 2000s see: Taehan Pulgyo Chogyejong Kyoyugwŏn, "Che 34 ki haengja kyoyuk kyehoeksŏ."

60 Lori Meeks suggested that conferring the precepts on laypeople was an attempt to better integrate them into the social and economic structures of the monasteries. See: Meeks, "Vows for the Masses: Eison and the Popular Expansion of Precept-Conferral Ceremonies in Premodern Japan."

61 In the 1990s the postulant program took place either in Chikchisa or in other major monasteries, such as T'ongdosa, Haeinsa, Songgwangsa, or Pŏmŏsa. In the last decade or so both the postulant program and the full ordinations of the Chogye Order have been fixed to Chikchisa.

62 Test preparation manuals and sample questions are periodically posted on the Chogye Order website and I have used this resource in order to assemble some of the questions presented in this book.

63 Kim Wŏn-u, "4 kŭp sŭngga kosi ch'ulche pangyang hwakchŏng."

64 For the promotion of Kanhua Chan as the hallmark of Korean Buddhism by the Chogye Order see: Senécal, "A Critical Reflection on the Chogye Order's Campaign for the Worldwide Propagation of Kanhwa Sŏn 看話禪."

65 Taehan Pulgyo Chogyejong Kyoyugwŏn, *4 kŭp sŭngga kosi yesang munjejip.*

66 This debate is demonstrated in an essay by Haeinsa's seminary head teacher at the time, Chio, "Kibon kyoyuk kwajŏng isu injŏngŭro ŭi 4 kŭp sŭngga kosi."

67 Yŏ Su-ryŏng, "Sŭngga kosi, kaep'yŏn kyogwa panyŏng sŭpŭi kanghwa."
68 Ibid.
69 For recent attempts to "revive" the *uposatha* system in Korea see: Kaplan, "Updating the Vinaya."
70 Taehan Pulgyo Chogyejong Kyoyugwŏn, "2002–3 yŏn sŭngga kyoyuk hyŏnhwang," 58.
71 According to the Buddhist media, in 2002, 290 monastics passed and 44 failed this exam; in 2003, 320 passed and 43 failed, and in 2004, 93 passed and 12 failed.
72 Taehan Pulgyo Chogyejong Kyoyugwŏn, *Sŭngga kibon kyoyuk kigwan mit chŏnmun kyoyuk kigwan chojŏngan maryŏn ŭl wihan kongch'ŏngoe.*
73 Taehan Pulgyo Chogyejong Kyoyugwŏn, "2002–3 yŏn sŭngga kyoyuk ŭi chindan kwa kwaje," 33.
74 The most recent list of all 263 possible short questions for the third-level exam is available in: Taehan Pulgyo Chogyejong Kyoyugwŏn, "2014 yŏn 3 kŭp sŭngga kosi tandaphyŏng munjejip."
75 The Chogye Order publishes a list of possible exam questions on its website several months before an exam is scheduled to take place.
76 See, for example: Sin Sŏng-min, "Chogyejong, naenyŏn ch'ŏt 1kŭp sŭngga kosi silsi."
77 Ŏ Hyŏn-gyŏng, "Kosiwiwŏnhoe, 1kŭp sŭngga kosi sihaeng . . . 51myŏng ŭngsi."
78 Taehan Pulgyo Chogyejong Kyoyugwŏn, "Sŭngga kyoyuk ŭi tangmyŏn kwaje e taehayŏ," 28. Note, in addition, that in 1996 the rate of monastic bureaucrats participating in such continuing education programs rose to 68 percent (1090 of 1569 eligible monastics); in 1997, 53 percent participated (1141 of 2147); and in 1998, 60 percent (1007 of 1684) participated in at least one of the courses.
79 The seminars for foreign monks often involve lectures on Korean temple etiquette, rituals, chants, and Chan Hall regulations. They also provide a chance for all foreign monastics on the peninsula to get together for a couple of days and catch up. Schedules for the 2002 foreign monastic seminar are available in: Taehan Pulgyo Chogyejong Kyoyugwŏn, *Educational Retreat of Basic Seminary for Foreign National Suhnims.*
80 Note that, as is the case with the seminary curricula, it was monastics associated with the monasteries of T'ongdosa and Pŏmŏsa in particular who have rebelled against the Order and participated much less in its seminars. Overall, opinion surveys demonstrated that 84 percent of the Chogye Order's abbots thought the continuing education seminars were a good idea and should be mandatory. See: Taehan Pulgyo Chogyejong Kyoyugwŏn, "Pon-malsa chuji yŏnsu sŏlmun chosa pogosŏ," 93–140.
81 Taehan Pulgyo Chogyejong Kyoyugwŏn, "Sŭngga chaegyoyuk kyebal kŏmt'osŏ."
82 Ch'oe Ho-sŭng, "Chogyejong, naenyŏn pŏpkye pyŏl kyoyuk sibŏm unyŏng."
83 Schedules for the last several years can be found on the Chogye Order website.
84 For a detailed discussion of the recent coffee trend in Korean Buddhist circles see: Uri Kaplan, "From the Tea to the Coffee Ceremony: Modernizing Buddhist Material Culture in Contemporary Korea."
85 See, for example, a news article on the tenth T'aego Order exams, which took place in 2007: Kim Wŏn-u, "T'aegojong che 10 ch'a pŏpkye kosi."

CONCLUSIONS

1 Michael Seth, *Education Fever: Society, Politics, and the Pursuit of Schooling in South Korea*, 1.
2 Such "education fever" and "examination mania" is sometimes attributed to the Confucian value of "loving study" (*haoxue* 好學), which appears several times in the *Analects*.
3 Ilchin, "Chijŏng t'oron," 48. The emphasis is my own.

Bibliography

Achrya, Chowang. "Aspects of Monastic Education in Sikkim." *Bulletin of Tibetology* 2 (1998): 1–6.

Ahn, Juhn. *Buddhas and Ancestors: Religion and Wealth in Fourteenth-Century Korea.* Seattle: University of Washington Press, 2018.

——. "Gongan Collections." In *The Collected Works of Korean Buddhism,* vol. 7, edited by John Jorgensen. Seoul: The Chogye Order of Korean Buddhism, 2012.

An Chae-ch'ŏl. *Ch'imun kyŏnghun* 緇門警訓 [Admonitions to the gray-robed monks]. Seoul: Tongbang Pulgyo Taehak, 2004.

Anonymous. "Chosŏn Pulgyo ch'ongbo." 1918.

App, Urs. *The Birth of Orientalism.* Philadelphia: University of Pennsylvania Press, 2010.

Baker, Don. "Privatization of Buddhism in the Chosŏn Dynasty." *Sungkyun Journal of East Asian Studies* 14, no. 2 (2014): 153–169.

Baudrillard, Jean. *The Gulf War Did Not Take Place.* Bloomington: Indiana University Press, 1991.

Bayer, Achim. "A Case for Celibacy: The Sudinna Story in the in the Pāli Vinaya and Its Interpretation." Paper presented at the Buddhist Narratives and Beyond conference. Bangkok, 2010.

Bebbington, David. "The Secularization of British Universities since the Mid-Nineteenth Century." In *The Secularization of the Academy,* edited by George Marsden and Bradley Longfield, 259–277. New York: Oxford University Press, 1992.

Benn, James. "Another Look at the Pseudo-Śūraṃgama Sūtra." *Harvard Journal of Asiatic Studies* 68, no. 1 (2008): 57–89.

Berkwitz, Stephen. "Textbook Buddhism: Introductory Books on the Buddhist Religion." *Religion* 46, no. 2 (2016): 221–246.

Birnbaum, Raoul. "Buddhist China at the Century's Turn." *The China Quarterly* 174 (2003): 428–450.

Blackburn, Anne M. *Buddhist Learning and Textual Practice in Eighteenth-Century Lankan Monastic Culture.* Princeton: Princeton University Press, 2001.

——. "Looking for the Vinaya: Monastic Discipline in the Practical Canons of the Theravada." *Journal of the International Association of Buddhist Studies* 22, no. 2 (1992): 281–311.

Blanchard, Jane. *Women of the Way: Embracing the Camino.* Self-published: Kindle Direct Publishing, 2012.

Borchert, Thomas Adams. "Educating Monks: Buddhism, Politics and Freedom of Religion on China's Southwest Border." PhD diss., University of Chicago, 2006.

Borup, Jørn. "Contemporary Buddhist Priests and Clergy." In *Handbook of Contemporary Japanese Religions,* edited by Inken Prohl and John Nelson, 107–132. Leiden: Brill, 2012.

——. *Japanese Rinzai Zen Buddhism: Myoshinji, a Living Religion.* Boston: Brill, 2008.

———. "Zen and the Art of Inverting Orientalism: Religious Studies and Genealogical Networks." In *New Approches to the Study of Religion,* vol. 1, edited by Peter Antes, Armin W. Geertz, and Randi R. Warne, 451–487. Berlin: Verlag de Gruyter, 2004.

Bowring, Richard. *The Religious Traditions of Japan 500–1600*. Cambridge: Cambridge University Press, 2008.

Broughton, Jeffrey Lyle. *The Letters of Chan Master Dahui Pujue*. Oxford: Oxford University Press, 2017.

———. *Zongmi on Chan*. New York: Columbia University Press, 2009.

Buddhist Texts Translation Society. *The Śūraṅgama Sūtra: With Excerpts from the Commentary by the Venerable Master Hsüan Hua*. Ukiah, CA: Buddhist Text Translation Society, 2009.

Buswell, Robert. "Admonitions to Neophytes (Kye ch'osim hagin mun 誡初心學人文)." In *The Collected Works of Korean Buddhism,* vol. 2, edited by Robert Buswell, 195–205. Seoul: The Chogye Order of Korean Buddhism, 2012.

———. "Arouse Your Mind and Practice!" In *Sourcebook of Korean Civilization,* vol. 1: *From Early Times to the Sixteenth Century,* edited by Peter H. Lee, 154–157. New York: Columbia University Press, 1993.

———. "The Identity of the Pŏpchip pyŏrhaeng nok" [Dharma collection and special practice record]. *Korean Studies* 6 (1982): 1–16.

———. "Imagining 'Korean Buddhism': The Invention of a National Religious Tradition." In *Nationalism and the Construction of Korean Identity,* edited by Hyung Il Pai and Timothy R. Tangherlini, 73–107. Berkeley: University of California Press, 1998.

———. *The Korean Approach to Zen: The Collected Works of Chinul*. Honolulu: University of Hawai'i Press, 1983.

———. *Numinous Awareness Is Never Dark: The Korean Buddhist Master Chinul's Excerpts on Zen Practice*. Honolulu: University of Hawai'i Press, 2016.

———. "Preface and Conclusion from Condensation of the Exposition of the Avataṃsakasūtra (Hwaŏm non chŏryo 華嚴論節要)." In *The Collected Works of Korean Buddhism,* vol. 2, edited by Robert Buswell, 355–367. Seoul: The Chogye Order of Korean Buddhism, 2012.

———. *Tracing Back the Radiance: Chinul's Korean Way of Zen*. Honolulu: University of Hawai'i Press, 1991.

———. "The Transformation of Doubt (Ŭijŏng 疑情) in Kanhwa Sŏn 看話禪: The Testimony of Gaofeng Yuanmiao 高峰原妙 (1238–1295)." In *Kanhwasŏn, kŭ wŏlli wa kujo* 간화선, 그 원리와 구조 [Kanhwa-Chan, its principle and structure]. Seoul: Dongguk University Press, 2011.

———. *The Zen Monastic Experience*. Princeton: Princeton University Press, 1992.

Buswell, Robert, and Donald Lopez. *The Princeton Dictionary of Buddhism*. Princeton: Princeton University Press, 2013.

Chandler, Stuart. *Establishing a Pure Land on Earth: The Foguang Buddhist Perspective on Modernization and Globalization*. Honolulu: University of Hawai'i Press, 2004.

Chang Yŏng-sŏp. *Ttŏnamyŏn kŭman inde* 떠나면 그만인데 [If you leave, that is enough]. Seoul: Goodbook Press, 2008.

Changik. "Hyŏndae Pulgyo ch'ulgacha toje kyoyuk ŭi kwaje" 현대불교 출가자 도제교육의 과제 [The issue of contemporary Buddhist apprentice education]. *Chonggyo kyoyukhak yŏn'gu* 32 (2010): 109–128.

Chappell, David. *T'ien-t'ai Buddhism: An Outline of the Fourfold Teachings*. Honolulu: University of Hawai'i Press, 1984.

Chehaeng. "Taechung saenghwal kwa hagŏp sŏngch'wido" 대중생활과 학업성취도 [Communal living and the way of fulfilling one's education]. In *Sŭngga kyoyuk kwa Han'guk Pulgyo* 승가교육과 한국불교 [Sangha education and Korean Buddhism], edited by Kaksan. Taegu: Chŏn'guk kangwŏn yŏnhap Pulgyo haksul taehoe chunbi wiwŏnhoe, 2003.

Ch'en, Kenneth. *Buddhism in China: A Historical Survey*. Princeton: Princeton University Press, 1972.

Chia, Jack Meng Tat. "Teaching Dharma, Grooming Sangha: The Buddhist College of Singapore." *Sojourn: Journal of Social Issues in Southeast Asia* 24, no. 1 (2009): 122–138.

Chihwan. "Paramjikhan suhaengjasang hwangnip ŭl wihan haengja kyoyuk naeyong" 바람직한 수행자상 확립을 위한 행자교육 내용 [Postulant education contents for nurturing advantageous practitioners]. *Sŏnu toryang* 2 (1992): 277–307.

Chimun. "Sŭngga kyoyuk ŭi hyŏndaehwa" 僧伽教育의 現代化 [Modernization of sangha education]. In *Sŭngga kyoyuk kwa Han'guk Pulgyo* 승가교육과 한국불교 [Sangha education and Korean Buddhism], edited by Kaksan. Taegu: Chŏn'guk kangwŏn yŏnhap Pulgyo haksul taehoe chunbi wiwŏnhoe, 2003.

Chio. "Kibon kyoyuk kwajŏng isu injŏngŭro ŭi 4 kŭp sŭngga kosi" 기본교육 과정 이수 인정으로의 4급 승가고시 [The fourth-level sangha examinations as confirming the completion of the basic education course]. In 4 kŭp sŭngga kosi chedo kaesŏn ŭl wihan t'oronhoe charyojip 4급 승가고시 제도 개선을 위한 토론회 자료집 [Collection of materials regarding the debates on reforming the fourth-level sangha examination system]. Unpublished report, 2000.

Cho, Eun-su (Cho Ŭn-su). "Female Buddhist Practice in Korea: A Historical Account." In *Korean Buddhist Nuns and Laywomen: Hidden Histories, Enduring Vitality,* edited by Eun-su Cho. Albany: SUNY Press, 2011.

———. "Han'guk Pulgyo chŏnsŏ ŭi p'yŏnch'an kwa kwaje" 한국불교전서의 편찬과 과제 [The Compilation of the complete works of Korean Buddhism and further challenges]. *Han'guk Pulgyohak* 69 (2014): 99–132.

———. "The Uses and Abuses of Wŏnhyo and the 'T'ong Pulgyo' Narrative." *The Journal of Korean Studies* 9, no. 1 (2004): 33–59.

Cho Ki-yong. "Taehan Pulgyo Chogyejong kaehyŏk chongdan ŭi inyŏm chŏngch'esŏng kwa sŭngga kyoyugŭi chŏngyang" 대한불교조계종 개혁종단의 이념 정체성과 승가교육의 정향(定向) [The ideological identity of the reform group within the Korean Chogye Order and the orientation of monastic education]. *Sŏnhak* 50 (2018): 9–40.

Cho Pyŏng-hwal. "Segye sŭngga kyoyuk ŭi ŏje wa onŭl" 세계 승가교육의 어제와 오늘 [The past and present of sangha education in the world]. In *Sŭngga kyoyuk 4,* edited by Taehan Pulgyo Chogyejong Kyoyugwŏn, 264–285. Seoul: Chogyejong Ch'ulp'ansa, 2002.

Cho Sŏng-t'aek (Cho Sungtaek). *Pulgyo wa Pulgyohak: Pulgyo ŭi yŏksajŏk ihae* 불교와 불교학: 불교의 역사적 이해 [Buddhism and Buddhist Studies: The historical understanding of Buddhism]. Seoul: Tolbegae, 2012.

Ch'oe Ho-sŭng. "Chogyejong, naenyŏn pŏpkye pyŏl kyoyuk sibŏm unyŏng" 조계종, 내년 법계별 교육 시범운영 [Model operation for the Chogye Order's next year's education according to rank]. *Pŏppo sinmun*. October 28, 2013. http://www.beopbo.com/news/articleView.html?idxno=77594. Accessed in March 2018.

Ch'oe, Yŏng-ho. *The Civil Examinations and the Social Structure in Early Yi Dynasty Korea: 1392–1600*. Seoul: The Korean Research Center, 1987.

Ch'ŏlun. "Kangwŏn kyoyuk kwa chedo kaesin" 講院教育과 制度改新 [Seminary education and system reform]. *Pulgyo* 93 (1932).

Chŏn Chae-gang. "Sŏnyo haesŏk ŭi oryu wa parŭn haesŏk" 선요 해석의 오류와 바른 해석 [Mistakes and corrections in the Chan Essentials analysis]. In *Sŭngga kyoyuk 7,* edited by Taehan Pulgyo Chogyejong Kyoyugwŏn. Seoul: Chogyejong Ch'ulp'ansa, 2008.

Chŏng Pyŏng-jo. "Han'guk Pulgyo ŭi hyŏnhwang kwa munjejŏm" 한국불교의 현황과 문제점 [The present situation and the problematic issues of Korean Buddhism]. *Pulgyo yŏn'gu* 2 (1986): 195–214.

Chŏng Yŏng-hoe. *Kaehwagi chonggyogye ŭi kyoyuk undong yŏn'gu* 개화기 종교계의 교육운동 연구 [Research of religious educational movements in the modern age]. Seoul: Hyean Press, 1999.

Chongbŏm. "Kangwŏn ŭi kyoyuk ch'egye wa kaesŏn panghyang" 강원의 교육체계와 개선방향 [The educational system and reform objectives of monastic seminaries]. In *Kangwŏn ch'ongnam* 강원총람 [A comprehensive survey of monastic seminaries], edited by Taehan Pulgyo Chogyejong Kyoyugwŏn. Seoul: Chogyejong Ch'ulp'ansa, 1997.

Chŏnggak. *Ch'ŏnsu kyŏng yŏn'gu* 천수경 연구 [A study of the Thousand Hands Sutra]. Seoul: Unjusa, 1996.

Chongmuk. "Ch'ongnim ŭi chindan, naagal panghyang: Haein ch'ongnim chungsim ŭro" 총림의 진단, 나아갈 방향: 해인총림 중심으로 [Diagnosis of the Chan community and objectives for its development: Focusing on the Haeinsa community]. In *Chogyejong ch'ongnim ŭi yŏksa wa munhwa* 조계종 총림의 역사와 문화 [The history and culture of the Chogye Order's Chan communities], edited by Taehan Pulgyo Chogyejong Kyoyugwŏn, 170–246. Seoul: Chogyejong Ch'ulp'ansa, 2009.

——. "Sŭngga taehak (kangwŏn) kyogwa kwajŏng unyŏng e kwanhan sogo" 승가대학(강원) 교과과정 운영에 관한 소고 [Some thoughts on the operation of the curriculums in sangha universities]. Paper presented at the Korean Buddhism Seminar. Haeinsa, 2006.

Chung, Inyoung. "Crossing Over the Gender Boundary in a Gray Robe: The Life of Myoŏm a Korean Buddhist Nun." PhD diss., University of Virginia, 2008.

Cleary, J. C. *Buddha from Korea: The Zen Teachings of T'aego*. Boston: Shambala, 2001.

Cleary, Thomas. *The Flower Ornament Scripture: A Translation of the Avatamsaka Sutra*. Boston: Shambala Publications, 1993.

Cole, Alan. *Mothers and Sons in Chinese Buddhism*. Stanford: Stanford University Press, 1998.

Collins, Samuel. "Who's This Tong-il? English, Culture, and Ambivalence in South Korea." *Changing English* 12, no. 3 (2005): 417–429.

Collins, Steven. "On the Very Idea of the Pāli Canon." *Journal of the Pāli Text Society* 15 (1990): 89–126.

Corporate Body of the Buddha Educational Foundation. *Sangha Talk*. Taiwan: Corporate Body of the Buddha Educational Foundation, 1998.

Denman, Brian, and Sigye Namgyel. "Convergence of Monastic and Modern Education in Bhutan?" *International Review of Education* 54 (2008): 475–491.

Dhammasami, Khammai. "Growing but as a Sideline: An Overview of Modern Shan Monastic Education." *Contemporary Buddhism* 10, no. 1 (2009): 39–49.

——. "Idealism and Pragmatism: A Dilemma in the Current Monastic Education Systems of Burma and Thailand." Paper presented at the Revisiting Buddhism and the spirit cult in Burma [and Thailand] seminar. Stanford University, 2004.

——. "The Impact of Political Instability on the Education of the Saṅgha in 17th Century Siam." *The Journal of the International Association of Buddhist Universities* 1 (2008): 171–200.

Doniger, Wendy. *On Hinduism*. Oxford: Oxford University Press, 2014.

Dreyfus, Georges. *The Sound of Two Hands Clapping: The Education of a Tibetan Buddhist Monk*. Berkeley: University of California Press, 2003.

Epstein, Ronald. "The Shurangama Sutra (T. 945): A Reappraisal of Its Authenticity." Paper presented at the Annual Meeting of the American Oriental Society. Philadelphia, 1976.

Ferrer, Jorge. "The Plurality of Religions and the Spirit of Pluralism: A Participatory

Vision of the Future of Religion." *International Journal of Transpersonal Studies* 28, no. 1 (2009): 139–151.
Ferrer, Jorge, and Jacob Sherman. *The Participatory Turn: Spirituality, Mysticism, Religious Studies*. Albany: SUNY Press, 2008.
Fine, Gary. "Ten Lies of Ethnography: Moral Dilemmas of Field Research." *Journal of Contemporary Ethnography* 22 (1993): 267–294.
Fisher, Gareth. "Fieldwork on East Asian Buddhism: Toward a Person-Centered Approach." *Fieldwork in Religion* 5, no. 2 (2010): 236–250.
——. *From Comrades to Bodhisattvas: Moral Dimensions of Lay Buddhist Practice in Contemporary China*. Honolulu: University of Hawai'i Press, 2014.
Foulk, Griffith. "The Zen Institution in Modern Japan." In *Zen: Tradition and Transition,* edited by Kenneth Kraft. New York: Grove Press, 1988.
Fox, Alan. "Dushun's Huayan Fajie Guan Men (Meditative Approaches to the Huayan Dharmadhatu)." In *Buddhist Philosophy: Essential Readings,* edited by William Edelglass and Jay L. Garfield, 73–83. Oxford: Oxford University Press, 2009.
Freiberger, Oliver. "The Buddhist Canon and the Canon of Buddhist Studies." *Journal of the International Association of Buddhist Studies* 27, no. 2 (2004): 261–283.
Gellner, David N. "Introduction: What Is the Anthropology of Buddhism About?" *Journal of the Anthropological Society of Oxford* 21, no. 2 (1990): 95–112.
Gosling, David. "Visions of Salvation: A Thai Buddhist Experience of Ecumenism." *Modern Asian Studies* 26, no. 1 (1992): 31–47.
Gregory, Peter. *Inquiry Into the Origin of Humanity: An Annotated Translation of Tsung-Mi's Yuan Jen Lun with a Modern Commentary*. Honolulu: University of Hawai'i Press, 1995.
——. "The Platform Sutra as the Sudden Teaching." *In Readings of the Platform Sutra,* edited by Morten Schlütter and Stephen Teiser, 77–108. New York: Columbia University Press, 2012.
——. "Sudden Enlightenment Followed by Gradual Cultivation: Tsung-mi's Analysis of Mind." In *Sudden and Gradual: Approaches to Enlightenment in Chinese Thought,* edited by Peter Gregory, 279–320. Honolulu: University of Hawai'i Press, 1987.
——. *Tsung-mi and the Sinification of Buddhism*. Princeton: Princeton University Press, 1991.
Griffiths, Paul. *Religious Reading: The Place of Reading in the Practice of Religion*. New York: Oxford University Press, 1999.
Groner, Paul. *Ryogen and Mount Hiei: Japanese Tendai in the Tenth Century*. Honolulu: University of Hawai'i Press, 2002.
——. "Training Through Debates in Medieval Tendai and Seizan-ha Temples." *Japanese Journal of Religious Studies* 38, no. 2 (2011): 233–261.
Ha Chŏng-nyong. "Sinpyŏn Sajip ŭi ŭiŭi wa kwaje" 新編 四集의 意義와 課題 [The significance and problems of the new edition of the Sajip]. In *Sŭngga kyoyuk 2,* edited by Taehan Pulgyo Chogyejong Kyoyugwŏn, 351–364. Seoul: Chogyejong Ch'ulpansa, 1998.
Haewŏl. "Kangwŏn kyoyuk, Pulgyo rŭl al su innŭn'ga" 講院教育, 불교를 알 수 있는가 [Is it possible to know Buddhism through the seminary education?]. In *Sŭngga kyoyuk kwa Han'guk Pulgyo* 승가교육과 한국불교 [Sangha education and Korean Buddhism], edited by Kaksan. Taegu: Chŏn'guk kangwŏn yŏnhap Pulgyo haksul taehoe chunbi wiwŏnhoe, 2003.
Hakeda, Yoshito S. *Awakening of Faith—Attributed to Aśvaghoṣa, with commentary by Yoshito S. Hakeda*. New York: Columbia University Press, 1967.
Han Myŏng-u. "Pŏpkye kubun hwijang naenyŏn put'ŏ ch'agyong" 법계구분 휘장 내년 부터 착용 [Using badges to differentiate monastic ranks beginning from next year]. *Hyŏndae Pulgyo*. October 2, 2002. http://www.hyunbulnews.com/news/articleView.html?idxno=121819. Accessed March 2018.

Han, Sangkil, and Matty Wegehaupt, "The Activities and Significance of Temple Fraternities in Late Chosŏn Buddhism." *Journal of Korean Religions* 3, no. 1 (2012): 29–63.

Hanh, Thich Nhat. *Peace in Every Step: The Path of Mindfulness in Everyday Life*. New York: Bantam, 1992.

Hardacre, Helen. "Fieldwork with Japanese Religious Groups." In *Doing Fieldwork in Japan,* edited by Theodore Bestor, Patricia Steinhoff, and Victoria Bestor, 71–88. Honolulu: University of Hawai'i Press, 2003.

Hawley, Samuel. *Inside the Hermit Kingdom: The 1884 Korea Travel Diary of George Clayton Foulk*. London: Lexington Books, 2008.

Hŏ Hŭng-sik. "Koryŏ sidae ŭi sŭnggwa chedo wa kŭ kinŭng" 高麗時代의 僧科制度와 그 機能 [The sangha examinations system and its function in the Koryŏ Dynasty]. *Yŏksa kyuyuk* 19 (1976): 103–138.

——. "Koryŏ ŭi sŭngjik kwa sŭngjŏng" 高麗의 僧職과 僧政 [Monastic offices and monastic governing in the Koryŏ Dynasty]. In *Sŭngga kyoyuk 3,* edited by Taehan Pulgyo Chogyejong Kyoyugwŏn, 167–177. Seoul: Chogyejong Ch'ulpansa, 2000.

Hō Sōkoku. "Kankoku Bukkyō shosi kenkyū" 韓国仏教書誌研究 [Bibliographic study of Korean Buddhism]. PhD diss., Taishō University, 2005.

Hobsbawm, Eric, and Terence Ranger. *The Invention of Tradition*. Cambridge: Cambridge University Press, 1992.

Hori, Victor Sogen. "Zen Koan Capping Phrase Books: Literary Study and the Insight 'Not Founded on words or Letters.'" In *Zen Classics: Formative Texts in the History of Zen Buddhism,* edited by Steven Heine and Dale Wright, 171–214. Oxford: Oxford University Press, 2006.

——. *Zen Sand: The Book of Capping Phrases for Koan Practice*. Honolulu: University of Hawai'i Press, 2003.

Huang, Chi-chiang. "Elite and Clergy in Northern Sung Hang-chou: A Convergence of Interest." In *Buddhism in the Sung,* edited by Peter Gregory and Daniel Getz, 295–339. Honolulu: University of Hawai'i Press, 1999.

Hubbard, Jamie. "Premodern, Modern, and Postmodern: Doctrine and the Study of Japanese Religion." *Japanese Journal of Religious Studies* 19, no. 1 (1992): 3–27.

Hwang Kŭm-yŏn. "Taehye Chonggo sŏnsa ŭi Sŏjang yŏn'gu" 大慧宗杲禪師의 書狀 연구 [Research of Dahui's *Letters*]. PhD diss., Dongguk University, 2010.

Hwarang. "Pŏmŏsa kangwŏn ŭi yŏksa wa munhwa" 범어사 강원의 역사와 문화 [The history and culture of Pŏmŏsa's seminary]. Paper presented at Sŭngga taehak ŭi yŏksa wa munhwa 승가대학의 역사와 문화 [The histories and cultures of sangha universities] seminar. Chogyesa, November 2009.

Hyewŏn. "Hyŏndae Han'guk sŏnwŏn Ch'ŏnggyu ŭi mosŭp kwa naagal pangyang" 현대 한국 선원 청규의 모습과 나아갈 방향 [The shape of modern Korean Chan Halls' Pure Rules and future objectives]. In *Sŭngga kyoyuk 5,* edited by Taehan Pulgyo Chogyejong Kyoyugwŏn, 259–275. Seoul: Chogyejong Ch'ulpansa, 2004.

Hyŏnŭng. "Chogye chongdan sŭngga kyoyuk ŭi tangmyŏn kwaje e tehayŏ" 조계종단 승가 교육의 당면과제에 데하여 [The present problems of the Chogye Order's sangha education]. In *Sŭngga kyoyuk 1,* edited by Taehan Pulgyo Chogyejong Kyoyugwŏn. Seoul: Chogyejong Ch'ulpansa, 1995.

——. "Chonghŏn-chongbŏp kwa sŭngga kyoyuk" 종헌-종법과 승가교육 [The Order's laws and constitution and sangha education]. *Sŏnu toryang* 6 (1994): 110–129.

Ilchin. "Chijŏng t'oron" 지정토론 [Designated discussant]. Paper presented at Chogyejong sŭngga kyoyuk kaesŏn pangan 조계종 승가교육 개선방안 [Development plans of the Chogye Order's monastic education] seminar. Chogyesa, July 2018.

Irvine, Richard. "The Experience of Ethnographic Fieldwork in an English Benedictine Monastery: Or, Not Playing at Being a Monk." *Fieldwork in Religion* 5, no. 2 (2010): 221–235.

Ishii, Yoneo. *Sangha, State, and Society: Thai Buddhism in History*. Honolulu: University of Hawai'i Press, 1986.

Jaffe, Richard. *Neither Monk nor Layman: Clerical Marriage in Modern Japanese Buddhism*. Princeton: Princeton University Press, 2001.

——. *Seeking Sakyamuni: South Asia in the Formation of Modern Japanese Buddhism*. Chicago: University of Chicago Press, 2019.

——. "Seeking Sakyamuni: Travel and the Reconstruction of Japanese Buddhism." *The Journal of Japanese Studies* 30, no. 1 (2004): 65–96.

Jansen, Berthe. "The Disciplinarian (*dge skos/ dge bskos/ chos khrims pa/ zhal ngo*) in Tibetan Monasteries: His Role and His Rules." *Revue d'Etudes Tibetaines* 37 (2016): 145–161.

Jing, Jun. *The Temple of Memories: History, Power, and Morality in a Chinese Village*. Stanford: Stanford University Press, 1996.

Joo, Ryan Bongseok. "Countercurrents from the West: 'Blue-Eyed' Zen Masters, Vipassana Meditation, and Buddhist Psychotherapy in Contemporary Korea." *Journal of the American Academy of Religion* 79, no. 3 (2011): 614–638.

Jorgensen, John. *A Handbook of Korean Zen Practice: A Mirror on the Sŏn School of Buddhism (Sŏn'ga kwigam)*. Honolulu: University of Hawai'i Press, 2015.

——. "Minjung Buddhism: A Buddhist Critique of the Status Quo." In *Makers of Modern Korean Buddhism,* edited by Jin Y. Park, 275–313. Albany: SUNY Press, 2010.

Jory, Patrick. "Thai and Western Buddhist Scholarship in the Age of Colonialism: King Chulalongkorn Redefines the Jatakas." *The Journal of Asian Studies* 61, no. 3 (2002): 891–918.

Kang Ho-sŏn. "Chosŏn chŏn'gi Mongsan hwasang yukto posŏl kanhaeng ŭi paegyŏng kwa ŭimi" 조선전기 몽산화상육도보설 (蒙山和尙六道普說) 간행의 배경과 의미 [The historical background and meaning of the publication of Mengshan heshang liudao pushuo in the early Chosŏn]. *Tongguk sahak* 56 (2014): 93–129.

Kaplan, Uri. "Assembling the Laity: Standardizing Lay Buddhist Affiliation via Education in Contemporary Korea." *The Journal of Korean Studies* 22, no. 1 (2017): 143–176.

——. *Buddhist Apologetics in East Asia: Countering the Neo-Confucian Critiques in the* Hufa lun *and the* Yusŏk chirŭi non. Leiden: Brill, 2019.

——. "From the Tea to the Coffee Ceremony: Modernizing Buddhist Material Culture in Contemporary Korea." *Material Religion* 13, no. 1 (2017): 1–22.

——. "Images of Monasticism: The Temple Stay Program and the Re-branding of Korean Buddhist Temples." *Korean Studies* 34 (2010): 127–146.

——. "The Present-day Korean Confucian Primer: Annotated Translation of the Four-Character Elementary Learning (*Saja sohak,* 四字小學)." *Acta Koreana* 19, no. 2 (2016): 239–253.

——. "Updating the Vinaya: Writing Monastic Laws and Pure Rules in Contemporary Korea." *Contemporary Buddhism* 17, no. 2 (2016): 252–274.

Kim Chi-hyŏn. "Chogyejong kibon kyoyuk kigwan p'yojun kyogwa kwajŏng e taehan yŏn'gu" 조계종 기본교육기관 標準敎科課程에 대한 硏究 [Research regarding the standard curriculum of the Chogye Order's basic education institutions]. *Han'guk Pulgyohak* 65 (2013): 313–340.

Kim Chin-yŏl. *Nŭngŏm kyŏng yŏn'gu immun* 능엄경연구입문 [Introductory research of the *Śūraṃgama Sutra*]. Seoul: Unjusa, 1993.

Kim Chŏng-ja. "Unmunsa haginsŭng ŭi suhaeng mit kyoyuk ch'egye yŏn'gu" 운문사 학인승의 수행 및 교육체계 연구 [Research regarding the educational system and practice of Unmunsa's monastic students]. *Tongbuka munhwa yŏn'gu* 24 (2010): 189–214.

Kim Hun. "Taehan Pulgyo Ch'ŏnt'aejong ŭi chonggyo kyoyuk e taehan koch'al" 대한불교

천태종의 종교교육에 대한 고찰 [A study of religious education in the Ch'ŏnt'ae Order]. *Sinjonggyo yŏn'gu* 24 (2011): 303–325.

Kim, Hwansoo Ilmee. "Buddhism during the Chosŏn Dynasty (1392–1910): A Collective Trauma?" *The Journal of Korean Studies* 22, no. 1 (2017): 101–142.

——. *Empire of the Dharma: Korean and Japanese Buddhism, 1877–1912*. Cambridge, MA: Harvard University Asia Center, 2012.

——. *The Korean Buddhism Empire: A Transnational History (1910–1945)*. Cambridge, MA: Harvard University Asia Center, 2018.

Kim, Jongmyung. "Yi Nŭnghwa, Buddhism, and the Modernization of Korea." In *Makers of Modern Korean Buddhism,* edited by Jin Y. Park, 91–107. Albany: SUNY Press, 2010.

Kim Kwang-sik. "1930 yŏndae Pulgyogye ŭi kangwŏn chedo kaesŏn munje" 1930년대 佛教界의 講院制度 개선문제 [Problems in reforming the Buddhist seminary system in the 1930s]. In *Kŭnhyŏndae Pulgyo ŭi chaejomyŏng* 근현대불교의 재조명 [Re-illuminating modern and contemporary Buddhism], edited by Kwang-sik Kim. Seoul: Minjoksa, 2000.

——. "Hwaŏmsa sŭngga taehak ŭi yŏksa" 화엄사 승가대학의 역사 [The history of Hwaŏmsa's sangha university]. Paper presented at Sŭngga taehak ŭi yŏksa wa munhwa 승가대학의 역사와 문화 [The histories and cultures of sangha universities] seminar. Chogyesa, November 2009.

Kim Kyu-bo. "Chŏngwŏn midal sŭngga taehak, taehagwŏn ŭro chŏnhwan hwallo mosaek" 정원미달 승가대학, 대학원으로 전환 활로 모색 [Looking for ways to transform seminaries that do not meet the minimum student quotas into graduate schools]. *Pŏppo sinmun*. February 7, 2014. http://www.beopbo.com/news/articleView.html?idxno=80507. Accessed March 2018.

Kim Pang-yong. "Kojungse Han'guk sŏnwŏn Ch'ŏnggyu ŭi t'ŭkching kwa ŭiŭi" 고중세 한국 선원 청규의 특징과 의의 [The special features and significance of Pure Rules in Korean Chan halls in ancient times and in the Middle Ages]. In *Sŭngga kyoyuk 5,* edited by Taehan Pulgyo Chogyejong Kyoyugwŏn. Seoul: Chogyejong Ch'ulpansa, 2004.

Kim Pong-jun. "94 yŏn Pulgyo kaehyŏk undong ŭi pansŏngjŏk chŏmgŏm" 94년 불교개혁 운동의 반성적 점검 [A reflective examination of the 1994 Buddhist reform movement]. *Pulgyo p'yŏngnon* 8 (2001): 216–234.

Kim, Seong-uk. "Korean Confucianization of Zen: Ch'oui Uisun's Affirmation of a Confucian Literati Approach to Buddhsim in Late Chosŏn." *Acta Koreana* 19, no. 1 (2016): 217–240.

Kim Suk-hyŏn. "Kobong hwasang Sŏnyo yŏn'gu" 高峰和尙禪要 硏究 [Research on Gaofeng's Chan Essentials]. PhD diss., Dongguk University, 2013.

Kim Sun-sŏk. "1994 yŏn Taehan Pulgyo Chogyejong kaehyŏk chongdan ŭi sŏngnip kwa ŭiŭi" 1994년 대한불교조계종 개혁종단의 성립과 의의 [The establishment and significance of the 1994 reformed Chogye Order]. *Taegak sasang* 20 (2013): 327–359.

Kim, Sung-Eun Thomas. "Buddho-Confucian Rituals, Filial Piety, and Ritual Monks: Sketching the Social-Cultural Dynamics of Later Joseon Buddhism." *The Review of Korean Studies* 17, no. 1 (2014): 189–211.

Kim Wŏn-u. "4 kŭp sŭngga kosi ch'ulche pangyang hwakchŏng" 4급 승가고시 출제방향 확정 [Determining the fourth-level sangha examination questions]. *Hyŏndae Pulgyo*. September 27, 2000. http://www.hyunbulnews.com/news/articleView.html?idxno=179451. Accessed March 2018.

——. "T'aegojong che 10 ch'a pŏpkye kosi" 태고종 제10차 법계고시 [The 10th T'aego Order rank-examinations]. *Hyŏndae Pulgyo*. July 6, 2007. http://www.hyunbulnews.com/news/articleView.html?idxno=246346. Accessed March 2018.

Kim, Yong-tae. *Glocal History of Korean Buddhism*. Seoul: Dongguk University Press, 2015.

Ko Hŭi-suk. "Han'guk Pulgyo kangwŏn samigwa kyoje ŭi sŏjijŏk yŏn'gu" 韓國佛敎 講院 沙彌科 敎材의 書誌的 硏究 [A bibliographic research of the study materials of the novice course in Korean Buddhist seminaries]. *Sŏjihak yŏn'gu* 10 (1994): 883–932.

Ko Pyŏng-ch'ŏl. "Taehan Pulgyo Chogyejong kyoyuk ŭi t'ŭkching kwa chŏnmang" 대한불교조계종 교육의 특징과 전망 [The special characteristics and prospects of the Korean Buddhist Chogye Order's education]. *Chonggyo yŏn'gu* 62 (2011): 201–235.

Ko Yŏng-sŏp. "Haein kangwŏn: Haeinsa sŭngga taehak (1900–2009) ŭi yŏksa wa munhwa" 해인강원-해인사승가대학 (1900–2009) 의역사와 문화 [The history and culture of Haeinsa seminary 1900–2009]. *Pulgyo hakpo* 53 (2009): 77–116.

———. "Pulgyogye ŭi Haein-masan taehak (1946–1967) kyŏngyŏng" 불교계의 해인-마산대학 (1946–1967) 경영 [The operation of the Buddhist Haein-Masan Univesrity between 1946–1967]. *Han'guk sŏnhak* 22 (2009): 387–441.

Kwangmyŏng. "Suhaengmyŏn esŏ pon kangwŏn kyoyuk" 修行面에서 본 講院敎育 [Seminary education from the perspective of practice]. In *Sŭngga kyoyuk kwa Han'guk Pulgyo* 승가교육과 한국불교 [Sangha education and Korean Buddhism], edited by Kaksan. Taegu: Chŏn'guk kangwŏn yŏnhap Pulgyo haksul taehoe chunbi wiwŏnhoe, 2003.

Kwŏn O-min. "Kyohak kwa chongak—hyŏnhaeng Pulgyo kangwŏn ŭi kyogwa kwajŏng e taehae tasi saenggak handa" 교학과 종학—현행 불교강원의 교과과정에 대해 다시 생각한다 [Doctrinal and religious learning—Rethinking the Buddhist seminary currciulum]. Paper presented at the Han'guk Pulgyo hakhoe che 42 hoe ch'un'gye chŏn'guk pulgyo haksul palp'yo taehoee 한국불교학회 제42회 춘계전국불교학술 발표대회 [The 42nd Korean national Buddhist academic conference]. Chogyesa, April 2005.

Kyaw, Pyi Phyo. "Foundations of Criticality: Applications of Traditional Monastic Pedagogy in Myanmar." *Contemporary Buddhism* 16, no. 2 (2015): 401–427.

Kyesŏng. "Chŏn'gyeda hwasang Pŏmnyong sŭnim" 전계다화상 범룡 (梵龍)스님 [An interview with Pŏmnyong sŭnim]. In *Sŭngga kyoyuk 3,* edited by Taehan Pulgyo Chogyejong Kyoyugwŏn, 300–314. Seoul: Chogyejong Ch'ulpansa, 2000.

Lai, Lei Kuan Rongdao. "Praying for the Republic: Buddhist Education, Student-Monks, and Citizenship in Modern China (1911–1949)." PhD diss., McGill University, 2013.

———. "The Wuchang Ideal: Buddhist Education and Identity Production in Republican China." *Studies in Chinese Religions* 3.1 (2017): 55–70.

Lampert, Michael. *Discipline and Debate: The Language of Violence in a Tibetan Buddhist Monastery.* London: University of California Press, 2012.

Lancaster, Lewis, and Sung-bae Park. *The Korean Buddhist Canon: A Descriptive Catalogue.* Berkeley: University of California Press, 1979.

Lee, Byong Won. "A Short History of Pomp'ae: Korean Buddhist Ritual Chant." *Journal of Korean Studies* 1, no. 2 (1971): 109–121.

Lee Jong-su (Yi Chong-su). "Chosŏn hugi Pulgyo illyŏk kwamok ŭi sŏnjŏng kwa kŭ ŭimi" 조선후기 불교 履歷科目의 선정과 그 의미 [The selection of the Buddhist curriculum in late Chosŏn and its significance]. *Han'guksa yŏn'gu* 150 (2010): 115–142.

———. "Monastic Education and Educational Ideology in Late Chosŏn Buddhism." *Journal of Korean Religions* 3, no. 1 (2012): 65–84.

Letts, Dennis. *In Pursuit of Status: The Making of South Korea's "New" Urban Middle Class.* Cambridge, MA: Harvard University Press, 1998.

Levering, Miriam. "Ch'an Enlightenment for the Laymen: Ta-hui and the New Religious Culture of the Sung." PhD diss., Harvard University, 1978.

———. "Dahui Zonggao (1089–1163): The Image Created by His Stories about Himself and by His Teaching Style." In *Zen Masters,* edited by Dale Wright and Steven Heine, 91–116. Oxford: Oxford University Press, 2010.

——. "Dahui Zonggao and Zhang Shangying: The Importance of a Scholar on the Education of a Song Chan Master." *Journal of Song-Yuan Studies* 30 (2000): 115–139.

Levine, Sarah, and David N. Gellner. *Rebuilding Buddhism: The Theravada Movement in Twentieth Century Nepal.* Cambridge, MA: Harvard University Press, 2005.

Long, Darui. "Buddhist Education in Sichuan." *Educational Philosophy and Theory* 34, no. 2 (2002): 185–206.

Lopez, Donald. *Curators of the Buddha: The Study of Buddhism Under Colonialism.* Chicago: University of Chicago Press, 1995.

Madsen, Richard. *Democracy's Dharma: Religious Renaissance and Political Development in Taiwan.* Berkeley: University of California Press, 2007.

Makoto, Hayashi. "Religious Studies and Religiously Affiliated Universities." In *Modern Buddhism in Japan,* edited by Hayashi Makoto, Otani Eiichi, and Paul Swanson, 163–193. Nagoya: Nanzan Institute for Religion and Culture, 2014.

Makransky, John. "The Emergence of Buddhist Critical-Constructive Reflection in the Academy as a Resource for Buddhist Communities and for the Contemporary World." *Journal of Global Buddhism* 9 (2008): 113–153.

Marcus, George. *Ethnography through Thick and Thin.* Princeton: Princeton University Press, 1998.

Marcus, George, and Michael Fischer. *Anthropology as Cultural Critique: An Experimental Moment.* Chicago: University of Chicago Press, 1986.

Marsden, George. "The Soul of the American University: A Historical Overview." In *The Secularization of the Academy,* edited by George Marsden and Bradley Longfield, 9–45. New York: Oxford University Press, 1992.

Masuzawa, Tomoko. *The Invention of World Religions: Or, How European Universalism Was Preserved in the Language of Pluralism.* Chicago: University of Chicago Press, 2005.

Mathews, Bruce. "Buddhism in Extremis: The Case of Cambodia." In *Buddhism and Politics in Twentieth-Century Asia,* edited by Ian Harris, 54–78. London: Continuum, 1999.

McBride, Richard. *Domesticating the Dharma: Buddhist Cults and the Hwaom Synthesis in Silla.* Honolulu: University of Hawai'i Press, 2008.

——. "Watch Yourself! (Jagyeongmun 自警文) By Yaun." In *The Collected Works of Korean Buddhism,* vol. 6, edited by The Chogye Order of Korean Buddhism. Seoul: The Chogye Order of Korean Buddhism, 2012.

McDaniel, Justin Thomas. *Gathering Leaves and Lifting Words: Histories of Buddhist Monastic Education in Laos and Thailand.* Seattle: University of Washington Press, 2008.

McMahan, David. *The Making of Buddhist Modernism.* Oxford: Oxford University Press, 2008.

Meeks, Lori. "Vows for the Masses: Eison and the Popular Expansion of Precept-Conferral Ceremonies in Premodern Japan." *Numen* 56, no. 1 (2009): 1–43.

Mizumura, Minae. *The Fall of Language in the Age of English.* New York: Columbia University Press, 2015.

Mochizuki Kaie. "Gendai Chūgoku niokeru Bukkyō kyōiku kikan no chōsa hōkoku" 現代中国における仏教教育機関の調査報告 [Survey report of Buddhist educational facilities in contemporary China]. *Minobusan daigaku tōyō bunka kenkyūjo hō* 11 (2007): 41–54.

Mohan, Pankaj. "The Roles of Monks Won'gwang and Chajang in the Formation of Early Silla Buddhism." In *Religions of Korea in Practice,* edited by Robert Buswell, 51–64. Princeton: Princeton University Press, 2008.

Mubi. "4 kŭp sŭngga kosi ŭi hyŏnhwang kwa palchŏn panghyang" 4급 승가고시의 형황과 발전 방향 [The current situation and possible development of the fourth-level sangha examinations]. In 4 kŭp sŭngga kosi chedo kaesŏn ŭl wihan t'oronhoe Charyojip 4급 승가고시 제도 개선을 위한 토론회 자료집 [Collection of materials

regarding the debates on reforming the fourth-level sangha examination system]. Unpublished report, 2000.
Mueller, Mark, Won-yoong Sunim, and Mujin Sunim. *Mirror of Zen: A Korean Buddhist Classic by Sŏsan*. Seoul: Propagation Ministry of the Korean Buddhist Chogye Order, 1995.
Mugwan. "Chibang sŭngga taehak kyoyuk chedo palchŏn kwaje wa panghyang" 지방 승가대학 교육제도 발전과제와 방향 [The development and the objectives of the education system at regional sangha universities]. In *Sŭngga kyoyuk 1,* edited by Taehan Pulgyo Chogyejong Kyoyugwŏn. Seoul: Chogyejong Ch'ulpansa, 1995.
Muller, Charles. "Awaken Your Mind and Practice (Balsim suhaeng jang) 發心修行章." In *The Collected Works of Korean Buddhism,* vol. 1, edited by Charles Muller. Seoul: The Chogye Order of Korean Buddhism, 2012.
———. "A Korean Contribution to the Zen Canon: The Oga Hae Seorui (Commentaries of Five Masters on the Diamond Sutra)." In *Zen Classics: Formative Texts in the History of Zen Buddhism,* edited by Dale Wright and Steven Heine, 43–64. Oxford: Oxford University Press, 2006.
———. *The Sutra of Perfect Enlightenment: Korean Buddhism's Guide to Meditation*. Albany: SUNY Press, 1999.
Mun, Chanju. "Kim Ilta's (1929–99) Systemization of the Current Jogye Order's Orthopraxy." *Taegak Sasang* 18 (2012).
———. *Purification Buddhist Movement 1954–1970: The Struggle to Restore Celibacy in the Jogye Order of Korean Buddhism*. South Carolina: Blue Pine Books, 2011.
Munhwa Ch'eyuk Kwan'gwangbu [Ministry of Culture, Sports, and Tourism]. *Han'guk ŭi chonggyo hyŏnhwang* 한국의 종교현황 [The present situation of religions in Korea]. Seoul: Munhwa Ch'eyuk Kwan'gwangbu, 2012.
Myŏngbŏp. "Suhaengja paech'ul esŏ kangwŏn ŭi silsang kwa kaesŏnjŏm" 수행자 배출에서 강원의 실상과 개선점 [The actual state of seminaries and reform ideas from the perspective of nurturing practitioners]. In *Sŭngga kyoyuk 2,* edited by Taehan Pulgyo Chogyejong Kyoyugwŏn. Seoul: Chogyejong Ch'ulpansa, 1998.
Nam, Hee-sook, and Inga Diederich. "Publications of Buddhist Literary Texts: The Publication and Popularization of Mantra Collections and Buddhist Ritual Texts in the Late Chosŏn Dynasty." *Journal of Korean Religions* 3, no. 1 (2012): 9–27.
Nam, Jung Mi. "The Changing Role of English in Korea: From English as a Tool for Advancement to English for Survival." *Pan-Pacific Association of Applied Linguistics* 9, no. 2 (2005): 227–240.
Nam To-yŏng. "Ch'ŏnt'ong munhwa wa kyoyuk: Sach'al kyoyuk ŭl chungsimŭro" 전통문화와 교육: 사찰교육을 중심으로 [Traditional culture and education: Focusing on monastic education]. *Kyoyuk nonch'ong* 10 (1990): 534–545.
———. "Han'guk Pulgyo chŏnsŏ rŭl chungsimŭro pon Chosŏn sidae sawŏn kyoyuk" 한국불교전서를 중심으로 본 조선시대 사원교육 [Temple education in the Chosŏn period seen through the Complete Works of Korean Buddhism]. In *Kangwŏn ch'ongnam* 강원총람 [A comprehensive survey of seminaries], edited by Taehan Pulgyo Chogyejong Kyoyugwŏn, 738–761. Seoul: Chogyejong Ch'ulpansa, 1997.
———. "Han'guk sach'al kyoyuk chedo" 韓國寺院 教育制度 [The education system of Korean monasteries]. *Yŏksa kyoyuk* 28 (1980): 25–66.
Nathan, Mark Andrew. "Buddhist Propagation and Modernization: The Significance of P'ogyo in Twentieth-Century Korean Buddhism." PhD diss., UCLA, 2010.
———. *From the Mountains to the Cities: A History of Buddhist Propagation in Modern Korea*. Honolulu: University of Hawai'i Press, 2018.
Nelson, John. *Experimental Buddhism: Innovation and Activism in Contemporary Japan*. Honolulu: University of Hawai'i Press, 2013.
Nguyen, Minh Thi. "Buddhist Monastic Education and Regional Revival Movements in Early Twentieth Century Vietnam." PhD diss., University of Wisconsin–Madison, 2007.

Nicoloff, Philip. *Sacred Kōyasan: A Pilgrimage to the Mountain Temple of Saint Kobo Daishi and the Great Sun Buddha*. Albany: SUNY Press, 2008.

Nithiyanandam, V. *Buddhist System of Education*. Delhi: Global Vision Publishing House, 2004.

Nonomura, Kaoru. *Eat Sleep Sit*. New York: Kodashana International, 1996.

Nŭnghŏ. "Sŏnjisik ŭl ch'ajasŏ ch'odae kyoyukwŏnjang Wŏnsan sŭnim" 선지식을 찾아서 초대교육원장 원산스님 [Finding a Dharma friend in the first head of the education department, Rev. Wŏnsan]. In *Sŭngga kyoyuk 4,* edited by Taehan Pulgyo Chogyejong Kyoyugwŏn, 395–413. Seoul: Chogyejong Ch'ulpansa, 2002.

Ŏ Hyŏn-gyŏng. "Kosiwiwŏnhoe, 1kŭp sŭngga kosi sihaeng...51myŏng ŭngsi" 고시위원회, 1급 승가고시 시행...51명 응시 [51 people sat for the first-level examinations administered by the examination committee]. *Pulgyo sinmun*. April 11, 2016. http://www.ibulgyo.com/news/articleView.html?idxno=148063. Accessed March 2018.

——. "Sinnyŏn hoegyŏn ŭro pon 2014 sŭngga kyoyuk pangyang" 신년회견으로 본 2014 승가교육 방향 [New Years' conference on the prospects of sangha education in 2014]. *Pulgyo sinmun*. January 27, 2014. http://www.ibulgyo.com/news/articleView.html?idxno=131396. Accessed March 2018.

O Yong-sŏp. "Hyesun i kanhaengan Yongboksa Pulsŏ" 혜순이 간행한 용복사 불서 [The Buddhist texts published by Hyesun in Yongboksa]. *Sŏjihak yŏn'gu* 63 (2015): 119–148.

Onoda Shunzō. "Meiji jidai no Bukkyō sō ga suishin shita Bukkyō kyōiku seido no kaikaku" 明治時代の仏教僧が推進した仏教教育制度の改革 [Reforms in the Buddhist education system advanced by Buddhist monks during the Meiji period]. *Hotoke kyō daigaku shūkyō bunka myūjiamu kenkyū kiyō* 12 (2016): 1–8.

Pak Il-sŭng. "Sŭngga ŭi taehak kyoyungnon" 僧伽의 大學教育論 [Educational theory for monastic higher education]. *Sŏngnim* 9 (1975): 339–349.

Pak Kyŏng-hun. "Kŭndae Pulgyo ŭi sŭngjik chedo" 근대불교의 僧職제도 [The monastic bureaucratic system in modern Buddhism]. In *Sŭngga kyoyuk 3,* edited by Taehan Pulgyo Chogyejong Kyoyugwŏn, 201–213. Seoul: Chogyejong Ch'ulpansa, 2000.

Pak Sang-guk. *Chŏn'guk sach'al sojang mokp'an chip* 全國寺刹所藏木板集 [Collection of the entire country's temple woodblock possessions]. Seoul: Munhwajae kwalliguk, 1987.

Pak Sŏng-bae. "Sŏngch'ŏl sŭnim ŭi tono chŏmsusŏl pip'an e taehayŏ" 성철스님의 돈오점수설 비판에 대하여 [On Rev. Sŏngch'ŏl's critique of the sudden awakening followed by gradual cultivation theory]. In *Kkaedarŭm, tono chŏmsu inga tono tonsu inga* 깨달음, 돈오점수인가 돈오돈수인가 [Enlightenment: Sudden awakening followed by gradual cultivation or sudden awakening and sudden cultivation], edited by Kang Kŏn-gi and Kim Ho-sŏng. Seoul: Minjoksa, 1992.

Paramore, Kiri. *Japanese Confucianism: A Cultural History*. Cambridge: Cambridge University Press, 2016.

Park, Jin-kyu. "English Fever in South Korea: Its History and Symptoms." *English Today* 25, no. 1 (2009): 50–57.

Park, Pori. "The Establishment of Buddhist Nunneries in Contemporary Korea." In *Korean Buddhist Nuns and Laywomen: Hidden Histories, Enduring Vitality,* edited by Eun-su Cho, 165–181. Albany: SUNY Press, 2011.

——. "Korean Buddhist Reforms and Problems in the Adoption of Modernity during the Colonial Period." *Korea Journal* 45, no. 1 (2005): 87–113.

——. *Trial and Error in Modernist Reforms: Korean Buddhism under Colonial Rule*. Berkeley: Institute of East Asian Studies, 2009.

Pine, Red. *The Lankavatara Sutra: A Zen Text*. Berkeley: Counterpoint, 2012.

——. *The Zen Teaching of Bodhidharma*. Washington: Empty Bowl, 1987.

Pittman, Don Alvin. *Toward a Modern Chinese Buddhism: Taixu's Reforms*. Honolulu: University of Hawai'i Press, 2001.

Pŏbin. "Sŭngga kyoyuk, sahoi wa sot'ong hago yŏksa e puhap haeya" 승가교육, 사회와 소통하고 역사에 부합해야 [Sangha education should correspond with society and conform with history]. *Pulgyo p'yŏngnon* 12, no. 1 (2010): 274–292.

Poceski, Mario. "Guishan Jingce and the Ethical Foundations of Chan Practice." In *Zen Classics: Formative Texts in Zen Buddhism,* edited by Steven Heine and Dale Wright, 15–42. New York: Oxford University Press, 2006.

Pogwang. "Taehan Pulgyo Chogyejong ŭi ch'ulgaja hyŏnhwang kwa ch'ulga chedo ŭi kaesŏn pangan" 대한불교조계종의 출가자 현황과 출가 제도의 개선방안 [The present situation of the home-leavers of the Korean Buddhist Chogye Order and plans for improving the system of leaving home]. *Taegak sasang* 17 (2012): 209–243.

Pon'gak. "4 kŭp sŭngga kosi chedo ŭi kaesŏn ŭl wihan chean" 4급 승가고시 제도의 개선을 위한 제안 [Proposals for reforming the fourth-level sangha examination system]. In *4 kŭp sŭngga kosi chedo kaesŏn ŭl wihan t'oronhoe charyojip* 4급 승가고시 제도 개선을 위한 토론회 자료집 [Collection of materials regarding the debates on reforming the fourth-level sangha examination system]. Unpublished report, 2000.

Pŏpchang. "Kangwŏn kyogwa kwajŏng chŏnban e taehan munjejŏm mit kaesŏnan" 강원교과과정 전반에 대한 문제점 및 개선안 [Problems in the entire seminary curriculum and reform plans]. In Kangwŏn kyogwa t'ongil mit kaesŏn ŭl wihan kyoyuk kwagyecha yŏnch'anhoi 강원 교과통일 및 개선을 위한 교육관계자 연찬회 [Workshop for educators regarding the unification and reform of seminary courses]. Unpublished report, 2000.

——. "T'ongil toen haengja kyoyugŭi chedo hwangnip pangyang" 통일된 행자교육의 제도 확립 방향 [Establishing a unified postulant education system]. *Sŏnu toryang* 2 (1992): 318–338.

Pŏpchŏng. "Haengja kyoyuk ŏttŏk'e hal kŏdin'ga" 행자교육 어떻게 할 것인가 [How should we conduct postulant education?]. *Sŏnu toryang* 2 (1992): 274–276.

Pŏpsan. "Han'guk Pulgyo sŭngga-pŏpkye chedo ŭi koch'al kwa chongdan sŭngga kosi chedo ŭi sihaeng" 한국불교 승과-법계제도의 고찰과 종단 승가고시제도의 시행 [Consideration of the Korean Buddhist sangha rank system and operation of the Order's sangha examination system]. In *Sŭngga kyoyuk 2,* edited by Taehan Pulgyo Chogyejong Kyoyugwŏn, 205–233. Seoul: Chogyejong Ch'ulpansa, 2002.

——. "T'ŭksu hakkyo kaesŏl kwa kwalli unyŏng e taehayŏ" 특수학교 개설과 관리운영에 대하여 [On establishing and managing specialized schools]. In *Sŭngga kyoyuk 1,* edited by Taehan Pulgyo Chogyejong Kyoyugwŏn. Seoul: Chogyejong Ch'ulpansa, 1995.

Pŏpsŏng. "Sŭngga kibon kyoyuk ŭi ch'egyehwa rŭl wihayŏ" 승가 기본교육의 체계화를 위하여 [On the systematization of basic sangha education]. In *Sŭngga kyoyuk 1,* edited by Taehan Pulgyo Chogyejong Kyoyugwŏn. Seoul: Chogyejong Ch'ulpansa, 1995.

Pullim. "Ch'ŏnamsa sŭngga taehak ŭi pyŏnch'ŏnsa mit apŭro ŭi palchŏn panghyang" 천암사승가대학의 변천사 및 앞으로의 발전 방향 [The history of the changes and the future developmental objectives of Ch'ŏnamsa's sangha university]. In *Piguni sŭngga taehak ŭi yŏksa wa munhwa* 비구니 승가대학의 역사와 문화 [The history and culture of nun seminaries], edited by Taehan Pulgyo Chogyejong Kyoyugwŏn, 137–204. Seoul: Chogyejong Ch'ulpansa, 2009.

Reader, Ian. "Buddhism and the Perils of Advocacy." *Journal of Global Buddhism* 9 (2008): 83–112.

Rowe, Mark, and Hiroki Kikuchi. "Round-Table Discussion: The Current State of Sectarian Universities." *Japanese Journal of Religious Studies* 31, no. 2 (2004): 429–464.

Samuels, Jeffrey. "Toward an Action-Oriented Pedagogy: Buddhist Texts and Monastic Education in Contemporary Sri Lanka." *Journal of the American Academy of Religion* 72, no. 4 (2004): 955–971.

Sangjŏng. "Kangwŏn, kwayŏn kibon kyoyuk in'ga" 강원, 과연 기본교육인가 [Do seminaries constitute basic education after all?]. In *Sŭngga kyoyuk kwa Han'guk Pulgyo* 승가교육과 한국불교 [Sangha education and Korean Buddhism], edited by Kaksan. Daegu: Chŏn'guk kangwŏn yŏnhap Pulgyo haksul taehoe chunbi wiwŏnhoe, 2003.

Sasaki, Ruth Fuller. *The Record of Linji.* Honolulu: University of Hawai'i Press, 2009.

Schedneck, Brooke. "Religious Encounters in Thailand: The Integration of Foreign Monks into Thai Monastic Life." Paper presented at the Conference of the Association of Asian Studies, The University of Colorado. September 2008.

Schickentanz, Eric. "Wang Hongyuan and the Import of Japanese Esoteric Buddhism to China during the Republican Period." In *Buddhism across Asia: Networks of Material, Intellectual and Cultural Exchange,* edited by Tansen Sen, 403–427. Singapore: Institute of Southeast Asian Studies, 2014.

Schlütter, Morten. *How Zen Became Zen: The Dispute over Enlightenment and the Formation of Chan Buddhism in Song-Dynasty China.* Honolulu: University of Hawai'i Press, 2008.

Senécal, Bernard. "A Critical Reflection on the Chogye Order's Campaign for the Worldwide Propagation of Kanhwa Sŏn 看話禪." *Journal of Korean Religions* 2, no. 1 (2011): 75–105.

Seth, Michael. *Education Fever: Society, Politics, and the Pursuit of Schooling in South Korea.* Honolulu: University of Hawai'i Press, 2002.

Sharf, Robert. "The Scripture in Forty-two Sections." In *Religions of China in Practice,* edited by Donald Lopez, 360–371. Princeton: Princeton University Press, 1996.

Shiina Kōyū. "Shimon keikun no bunken shi teki kōsatsu" 『緇門警訓』の文献史的考察 [A study of the textual history of the Admonitions to the Gray-Robed Monks]. *Indogaku Bukkyōgaku kenkyū* 59, no. 2 (2011): 623–630.

Shim, Jae-ryong. *Korean Buddhism: Tradition and Transformation.* Seoul: Jimoondang International, 1999.

Shin, Gi-Wook. *Ethnic Nationalism in Korea: Genealogy, Politics, and Legacy.* Stanford: Stanford University Press, 2006.

Shore, Jeff. *Great Doubt: Practicing Zen in the World.* Boston: Wisdom Publications, 2016.

Sin Hoe-jŏng. "Ch'imun kyŏnghunju ŭi kyoyukchŏk kach'i e kwanhan yŏn'gu" 緇門警訓註의 교육적 가치에 관한 연구 [Research on the educational value of the Commentary to the Admonitions to the Gray-Robed Monks]. MA thesis, Dongguk University, 2007.

Sin Sŏng-min. "Chogyejong ch'ongmuwŏnjang sŏngŏ indan hwaktae toena" 조계종 총무원장 선거인단 확대되나 [Can we expand the number of voters in the elections for the head of the Chogye Order's main office?]. *Hyŏndae Pulgyo.* May 23, 2014. http://www.hyunbulnews.com/news/articleView.html?idxno=279631. Accessed March 2018.

———. "Chogyejong, naenyŏn ch'ŏt 1kŭp sŭngga kosi silsi" 조계종, 내년 첫 1급 승가고시 실시 [The Chogye Order to implement the first first-level sangha examinations next year]. *Hyŏndae Pulgyo.* December 19, 2014. http://www.hyunbulnews.com/news/articleView.html?idxno=282019. Accessed March 2018.

Singh, Nisha. *The Origin and Development of Buddhist Monastic Education in India.* Delhi: Indo-Asian Publication House, 1997.

Smith, Christian. "Secularising American Higher Education: The Case Study of Early American Sociology." In *The Secular Revolution: Power, Interests, and Conflict in the Secularization of American Public Life,* edited by Christian Smith, 97–159. Berkeley: University of California Press, 2003.

Smith, J. Z. "Canons, Catalogues, and Classics." In *Canonization and Decanonization: Papers Presented to the International Conference of the Leiden Institute for the Study of Religions,* edited by Arie van der Kooij and Karel van der Toorn, 295–311. Leiden: Brill, 1998.

Son Sŏng-p'il. "16–17 segi Pulgyo chŏngch'aek kwa Pulgyogye ŭi tonghyang" 16-17세기 불교정책과 불교계의 동향 [Buddhist policies and tendencies in the sixteenth and seventeenth centuries]. PhD diss., Dongguk University, 2013.

——. "16 segi chŏnban Pulgyogye ŭi silt'ae: Chŏllado chiyŏk ŭl chungsim ŭro" 16세기 전반 불교계의 실태: 전라도 지역을 중심으로 [The real situation of Buddhism in the early sixteenth century: Focusing on the Cholla Province]. *Chosŏn sidae sa hakpo* 77 (2016): 125–172.

——. "16 segi Chosŏn ŭi Pulsŏ kanhaeng" 16世紀朝鮮의 佛書刊行 [Buddhist text printing in sixteenth-century Chosŏn]. MA thesis, Dongguk University, 2007.

Sŏngbon. "Kibon kyoyuk kigwan kongt'ong kyogwamok sŏnjŏng kwa sŭngga kyoyuk ŭi munjejŏm" 기본교육기관 공통교과목 선정과 승가교육의 문제점 [Selection of unified curriculums for basic education facilities and the problems with sangha education]. In *Sŭngga kyoyuk 7,* edited by Taehan Pulgyo Chogyejong Kyoyugwŏn. Seoul: Chogyejong Ch'ulpansa, 2008.

Sŏran. "Han'guk Pulgyo sŭngga kyoyuk ŭi palchŏn panghyang e taehan yŏn'gu" 한국불교 승가교육의 발전방향에 대한 연구 [Research on the development of Korean Buddhist sangha education]. In *Sŭngga kyoyuk 1,* edited by Taehan Pulgyo Chogyejong Kyoyugwŏn. Seoul: Chogyejong Ch'ulpansa, 1995.

Starling, Jessica. "Family Temples and Religious Learning in Contemporary Japanese Buddhism." *Lewis & Clark College Journal of Global Buddhism* 16 (2015): 144–156.

Sueki Fumihiko. "Gendai Chūgoku Bukkyō no kenkyū" 現代中国仏教の研究 [Research of contemporary Chinese Buddhism]. *Tōyō bunka kenkyūjo kiyō* 119 (1992): 273–352.

Sugyŏng. "Samsŏn kangwŏn ŭi paltalsa" 삼선강원의 발달사 [The history of the development of Samsŏn Buddhist College]. In *Piguni sŭngga taehak ŭi yŏksa wa munhwa* 비구니 승가대학의 역사와 문화 [The history and culture of nun seminaries], edited by Taehan Pulgyo Chogyejong Kyoyugwŏn, 205–283. Seoul: Chogyejong Ch'ulpansa, 2009.

Sujŏng. "Tonghaksa sŭngga taehak ŭi yŏksa wa hyŏnhwang" 동학사승가대학의 역사와 현황 [The history and present situation of Tonghaksa's sangha university]. In *Piguni sŭngga taehak ŭi yŏksa wa munhwa* 비구니 승가대학의 역사와 문화 [The history and culture of nun seminaries], edited by Taehan Pulgyo Chogyejong Kyoyugwŏn, 53–82. Seoul: Chogyejong Ch'ulpansa, 2009.

T'aegyŏng. "Chongdan sŭngga chŏnmun illyŏk yuksŏng mit hwaryong pangan e taehayŏ" 종단 승가 전문인력 육성 및 활용 방안에 대하여 [On nurturing and utilizing monastic specialists in the Order]. In *Sŭngga kyoyuk 5,* edited by Taehan Pulgyo Chogyejong Kyoyugwŏn, 299–320. Seoul: Chogyejong Ch'ulpansa, 2004.

Taehan Pulgyo Chogyejong [The Korean Chogye Order]. *Ch'ulgaja, irŏk'e madihago indohamnida* 출가자, 이렇게 맞이하고 인도합니다 [Home-Leavers, this is how we receive and guide them]. Seoul: Chogyejong Ch'ulpansa, 2014.

——. "Pon-malsa chuji yŏnsu sŏlmun chosa pogosŏ" 본-말사 주지연수 설문조사 보고서 [Report of the survey among abbots of main and branch temples regarding continuing education]. In *Sŭngga kyoyuk 3,* edited by Taehan Pulgyo Chogyejong Kyoyugwŏn, 93–140. Seoul: Chogyejong Ch'ulpansa, 2000.

——. "Pŏpkye pŏp" 법계법 [Sangha rank law]. 1976.

——. *Sinp'yŏn ch'imun* 新編緇門 [New edition to the Admonitions to the Gray-Robed Monks]. Seoul: Chogyejong Ch'ulpansa, 2008.

Taehan Pulgyo Chogyejong Kyoyugwŏn [The Chogye Order Education Department]. *4 kŭp sŭngga kosi yesang munjejip* 4급 승가고시 예상문제집 [Prospective questions for the fourth-level sangha examinations]. Seoul: Chogyejong Ch'ulpansa, 2001, 2003, 2006.

———. *5 kŭp sŭngga kosi yesijip* 5급 승가고시 예시집 [Collection of preparation questions for the fifth-level sangha examinations]. Seoul: Chogyejong Ch'ulpansa, 2006.

———. "2000, 2001 yŏndo Kyoyugwŏn saŏp hyŏnhwang mit kwaje" 2000, 2001년도 교육원 사업현황 및 과제 [The tasks and current activities of the Education Department in 2000, 2001]. In *Sŭngga kyoyuk 4,* edited by Taehan Pulgyo Chogyejong Kyoyugwŏn. Seoul: Chogyejong Ch'ulpansa, 2002.

———. "2002–3 yŏn sŭngga kyoyuk hyŏnhwang" 2002–3년 승가교육 현황 [The state of sangha education in 2002–3]. In *Sŭngga kyoyuk 5,* edited by Taehan Pulgyo Chogyejong Kyoyugwŏn. Seoul: Chogyejong Ch'ulpansa, 2004.

———. "2002–3 yŏn sŭngga kyoyuk ŭi chindan kwa kwaje" 2002–3년 승가교육의 진단과 과제 [Diagnosis and problems in sangha education, 2002–3]. In *Sŭngga kyoyuk 5,* edited by Taehan Pulgyo Chogyejong Kyoyugwŏn, 21–40. Seoul: Chogyejong Ch'ulpansa, 2004.

———. "2014 yŏn 3 kŭp sŭngga kosi tandaphyŏng munjejip" 2014년 『3급 승가고시』 단답형 문제집 [Collection of short-answer questions for the 2014 third-level sangha examinations]. http://www.buddhism.or.kr/index.html. Accessed March 2018.

———. "2014 yŏndo sŭngga taehak p'yojun kyoyuk kwajŏng annae" 2014년도 승가대학 표준교육과정안내 [The 2014 information regarding the standard educational curriculum of sangha universities]. Unpublished report, 2014.

———. *Buddhist English,* vols. 1, 2. Seoul: Chogyejong Ch'ulpansa, 2012.

———. "Che 34 ki haengja kyoyuk kyehoeksŏ" 제34기 행자교육계획서 [Plan for the 34th postulant education program]. Unpublished report, 2008.

———. "Chigwan sŭnim int'ŏbyu" 지관 스님 인터뷰 [An interview with Venerable Chigwan]. In *Sŭngga kyoyuk 6,* edited by Taehan Pulgyo Chogyejong Kyoyugwŏn, 353–386. Seoul: Chogyejong Ch'ulpansa, 2006.

———. *Ch'ogi Pulgyo: kangŭi kyehoegan 1* 초기불교: 강의계획안 1 [Syllabi 1 for early Buddhism]. Seoul: Chogyejong Ch'ulpansa, 2012.

———. "Ch'ogi Pulgyo kyosupŏp yŏnch'anhoe" 초기불교 교수법 연찬회 [Workshop regarding the teaching of early Buddhism]. Unpublished report, 2012.

———. "Chogyejong sŭngga kyoyuk hyŏnhwang" 조계종 승가교육 현황 [The present situation of the Chogye Order's sangha education]. In *Sŭngga kyoyuk 2,* edited by Taehan Pulgyo Chogyejong Kyoyugwŏn. Seoul: Chogyejong Ch'ulpansa, 1998.

———. *Chogyejongsa: kŭnhyŏndae p'yŏn* 曹溪宗史: 근현대편 [The history of the Chogye Order: Modern and contemporary]. Seoul: Chogyejong Ch'ulpansa, 2007.

———. "Chongdan sat'ae ŭi kyohun kwa sŭngga ŭi kwaje" 종단사태의 교훈과 승가의 과제 [The lesson from the Order's incident and the task of the sangha]. In *Sŭngga kyoyuk 3,* edited by Taehan Pulgyo Chogyejong Kyoyugwŏn. Seoul: Chogyejong Ch'ulpansa, 2000.

———. *Educational Retreat of Basic Seminary for Foreign National Suhnims.* Seoul: Chogyejong Ch'ulpansa, 2002.

———. *Haengja kyobon* 행자교본 [Postulant textbook]. Seoul: Chogyejong Ch'ulpansa, 1995.

———. *Hanmun Pulchŏn: kangŭi kyehoegan 4* 한문불전: 강의계획안 4 [Syllabi 4 for Classical Chinese Buddhist texts]. Seoul: Chogyejong Ch'ulpansa, 2012.

———. "Irhwan sŭnim int'ŏbyu" 일환 스님 인터뷰 [Interview with Rev. Irhwan]. In *Sŭngga kyoyuk 6,* edited by Taehan Pulgyo Chogyejong Kyoyugwŏn, 389–440. Seoul: Chogyejong Ch'ulpansa, 2006.

———. "Kangwŏn kyogwa kwajŏng t'ongil mit kaesŏn ŭl wihan sŏlmun chosa punsŏk kyŏlgwa" 강원 교과과정 통일 및 개선을 위한 설문조사 분석결과 [Analysis of the results of the surveys regarding seminary curriculum unification and reform]. In Kangwŏn kyogwa t'ongil mit kaesŏn ŭl wihan kyoyuk kwan'gyeja yŏnch'anhoe 강

원 교과통일 및 개선을 위한 교육관계자 연찬회 [Educators' seminar on seminary curriculum unification and reform]. Unpublished report, 2000.
——. "Kangwŏn kyogwa kwajŏng t'ongil mit kaesŏn ŭl wihan sŏlmun chosa punsŏk pogosŏ" 강원교과과정 통일 및 개선을 위한 설문조사 분석보고서 [Analysis report of the survey regarding the unification and reform of the seminary curriculums]. In *Sŭngga kyoyuk 4,* edited by Taehan Pulgyo Chogyejong Kyoyugwŏn, 33–55. Seoul: Chogyejong Ch'ulpansa, 2002.
——. *Kyeyul kwa Pulgyo yulli: kangŭi kyehoegan 7* 계율과 불교윤리: 강의계획안 7 [Syllabi 7 for Vinaya and Buddhist ethics]. Seoul: Chogyejong Ch'ulpansa, 2012.
——. "Kyoyugwŏn 10 yŏn ŭi saŏp pogo mit ch'omgp'yŏng" 교육원 10년의 사업보고 및 총평 [Operation report and general review of the Education Department's activities in the past ten years]. In *Sŭngga kyoyuk 6,* edited by Taehan Pulgyo Chogyejong Kyoyugwŏn. Seoul: Chogyejong Ch'ulpansa, 2006.
——. "Kyoyuk kyoyŏkcha kyosubŏp yŏnch'anhoe" 교육교역자 교수법 연찬회 [Seminar on teaching methods for educators]. Unpublished report, 2012.
——. "Pon-malsa chuji yŏnsu sŏlmun chosa pogosŏ" 본-말사 주지연수 설문조사 보고서 [Report on the survey regarding continuing education among the abbots of main and branch monasteries]. In *Sŭngga kyoyuk 3,* edited by Taehan Pulgyo Chogyejong Kyoyugwŏn. Seoul: Chogyejong Ch'ulpansa, 2000.
——. *Pulgyosa: kangŭi kyehoegan 6* 불교사: 강의계획안 6 [Syllabi 6 for Buddhist history]. Seoul: Chogyejong Ch'ulpansa, 2012.
——. *Sŏn Pulgyo: kangŭi kyehoegan 3* 선불교: 강의계획안 3 [Syllabi 3 for Chan Buddhism]. Seoul: Chogyejong Ch'ulpansa, 2012.
——. *Sŏnwŏn Ch'ongnam* 선원 총람 [A comprehensive survey of Chan Halls]. Seoul: Chogyejong Ch'ulpansa, 2000.
——. "Sŭngga chaegyoyuk kyebal kŏmt'osŏ" 승가 재교육 계발 검토서 [Examination of the development of continuing education for the sangha]. In *Sŭngga kyoyuk 4,* edited by Taehan Pulgyo Chogyejong Kyoyugwŏn, 191–202. Seoul: Chogyejong Ch'ulpansa, 2002.
——. *Sŭngga kibon kyoyuk kigwan kyogwa kwajŏng mit kyogwamok kaep'yŏnan maryŏn ŭl wihan kongch'ŏngoe* 승가 기본교육기관 교과과정 및 교과목 개편안 마련을 위한 공청회 [Public hearing regarding reform plans for the curriculums in the sangha's basic educational facilities]. Seoul: Chogyejong Ch'ulpansa, 2010.
——. *Sŭngga kibon kyoyuk kigwan mit chŏnmun kyoyuk kigwan chojŏngan maryŏn ŭl wihan kongch'ŏngoe* 승가 기본교육기관 및 전문교육기관 조정안 마련을 위한 공청회 [Public hearing regarding regulation plans for basic and specialist educational facilities for the sangha]. Seoul: Chogyejong Ch'ulpansa, 2010.
——. "Sŭngga kyoyuk chedo kaesŏn ch'ujin wiwŏnhoe hwaltong kyŏnggwa" 승가교육제도개선 추진위원회 활동 경과 [Progress report of the activity of the committee for the promotion of systematic reforms in sangha education]. In *Sŭngga kyoyuk 6,* edited by Taehan Pulgyo Chogyejong Kyoyugwŏn. Seoul: Chogyejong Ch'ulpansa, 2006.
——. "Sŭngga kyoyuk kwajong mit kyoyuk kigwan annae" 승가교육 과정 및 교육기관 안내 [Information on the curriculum and educational institutions of the sangha]. Unpublished report, 2009.
——. "Sŭngga kyoyuk ŭi sŏnggwa wa chŏnmang" 승가교육의 성과와 전망 [The outcome and prospects of sangha education]. In *Sŭngga kyoyuk 4,* edited by Taehan Pulgyo Chogyejong Kyoyugwŏn, 236–261. Seoul: Chogyejong Ch'ulpansa, 2002.
——. "Sŭngga kyoyuk ŭi tangmyŏn kwaje e taehayŏ" 승가교육의 당면 과제에 대하여 [On the present problems in sangha education]. In *Sŭngga kyoyuk 2,* edited by Taehan Pulgyo Chogyejong Kyoyugwŏn. Seoul: Chogyejong Ch'ulpansa, 1998.
——. "Sŭngga poksik yut'ong hyŏnhwang kwa kaesŏn pangan sŏlmun chosa punsŏ pogosŏ" 승가복식 유통현황과 개선방안 설문조사 분서보고서 [Analysis report of the survey regarding the present circulation and reform plans of the sangha

attire]. In *Sŭngga kyoyuk 4,* edited by Taehan Pulgyo Chogyejong Kyoyugwŏn. Seoul: Chogyejong Ch'ulpansa, 2002.

——. *Taesŭng Pulgyo: kangŭi kyehoegan 2* 대승불교: 강의계획안 2 [Syllabi 2 for Mahāyāna Buddhism]. Seoul: Chogyejong Ch'ulpansa, 2012.

——. *Ŭngyong Pulgyo: kangŭi kyehoegan 5* 응용불교: 강의계획안 5 [Syllabi 5 for applied Buddhism]. Seoul: Chogyejong Ch'ulpansa, 2012.

——. "(Untitled Report)." In *Sŭngga Kyoyuk 1,* edited by Education Department, The Chogye Order, 57–61. Seoul: Chogyejong Ch'ulpansa, 1995.

——. "(Untitled Report)." In *Sŭngga kyoyuk 3,* edited by Taehan Pulgyo Chogyejong Kyoyugwŏn. Seoul: The Chogye Order, 1999.

Taehan Pulgyo Ch'ŏnt'aejong [The Korean Ch'ŏnt'ae Order]. *Ch'ŏnt'ae sinhaeng ŭi ch'ŏkkŏrŭm* 천태신행의 첫걸음 [First steps in the Ch'ŏnt'ae faith]. Seoul: Taehan Pulgyo Ch'ŏnt'aejong, 2003.

Tambiah, Stanley. *World Conqueror and World Renouncer: A Study of Buddhism and Polity in Thailand against a Historical Background.* Cambridge: Cambridge University Press, 1977.

Tarocco, Francesca. *The Cultural Practices of Modern Chinese Buddhism: Attuning the Dharma.* New York: Routledge, 2007.

Taussig, Michael. *Mimesis and Alterity: A Particular History of the Senses.* New York: Routledge, 1993.

Taylor, Charles. "Modes of Secularism." In *Secularism and Its Critics,* edited by Rajeev Bhargava, 31–53. Oxford: Oxford University Press, 1998.

——. *A Secular Age.* Cambridge, MA: Harvard University Press, 2007.

Taylor, Rodney. *The Confucian Way of Contemplation: Okada Takehiko and the Tradition of Quiet-Sitting.* Columbia: University of South Carolina Press, 1988.

——. *The Religious Dimensions of Confucianism.* Albany: SUNY Press, 1990.

Terwiel, B. J. "A Model for the Study of Thai Buddhism." *Journal of Asian Studies* 35, no. 3 (1976): 391–403.

Tikhonov, Vladimir. "The Japanese Missionaries and Their Impact on Korean Buddhist Developments (1876–1910)." In *Makers of Modern Korean Buddhism,* edited by Jin Y. Park, 245–274. Albany: SUNY Press, 2010.

——. "Militarized Masculinity with Buddhist Characteristics: Buddhist Chaplains and their Role in the South Korean Army." *The Review of Korean Studies* 18, no. 1 (2015): 7–33.

Tikhonov, Vladimir, and Owen Miller. *Selected Writings of Han Yongun.* London: Brill, 2008.

T'oehyu. "Taesŭng Pulgyo wa onŭl ŭi sŭngga kyoyuk" 대승불교와 오늘의 승가교육 [Mahāyāna Buddhism and sangha education today]. In Taesŭng Pulgyo, ŏttŏk'e karŭch'igo silch'ŏnhal kŏdin'ga 대승불교,어떻게 가르치고 실천할 것인가 [How to teach Mahāyāna Buddhism and put it into practice]. Unpublished report, 2012.

Tongguk Taehakkyo. *Han'guk Pulgyo chŏnsŏ* [The complete works of Korean Buddhism]. Seoul: Tongguk Taehakkyo ch'ulp'anbu, 1979.

——. *Tongguk Taehakkyo paengnyŏnsa* 동국대학교 백년사 [A hundred years of Dongguk University history], vol. 1. Seoul: Tongguk Taehakkyo ch'ulp'anbu, 2006.

Tuzzeo, Daniel Ryan. "Education, Invention of Orthodoxy, and the Construction of Modern Buddhism on Dharma Drum Mountain." MA thesis, Florida State University, 2012.

Unsan. "Unmun sŭngga taehak ŭi chŏnt'ong kwa hyŏnjaesŏng" 운문승가대학의 전통성과 현재성 [The traditional and present character of Unmunsa's sangha university]. In *Piguni sŭngga taehak ŭi yŏksa wa munhwa* 비구니 승가대학의 역사와 문화 [The history and culture of nun seminaries], edited by Taehan Pulgyo Chogyejong Kyoyugwŏn, 11–52. Seoul: Chogyejong Ch'ulpansa, 2009.

Vermeersch, Sem. *The Power of the Buddhas: The Politics of Buddhism during the Koryo Dynasty (918–1392).* Cambridge, MA: Harvard University Asia Center, 2008.

Vos, H. M. "The Canon as a Straitjacket." In *Canonization and Decanonization: Papers Presented to the International Conference of the Leiden Institute for the Study of Religions,* edited by Arie van der Kooij and Karel van der Toorn, 351–370. Leiden: Brill, 1998.

Walraven, Boudewijn. "A Re-Examination of the Social Basis of Buddhism in Late Chosŏn Korea." *Seoul Journal of Korean Studies* 20, no. 1 (2007): 1–20.

Wang Sŏn-yŏp. "Yŏngnamdae tosŏgwan tongbin mun'go sojang p'yohun sap'an Ch'imun kyŏnghun ŭi Sŏji mit Kugyŏl" 영남대도서관 동빈문고 소장 表訓寺板 『緇門警訓』 의 서지 및 구결 [A study of the bibliography and kugyŏl of Ch'imun kyŏnghun at Yŏngnam University central library]. *Minjok munhwa nonch'ong* 48 (2011): 147–167.

Wanniansi. *Zhejiang Fuxueyuan Tiantaizong Fuxueyuan* 浙江佛學院天台宗佛學院 [The Buddhist seminary of the Tiantai Order of Zhejiang]. Zhejiang: Wanniansi, 2013.

Weinstein, Stanely. *Buddhism Under T'ang*. New York: Cambridge University Press, 1987.

Welch, Holmes. *Buddhism Under Mao*. Cambridge, MA: Harvard University Press, 1972.

——. *The Buddhist Revival in China*. Cambridge, MA: Harvard University Press, 1968.

Welter, Albert. *Monks, Rulers, and Literati: The Political Ascendancy of Chan Buddhism*. Oxford: Oxford University Press, 2006.

——. *Yongming Yanshou's Conception of Chan in the Zongjing lu: A Special Transmission Within the Scriptures*. Oxford: Oxford University Press, 2011.

Williams, Paul. *Unexpected Way: On Converting from Buddhism to Catholicism*. London: Bloomsbury T&T Clark, 2002.

Wŏlho. "Chŏnt'ong kangwŏn kyoyuk kwa hyŏndaesik taehak kyoyuk e taehan pigyo koch'al" 전통 강원교육과 현대식 대학교육에 대한 비교 고찰 [Comparartive inquiry into traditional seminary education and modern university education]. In *Sŭngga kyoyuk 4,* edited by Taehan Pulgyo Chogyejong Kyoyugwŏn. Seoul: Chogyejong Ch'ulpansa, 2002.

Wŏn Ŭi-bŏm. "Sŭngga kyoyuk ŭi yŏksajŏk chŏn'gae" 僧伽教育의 歷史的展開 [The historical development of sangha education]. *Sŏngnim* 9 (1975): 334–338.

Wŏngyŏng. "Chŏnt'ong kangwŏn hagin ŭi kibon kyoyuk e taehan insik koch'al" 傳統講院 學人의 基本教育에 대한 認識考察 [Consideration of the basic education of the traditional seminary students]. In *Sŭngga kyoyuk kwa Han'guk Pulgyo* 승가교육과 한국불교 [Sangha education and Korean Buddhism], edited by Kaksan. Taegu: Chŏn'guk Kkngwŏn yŏnhap Pulgyo haksul taehoe chunbi wiwŏnhoe, 2003.

Wŏnil. "Ch'imun kyŏnghun e taehan sogo" 치문 경훈에 대한 소고 [Some thoughts on the Admonitions to the Gray-Robed Monks]. *Sudara* 2 (1987): 126–133.

Wu, Jiang. *Enlightenment in Dispute: The Reinvention of Chan Buddhism in Seventeenth-Century China*. New York: Oxford University Press, 2008.

——. "Knowledge for What? The Buddhist Concept of Learning in the Śūramgama Sūtra." *Journal of Chinese Philosophy* 33, no. 4 (2006): 491–503.

——. "The Rule of Marginality: Hypothesizing the Transmission of the Mengshan Rite for Feeding the Hungry Ghosts in Late Imperial China." *Pacific World* 3, no. 20 (2018): 131–167.

Wu, Jiang, and Ron Dziwenka. "Better Than the Original: The Creation of Goryeo Canon and the Formation of Giyang Bulgyo 祈禳佛教." In *Spreading the Buddha's Word in East Asia: The Formation and Transformation of the Chinese Buddhist Canon,* edited by Jiang Wu and Lucille Chia, 249–283. New York: Columbia University Press, 2016.

Yanggwan. "T'ongdosa sŭngga taehak ŭi yŏksa wa chŏnt'ong" 통도사 승가대학의 역사와 전통 [The tradition and culture of T'ongdosa's sangha university]. Paper presented at Sŭngga taehak ŭi yŏksa wa munhwa 승가대학의 역사와 문화 [The histories and cultures of sangha universities] seminar. Chogyesa, November 2009.

Yao, Xinzhong. *An Introduction to Confucianism*. Cambridge: Cambridge University Press, 2000.

Yi Ki-un. "Kŭndaegi Pulgyogye ŭi 30 ponsan kyoyuk ch'eje chŏngbi wa injae yangsŏng" 근대기 불교계의 30本山 교육체제 정비와 인재양성 [Consolidation of the education system and cultivating men of ability by the thirty Buddhist head temples in the modern period]. *Han'guk sŏnhak* 20 (2008): 431–60.

Yi Ki-yŏng. "Sŭngga kyoyuk ŭi chemunje" 僧伽敎育의 諸問題 [Various problems with sangha education]. *Sŏngnim* 9 (1975): 328–333.

Yi Kye-p'yo. "Songgwangsa kangwŏn ŭi yŏksa" 松廣寺 講院의 역사 [The history of Songgwangsa's seminary]. Paper presented at Sŭngga taehak ŭi yŏksa wa munhwa 승가대학의 역사와 문화 [The histories and cultures of sangha universities] seminar. Chogyesa, November 2009.

Yi Kyŏng-su. "Ilche sidae Pulgyo yuhaksaeng ŭi tongyang" 일제시대 불교 유학생의 동향 [Trends in Buddhists studying abroad during the Japanese colony]. In *Sŭngga kyoyuk 2,* edited by Taehan Pulgyo Chogyejong Kyoyugwŏn, 252–297. Seoul: Chogyejong Ch'ulpansa, 1998.

Yi Pong-ch'un. "Chosŏn sidae ŭi sŭngjik chedo" 조선시대의 僧職제도 [The monastic bureaucratic system of the Chosŏn era]. In *Sŭngga kyoyuk 3,* edited by Taehan Pulgyo Chogyejong Kyoyugwŏn, 178–200. Seoul: Chogyejong Ch'ulpansa, 2000.

Yi Tŏk-chin. "Taesŭng kyŏngjŏn i Sŏn Pulgyo e mich'in yŏnghyang" 대승경전이 선불교에 미친 영향 [The influence of Mahāyāna sutras on Chan Buddhism]. In Taesŭng Pulgyo, ŏttŏk'e karŭch'igo silch'ŏn hal kŏdin'ga 대승불교,어떻게 가르치고 실천할 것인가 [How to teach Mahāyāna Buddhism and put it into practice]. Unpublished report, 2012.

Yifa. *The Origins of Buddhist Monastic Codes in China*. Honolulu: University of Hawai'i Press, 2002.

Yinger, J. Milton. "Pluralism, Religion, and Secularism." *Journal for the Scientific Study of Religion* 6, no. 1 (1967): 17–28.

Yŏ Su-ryŏng. "Sŭngga kosi, kaep'yŏn kyogwa panyŏng sŭpŭi kanghwa" 승가고시, 개편 교과 반영 · 습의 강화 [Reflecting upon sangha examinations and curricular reforms and strengthening practice]. *Pulgyo p'ok'ŏsŭ,* 2010.

Yogyŏng. "Piguni kyoyuk toryang Pongnyŏngsa sŭngga taehak e taehan koch'al" 비구니 교육 도량 봉녕사승가대학에 대한 고찰 [Inquiry into the nun education at Pongnyŏngsa's sangha university]. In *Piguni sŭngga taehak ŭi yŏksa wa munhwa* 비구니 승가대학의 역사와 문화 [The history and culture of nun seminaries], edited by Taehan Pulgyo Chogyejong Kyoyugwŏn, 83–136. Seoul: Chogyejong Ch'ulpansa, 2009.

Yonghak. "Kangwŏn kyoyuk ŭi hyoyulchŏgin haksŭp ŭl wihan kangwŏn kyoje kaesŏnan" 강원 교육의 효율적인 학습을 위한 강원 교제 개선안 [Reform plan of seminary textbooks for efficient practice of seminary education]. In *Kangwŏn kyogwa t'ongil mit kaesŏn ŭl wihan kyoyuk kwan'gyeja yŏnch'anhoe* 강원 교과통일 및 개선을 위한 교육관계자 연찬회 [Public hearing for educators regarding the unification and reform of seminary curriculums], edited by Taehan Pulgyo Chogyejong Kyoyugwŏn. Seoul: Chogyejong Ch'ulpansa, 2000.

———. "Tosŏ ŭi ot'alcha chijŏk e taehan kyŏnhae" 도서의 오탈자 지적에 대한 견해 [Thoughts about misprints in the Chan Preface]. In *Sŭngga kyoyuk 7,* edited by Taehan Pulgyo Chogyejong Kyoyugwŏn. Seoul: Chogyejong Ch'ulpansa, 2008.

Yŏngjin. "Sagŭp sŭngga kosi kaesŏn panghyang e taehan kich'o sŏnwŏn ŭi ipchang" 四級僧伽考試 개선방향에 대한 基礎禪院의 입장 [The position of the Elementary Chan Hall regarding the reforms of the fourth-level sangha examinations]. In *4 kŭp sŭngga kosi chedo kaesŏn ŭl wihan t'oronhoe charyojip* 4급 승가고시 제도 개선을 위한 토론회 자료집 [Collection of materials regarding the debates on reforming the fourth-level sangha examination system]. Unpublished report, 2000.

Yu, Chun-fang. "Ch'an Education in the Sung: Ideals and Procedures." In *Neo-Confucian*

Education: The Formative Stage, edited by William Theodore de Bary, 57–104. Los Angeles: University of California Press, 1989.

——. *Passing the Light: The Incense Light Community and Buddhist Nuns in Contemporary Taiwan.* Honolulu: University of Hawai'i Press, 2013.

Yuh, Leighanne Kimberly. "The Royal Academy: Korea's First Instance of American-Style Education and the Making of Modern Korean Officials, 1886–1994." *Sungkyun Journal of East Asian Studies* 15, no. 1 (2015): 109–129

Yun, Woncheol. "Zen Master T'oe'ong Sŏngch'ŏl's Doctrine of Zen Enlightenment and Practice." In *Makers of Modern Koran Buddhism,* edited by Jin Y. Park, 199–226. Albany: SUNY Press, 2010.

Zack, Stephen J. "Buddhist Education Under Prince Wachirayan Warorot." PhD diss., Cornell University, 1978.

Zhe, Ji. "Buddhist Institutional Innovations." In *Modern Chinese Religions 1850–2015,* edited by Vincent Goossaret, Jan Kiely, and John Lagerwey, 731–766. Leiden: Brill, 2014.

Zurcher, Eric. "Buddhism and Education in T'ang Times." In *Neo-Confucian Education,* edited by Theodore De Bary and John Chaffee, 19–56. Los Angeles: University of California Press, 1989.

——. *The Buddhist Conquest of China: The Spread and Adaptation of Buddhism in Early Medieval China.* Leiden: Brill, 1959.

Index

About the Author

Uri Kaplan is a lecturer at the Hebrew University of Jerusalem. He is author of *Buddhist Apologetics in East Asia: Countering the Neo-Confucian Critiques in the* Hufa lun *and the* Yusŏk chirŭi non (2019).